SHAREWARE
HEROES

BY THE SAME AUTHOR

The Secret History of Mac Gaming

SHAREWARE HEROES

The renegades who redefined gaming
at the dawn of the Internet

RICHARD MOSS

unbound

First published in 2022

Unbound
Level 1, Devonshire House, One Mayfair Place, London W1J 8AJ
www.unbound.com

© Richard Moss, 2022

Text design by PDQ Digital Media Solutions Ltd.

A CIP record for this book is available from the British Library

ISBN 978-1-80018-109-0 (hardback)
ISBN 978-1-80018-174-8 (paperback)
ISBN 978-1-80018-110-6 (ebook)

Printed in Great Britain by Clays Ltd, Elcograf S.p.A.

1 3 5 7 9 8 6 4 2

With special thanks to the following superfriends for their generous support of this book

Joseph Agreda
Matt Alderman
Gui Ambros
Derek Balling
Clint 'LGR' Basinger
Rocco Buffalino
Jan Burda
Keith Burke
Brian Christensen
Barry Cooper
Colin Cornaby
Matt Croydon
Cythera Guides
  (Seth Polsley)
Damien & Tika
Lee Dare
Alexis Delgado
Scott Densmore
Jon Duckworth
Rob Eberhardt
Paul Eremenko
Harley Faggetter
Cameron Friend
Peter Geddeis
David Gow
Joshua Grimes
Alex H
Drew Hamlin
Scott Herriman
Adam Howell

Tim Jenness
Keith Kaisershot
Tanara Kuranov
Matt "Zebe" Lee
Benjamin Mak
Preston Maness
Steve Marmon
Anthony Micari
Bobby Mohan
Simon Moss
Joerg Mueller-Kindt
Nadiim 'Dimo' Nafei
Mike Nielsen
Dave Oshry
Justin Pauls
James Pederson
Fabrizio Pedrazzini
Matt Penna, III
Daniel G. Rego
Yannick Rochat
Rockey
Guido Rößling
Sabrina Seerey
Max Silbiger
Scott Spencer
Jim Stirrup
Steve Streza
Michael S. Tashbook
Richard Thames
Jonathan Wrigley

Contents

HIT SPACE BAR
TO CONTINUE

Introduction

Twenty-five-plus years ago – aeons, on the timescale of the modern Internet – we didn't have a single, simple, all-encompassing term to describe games published outside of conventional brick-and-mortar retail channels. There was no one generic name for independently made online-distributed games. Instead, there were several overlapping, unsatisfying terms.

For a period of the 1980s, we described it as the bedroom coder revolution. But that really only worked for the teenage whiz-kids who made their names with a few solo-created hits, and not the mortgaged 30-something garage tinkerers or the 20-something side hustlers. As a term it failed also to acknowledge the significant out-of-the-bedroom effort required to have a successful release – going to computer shows and swap meets, running demonstrations for magazine editors, packing and duplicating games for mail orders, and so on. It made success sound simple, almost a matter of luck.

The music industry had 'indie' or 'independent' labels and the movie industry had independent film, but it would be years before anybody thought to apply the word to games. Instead, from the late 1980s through to the early 2000s, we described them primarily according to their distribution model: commercial games were sold in boxes at retail stores, budget games were low-cost commercial games, freeware games were free to play and distribute non-commercially (but the author retained their copyright), public-domain games were free games where the author released their copyright, and shareware games were… well, there were a lot of shareware models, but essentially shareware games were free to try with a requested voluntary payment if you wanted to keep playing them.

(And often public domain was mistakenly used as a catch-all to describe the three non-commercial models all together.)

Shareware was the dominant of the three non-retail forms, and the one that best approximates what we call indie today. And it was a revolutionary concept – the idea that you could download a program off the nascent Internet, try it, then pay if you liked it. Its proponents all said that one day all software would be sold this way; its detractors laughed in their face, astounded at their apparent naivety. But slowly, little by little, shareware proved itself not only viable but also (potentially) profitable – before suddenly the term went extinct and the word 'indie' took over.

This book is about how (and why) shareware rose to prominence and then disappeared from common vernacular, but it's also about more than that. It's a book about people – the everyday heroes who made this revolution happen. Some of them got rich; many of them didn't. All played their part. The meteoric rise of indie games would come later, but here we see something of a dress rehearsal – a practice run wherein the kinks of independent marketing and distribution and sales and development of games could be smoothed out and tested with some of the best and worst games ever made (and lots of things in between).

In telling this story of a counter-cultural movement that changed both the games industry *and* the software business at large, I've tried to provide a solid cross-section of what was happening. I wanted to explore not only the big sweeping changes and innovations that drove shareware to prominence but also the personal stories, the minor victories, and the disappointing failures. There were literally thousands of shareware games, so I never had any hope of covering everything – but I hope I have at least provided a sense of what it was to be making and publishing games over the Internet back when the Internet was in its infancy (and before social media and microtransactions rewrote the rules again).

A note on sourcing

In the process of writing this book, I interviewed and consulted with several dozen people who were involved in the shareware scene. But memory is fallible, and many people were unavailable, dead, or couldn't be located, so I also turned to a raft of other sources to help me form as complete a picture of the history as I could. I pored over Usenet archives, dug up old and defunct websites in the Internet Archive's Wayback Machine, consulted articles and interviews and databases published on extant websites, read old magazines and newspapers, bought and borrowed old books, searched for archived documents, and, of course, studied the games themselves. (Though unfortunately one critical resource – the 1980s CompuServe forums – appears to have perished completely, which left a gaping hole in the early shareware history.)

I tried as much as possible to keep track of all these sources and have compiled those records into a page on a website, which you can find at sharewareheroes.com/sources (also available on the Internet Archive at https://archive.org/details/shareware-heroes-bibliography). Many of my web-based sources are also linked to from a database I made to help me write this book, with listings of various key people, games, and companies from the shareware games scene. You can find that at ragic.com/sharewareheroes

```
+=====================================+
|            s h a r e w a r e        |
|        User-Sponsored Software      |
+-------------------------------------+
| If you play this game and find it to|
| be enjoyable, your contribution ($10|
| suggested) will be appreciated. The |
| PASCAL source code will be sent with|
| a contribution of $50.              |
|         PC Research, Inc.           |
|         shareware - 3D              |
|         8 Village Lane              |
|         Colts Neck, NJ 07722        |
|                                     |
| You are encouraged to copy and share|
| this game with other users, on the  |
| conditions that the program is not  |
| distributed in modified form, that  |
| no fee or consideration is charged, |
| and that this notice is not removed.|
+=====================================+

Black/White or Color display (b or c)?
```

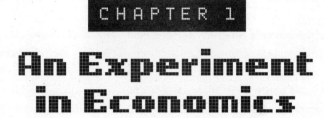

CHAPTER 1

An Experiment in Economics

Software used to be free. Back in the 1970s, its job was to sell computers. Occasionally it sold services. And even for the customers – the people whose businesses and institutions bought computers – software was considered a means to an end. It was a way to be more efficient, or more accurate. Or sometimes merely to further the needle – to venture deeper into the vast unknown of what computers could accomplish.

Nobody thought about making money from their code. Computers cost millions of dollars. Who in their right mind would be willing to pay that kind of money, only to be stung again for the tools that made their computer useful? No, software was free for everyone's benefit. And the most prolific users of computers, those same people who invariably wrote all the new computer programs, liked it that way.

To the idealistic programming whiz-kids profiled in journalist Steven Levy's book *Hackers: Heroes of the Computer Revolution*, code was meant to be uninhibited. Computers and everything connected to them were tools of learning. You derived value from them in the form of knowledge – knowledge gained through their use, but also through their misuse (or deconstruction) – that in turn enabled improvements to the systems.

If software cost money, even if it lacked copy protection, then its essential lessons were locked behind what they saw as an unnecessary barrier. And unnecessary barriers slowed the advancement of computer software and hardware design, which was the hackers' singular, fervent goal. The hacker ethic that fuelled the best computing innovations of the era – including the invention of personal computers such as the Apple II and Altair 8800 and of the BASIC programming language – demanded that information should be free. That it should flow, without obstacle, between machines and people so that anyone could come along and make things better – forever edging nearer to the perfect systems, the perfect programs, that improve the world around us.

The makers of popular computer games were no exception. Whereas games made for coin-operated arcade machines and TV-based consoles such as the Intellivision and Atari 2600 had been commercial products from the outset, games developed for mainframe and hobbyist computers emerged out of the same hacker ethic and collective spirit as other software.

The most popular computer games of the era – the likes of first-person shooter *Maze*, text-based spelunking game *Colossal Cave Adventure*, and space games *Empire*, *Star Trek*, and *Spacewar!* – were nearly all shared freely over the ARPANET, a US military-funded precursor to the Internet, and it wasn't unusual for the authors of computer games to allow anyone to add to or change the code to improve the experience in some way.

Maze, for instance, began life as an experiment. Three high school seniors on a work-study program at NASA Ames Research Center in 1973 took a routine they'd written to rotate a wireframe cube on a screen and expanded it into a three-dimensional maze built out of cubes. By the time they left for college, it had already begun its transformation into a multiplayer shooting game. But it then took on a life of its own after one of the three took it with him to MIT, where various members of the Dynamic Modeling Group optimised, enhanced, refined, and added to it progressively over the next few years.

They rewrote the code so that a mainframe computer could coordinate moves on each IMLAC mini-computer running the game, then they got it working across the ARPANET so that MIT and Stanford students could compete against each other late into the night. They made new mazes, multiple viewing modes, and robot players. One clever soul created a spectator program that allowed others to watch matches from an Evans & Sutherland LDS-1 graphics display computer in another room.

Many other early computer games, such as *Empire*, *Rogue*, and *Hack* (itself an attempt to remake *Rogue* from memory), went through similar evolutions as their source code passed through dozens of hands, each eager to make their mark upon it.

This was an environment of one-upmanship, where people cared more about showing off to friends than coming up with a commercial hook. Because, after all, friends were the only people anyone expected would actually play these games. As Brand Fortner, creator of the multiplayer combat flight simulator *Airfight*, explains, 'The thought that you could make money in software didn't occur to us in the 1970s.' (The following decade, in what Fortner thought was a 'mind-blowing' concept, *Airfight* would become a commercial product from which he received royalties.)

Acclaimed game designer Don Daglow (whose many works include *Utopia*, *Neverwinter Nights*, and the *Tony La Russa Baseball* series) puts a finer point on it:

> This is the point where computers still cost millions of dollars. They're expensive to operate. You need refrigerated rooms. The idea that anybody's ever getting paid money for this is still silly. You know, the growth of *Pong* and coin-ops

and stuff like that – that's a different world. That's not like what we do.

Slowly but surely, however, as more people took an interest in computers, the idea that you could make money from software began to spread around the industry.

The seed of the idea was planted in 1975 by Microsoft (then styled Micro-Soft) co-founders Bill Gates and Paul Allen, who broke from hacker norms by making a deal with Altair to distribute their BASIC interpreter as a commercial product called Altair BASIC. The hacker community resisted this effort to commercialise the industry, pirating the software en masse, but Gates persisted and Microsoft grew.

Other commercial software companies soon emerged, such as *Microchess* publisher VisiCorp (better known for the VisiCalc spreadsheet software) in 1976, relational database systems maker Software Development Laboratories (now Oracle Corporation), and word processing software developer MicroPro in 1978.

Computers had by this point stopped being the sole realm of hobbyists, academics, and big businesses. They'd become smaller and more powerful. By the late 1970s, microcomputers – computers powered by a microprocessor and small enough to fit on an average desk (what we now call personal computers) – were able to accomplish tasks like bookkeeping and word processing, and to run graphically rich software. This expanded their market; now computers were useful to working professionals and technologically inclined children. And they increasingly came preassembled, in cases, ready to use the moment you took them home.

From around 50,000 microcomputer sales by the end of 1976, mostly in the form of kit computers that hobbyists could assemble themselves, the market ballooned in size. In 1979 – the year Atari's 400 and 800 computers launched, and the Apple

II got its first 'killer app', spreadsheet program VisiCalc – there were around 580,000 machines sold worldwide. When the mass-market favourite Commodore 64 first rolled off the production line in 1982, just as the IBM PC started to pick up momentum, a further 2.8 million new microcomputers were sold around the world.

As microcomputer sales rose, so too did commercial software sales. Software companies like Microsoft, Ashton-Tate, and Quark, together with game companies like Muse Software and Infocom (founded by former MIT students, one of whom had worked on *Maze*), rose up to meet the demand for programs both productive and playful among this new brand of computer user. But there was a problem with distribution.

The software industry was so new that there weren't clear processes in place for getting programs from developer to end-user. Some developers made deals with computer retailers in their region to get products available in-store, which at this point usually meant putting a disk or cassette tape and manual inside a clear plastic bag that could be hung from a hook. Others chose mail-order systems, with their products listed in magazines and catalogues.

Free to share

A handful had the idea to try something different. They thought to forgo the usual retail channels altogether and instead embrace the sharing, communal nature of the early computing industry – an industry that cared little for such annoyances as copy protection and that gleefully passed around software of all kinds, commercial or not, across user groups and bulletin board systems (BBSs – online message boards accessed via dial-up modems).

One of these people was called Andrew Fluegelman.

Fluegelman operated a one-man independent book publisher – which doubled as an imprint for larger publishers – called The Headlands Press in Tiburon, California. Recognising the growing computer market and the computer's potential as a writing tool, he decided to produce and co-author a book about writing with computer technology.

He didn't actually *own* a computer at this moment, in 1981, but that was no matter – computers were still so new that he could just buy one and learn everything he needed to know in the process of writing the book.

He'd been thinking about computers for years. He later recalled in a 1982 interview with *PC* magazine that he'd attended one of the first computer fairs in San Francisco in 1977 or '78 to learn about this exciting new technology. But he'd left thoroughly intimidated, even by terms as basic as 'floppy disk'. 'I came away feeling that I was going to have to learn how to operate a soldering gun before I was ever going to get into the computer world,' he said in the interview.

Still, computers seemed important, so he'd kept trying to feel out the technology. He'd read computer books and magazines, visited computer stores, and tried using a friend's word processor, and then when IBM announced its PC in August 1981 – shortly after he signed on to work on *Writing in the Computer Age* – he knew that was the one for him.

In October he received the machine, along with programming tool BASIC, spreadsheet program VisiCalc, and, after a short delay, word processing program EasyWriter. By November he was knee-deep in learning to write his own programs in BASIC.

Fluegelman felt empowered by his computer. He described it as being like an extension of himself that effectively grafted '2,000 extra brains' onto his skull, to use however he saw fit.

He chose to use these ancillary brains to make his life easier. He wrote a communications program to help him swap drafts and edits back and forth with his co-author, and an accounting program to help with his bookkeeping.

As he and his co-author worked on their book, he enhanced his communications tool. He added a dialling directory, so that it could remember what number to dial for each online service and personal contact, and he created macros for automating common tasks. Every time he had an idea for something that would make the program more useful, he'd write code to add it in.

'In the process,' he later told *MicroTimes* magazine, 'I gave [the communications program] to a lot of my friends, and they started using it.' No other programs for the IBM PC at the time could match the functionality of this PC-Talk program, which could send and receive and preview files via a modem connection between an IBM PC and *any* other microcomputer or an online service such as CompuServe. His friends, recognising this, suggested he publish PC-Talk commercially. But he didn't like that idea.

He knew the publishing business. After working in book publishing for eight years, he was well versed in its drawbacks. He worried it would sap the fun – the exhilaration – out of software development, and maybe worse. There were already horror stories floating around of copy-protection schemes months in the making that would get defeated in an afternoon, thereby opening the door to mass piracy while simultaneously annoying legitimate customers.

Instead of searching for a publisher and risking derailment, whether from piracy or other business issues, he decided to self-publish. But not through conventional retail channels. He'd heard a local public TV station talk about 'user-supported television' during a pledge drive. He'd do the same thing with software.

User-supported software: free to share, free to use, funded by the generosity of its users. 'An experiment in economics,' he later remarked – a test of viral distribution and the willingness of people to voluntarily pay for the programs they enjoy – but not, he insisted, in altruism. He called it 'freeware', and out into the wild went PC-Talk – its only hope of financial reward resting in a simple run-time notice that explained the concept. Incredibly, it worked. Within six months he received more than $15,000 in payments for the program, with monthly registrations rapidly trending upwards.

At the same time, unbeknownst to Fluegelman, another person some 1,300 kilometres away in Bellevue, Washington, was conceiving his own user-supported-software revolution.

IBM employee Jim Knopf (a.k.a. Jim Button) had fallen in love with personal computing years earlier. He'd written two programs on his Apple II – one to print mailing labels for a local church congregation, the other to house general-purpose databases. Then when the IBM PC came out, he'd sold the Apple II, bought a PC, and converted the database program from the Apple dialect of BASIC to IBM BASIC.

He'd then shared this program, Easy File, with his colleagues at IBM, many of whom were taking their first steps into the world of personal computing. Before long, its use had spread beyond IBM's Seattle offices and into the wider Seattle area. Knopf had tried to track all these users by recording their details in his own copy of the program, so that he could notify them when he had updated Easy File with new fixes and improvements. But quickly his costs – both in time and in postage stamps – had begun to spiral out of control.

To help cover his expenses, Knopf added a message to the program that asked for donations – purely on a voluntary basis – of $10 from each user. In exchange for their donation, a user would gain access to his mailing list.

Knopf then bought a subscription to the online service CompuServe and posted a message in the forums to say that he would send a copy to anyone who mailed him a blank floppy disk with a pre-paid/pre-stamped return envelope.

Almost immediately, Knopf received a phone call. Another program, PC-Talk, included a similar message – maybe he should get in touch with its author Andrew Fluegelman to set up some kind of cross-promotion? It seemed worth checking out.

Impressed by PC-Talk, and Fluegelman's apparent belief in the potential of its unusual 'freeware' marketing method, Knopf soon sent him a letter. In July 1982, the pair agreed to collaborate. Knopf would rename Easy File as 'PC-File', to match the branding of PC-Talk, and he'd change his requested donation from $10 to $25 – also to match PC-Talk. Then for cross-marketing, each author would include a reference to the other's program on their distribution disks.

Knopf later wrote that his wife had called him 'a foolish old man' for thinking anyone would voluntarily send him money for the program. He'd felt more optimistic. That perhaps he'd even make several hundred dollars to help fund his personal computing hobby.

Both were wrong. 'My tiny post-office box was too small to receive the responses from a wildly enthusiastic public,' he later wrote.

It helped that the marketing method was so novel, which got people (and, most importantly, press) talking. But also it was critical that PC-File and PC-Talk were high-quality programs at budget prices, with unlimited time to try before you buy and a message that explicitly reversed the emerging norm of commercial software. Rather than warn against making copies to share with others, these programs *encouraged* people to make copies that others could use.

By August of 1984, two years after he'd made contact with Fluegelman, Knopf's PC-File income had climbed to around ten times his salary at IBM. Knopf had never planned to leave IBM. But work related to his hobby program had consumed his evenings and weekends for months, and he could stand no more. Something had to give, and it wasn't going to be PC-File, so he resigned from IBM.

Now all-in on his side business, PC-File's growth accelerated. He hired employees and put out additional programs, collectively garnering millions of dollars in revenue every year – all without a single title on retail shelves.

Play time

News of Knopf and Fluegelman's successes spread far and wide around the industry. Quickly others embraced this idea of free software you could pay for.

There were graphics editors, networking utilities, music composition tools, business programs, educational programs, and all manner of other productivity software – some filling gaps in the market that weren't catered to by the commercial software industry, others offering lower-cost (though not necessarily lower-functionality) alternatives to commercial tools. And, occasionally, there were games too.

One of the earliest, *3-Demon* (1983), called itself both shareware and 'user-sponsored software' – with a requested donation of $10 (or $50 if you wanted source code). It was an unlicensed *Pac-Man* clone in which players saw the world from Pac-Man's perspective, presented in a wireframe-3D maze, struggling to find all the pellets on the ground without getting eaten by a ghost (the mouth of which would engulf the screen if it caught you).

Released around the same time, text-based murder-mystery game *Sleuth* (1983–4) had a suggested contribution of

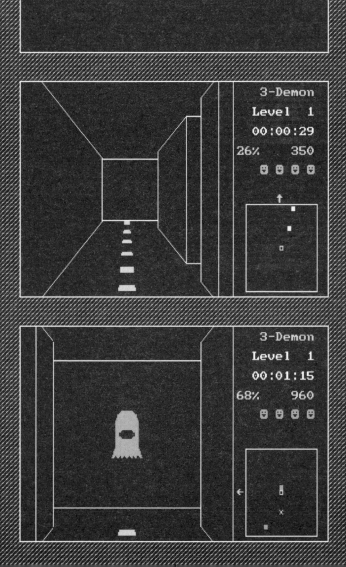

$15 if you enjoyed guiding your smiley-face square around a two-storey house, where the seemingly empty rooms gained life (and clues!) through text narration, in search of a killer who just might go in search of you.

Published a little later, but adapted from a 1983 mail-order Apple III release, Mac game *Cap'n Magneto* (1985) proved that shareware would not solely be an IBM PC phenomenon.

Developer Al Evans had been inspired to make a game after experimenting with a 'running horses' character-set animation demo that had come with the Apple III. He devised his concept for *Cap'n Magneto* from a frustration with the fantasy role-playing game (RPG) *Ultima*, which presented an immense world filled with castles and towns and dungeons but provided non-playable characters (like monsters and other people) that could be reasoned with only in towns. 'It seemed to me that it would be more fun if there were some possibility any creature you ran into would be friendly,' Evans says, 'and if the friendly ones would pass along useful information and be helpful in taking care of the unfriendly ones.'

His sci-fi adventure would be styled after *Ultima*'s overworld, with a top-down perspective of the player character. Players could wander about a large world encountering interesting people, places, things, and puzzles, all while collecting and using objects that might help in the quest to capture a mind-control device called the Crown of Control and thus put an end to rampant piracy on the planet Rigel IV.

With the right tools (mainly a *Star Trek*-inspired tricorder), players could engage with any of the creatures met along the way – each of which had a range of possible, partially randomised reactions to the player based on certain class attributes and limited perception. 'Humanoids are about 65 per cent likely to be friendly, about 60 per cent likely to be courageous, and about 40 per cent likely to be unpredictable as a class,' explains

Evans – who also used a pseudo-fractal dice roll algorithm he adapted from a *Scientific American* article to implement his randomness. Other classes of creature had different likelihoods of each reaction type.

Cap'n Magneto's original Apple III release had struggled to find an audience on the poor-selling, soon-discontinued computer it ran on, but its expanded Mac version – bolstered by improved graphics and creative use of the Mac's built-in speech synthesiser – proved very popular. Users groups, online newsgroups, and bulletin board system operators enthusiastically passed it around, while magazines and newsletters gave it rave (though largely belated) reviews too. Journalist Rusel DeMaria called it his favourite shareware game in a November 1987 issue of *Macworld* (which rarely mentioned shareware), for instance, praising its irreverent humour, offbeat plot, clever puzzles, and excellent blending of strategy with action. And in 1990 *MacUser* magazine declared it one of the 200 best Macintosh software products.

Registrations came from far and wide, arriving in unusually high numbers for an early shareware game. Over a period of several years following its initial release, Evans received around $10,000–$12,000 from the game – nowhere near enough for him to live off, but considerably more than the 'pizza and beer' money most of his peers in the shareware games business were earning (see Chapter 3 for more on the money question).

Other early standouts that have survived the passing of time include Mac-only *Wheel of Fortune* knock-off *Phraze Craze Plus* (1986), which was a favourite among Mac users for years afterwards, and DOS shoot-'em-up *Flightmare* (1984), which asked for 'a monetary thank you card of five to fifty dollars' if you found it entertaining. *Flightmare* is also notable for its novel approach to the idea of three-dimensional graphics. Many games had by this time dabbled in 3D, be it through vector line-drawing

– to give off a wireframe-3D look – or primitive (and slowly drawn) polygons, or just a first-person-perspective drawing of a scene. But *Flightmare* presented its world simultaneously in a side view *and* a top view, and it required its players to constantly refer to both of these. Shots fired would only hit an enemy if they were first aligned within both axes.

Many of the earliest attempts to distribute games through this payment-optional business model have all but (if not completely) vanished from the public record. Or their initial releases have been lost, as in the case of pirate-themed action-strategy game *Kaptajn Kaper i Kattegat* (a.k.a. *Privateer*) – a prototypical *Pirates!* (a popular commercial game from 1987) inspired by 1983 ZX Spectrum game *Plunder*, in which players captain a pirate ship, feed their crew, buy stuff with money made from selling loot, and raid and seize English merchant ships.

Kaptajn Kaper's earliest surviving version dates back to 1985, though developer Peter Ole Frederiksen may have first released it in '84, and it requested voluntary donations of 50 Danish kroner – despite Frederiksen's complete ignorance of the emerging movement Stateside.

What's in a name?

As much as this new form of software distribution had exploded in popularity among users, and in traction among developers, its successes were hamstrung by one simple problem: it didn't have an agreed-upon, industry-standardised name. Rather, it had *three* names: Fluegelman's 'freeware' (which was trademarked and so couldn't be used by anyone else), Knopf's 'user-supported software', and PC-Write author Bob Wallace's 'shareware'.

Wallace had left a job at Microsoft and formed a company called Quicksoft specifically to enter this burgeoning market

with his PC-Write word processor. Released in August 1983, PC-Write had three price points: $10 for an unregistered disk version, containing both the program and its documentation, direct from Wallace; $75 for a registered version with printed manual (in a binder), source code, phone support, and a copy of the next version of PC-Write; or free – nothing at all – for an unregistered version obtained via a friend or some other third party. And as a further incentive, he offered a one-time (i.e. first referral only) $25 commission to registered users whose friend registered a copy of their own.

He called this model 'commission shareware', or just shareware for short – the name adapted from a 30 May 1983 renaming of an *InfoWorld* magazine column by contributing editor Jay Lucas that covered public-domain software. (The column was called Freeware until *InfoWorld* learned of Fluegelman's trademark on the term ahead of publishing its eighth instalment, whereupon readers were invited to submit suggestions for a new name; at least a dozen people suggested 'Shareware', which *InfoWorld* adopted from the tenth entry onwards.)

With three prominent names and a host of lesser-known variants, the free-to-share, pay-to-register software marketing and distribution model had little chance of widespread success. It was just too confusing. Enter *Softalk-PC* columnist and software author Nelson Ford.

Ford had just begun a column in the magazine about public-domain software for the IBM PC, but he lacked a suitable (non-trademarked) term to describe works that fell into a 'quasi-public-domain' realm – programs that, unlike regular public-domain works, were supported post-release by their authors and that came with a suggested or requested user-contributed registration fee. So, in the May 1984 issue he asked his readers for their suggestions.

Two months later, in the July issue, Ford mentioned three of these: conscience-wear, so-called because 'the longer you use the software, the more it *wears* on your *conscience* if you do not pay'; tryware, which Ford thought a suitable name; and shareware, which he liked but worried was already in use by Quicksoft on PC-Write. Then, finally, in the following issue, Ford chose shareware as his winner, given its popularity among readers and its already widespread acceptance, after receiving clarification from Bob Wallace that Quicksoft claimed no ownership of the term.

Two years on from its invention, shareware finally had a name most people could agree on. The only trouble now was that the audience for software – the installed base of people who owned or used personal computers – was growing faster than the online networks through which shareware was distributed.

INSTRUCTIONS FOR SLEUTH

As you begin a game of SLEUTH a murder has just been committed. Your job is to mingle with the houseguests and to search the contents of the house until you feel you have solved the crime. Every game of SLEUTH is different so you must fully explore the house each time that you play.

You can move through the house by using the four cursor keys (←↑↓→) located on the numeric keypad. Be particularly careful when moving on the stairways since you must change direction each time you move from one floor to another.

You can search rooms, people and objects by using simple phrases such as EXAMINE DOOR, SEARCH VICTORIA, or LOOK AT JAR. When you want to SEARCH or ACCUSE a person you only need to type in their first name. To get more information from the guests you may QUESTION them, or ask for their ALIBIs. The characters tend to be rather moody and will not always answer your questions the first time around. They are also rather restless and will be moving around the house during the game.

PRESS ANY KEY TO CONTINUE

THE SHAREWARE BOOK
NEW RELEASES SUPPLEMENT
AND ADDENDUM

OCTOBER 1989

To be read in conjunction with, and where appropiate superceding catalogue 5.2

shareware

marketing

"ONE DAY ALL SOFTWARE WILL BE SOLD THIS WAY"

Published by:
Shareware Marketing
Beer,
England,
EX12 3HW
Tel 0297 24088   ISSN 0956 8433

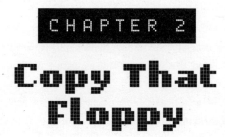

CHAPTER 2

Copy That Floppy

All successful software must conquer two mighty foes: distribution and discoverability. Without good distribution, people won't be able to access it; without easy discoverability, people won't know it exists.

Shareware tackled both problems through its virality – through positive buzz and word-of-mouth marketing, as both knowledge of the software and *the software itself* passed from person to person, the two ideas intrinsically intertwined. But this only worked to a certain extent.

It was a business model fit for the future, no doubt, but the future had yet to arrive. For now, shareware's great rise would be constrained by those very same strengths that made it flourish.

In the beginning, there were four main ways to acquire shareware: locally, copied to a floppy disk or hard drive by someone you knew; in person, bought or borrowed at a local computer users group meeting or a software show like the West Coast Computer Faire; direct from the author; or online, downloaded to your computer from a bulletin board system (BBS) or an online subscription-based service like CompuServe (which later added a service called SWREG where users could add the registration cost of a shareware program directly to their bill and the author would receive 80 per cent).

Shareware also had a fifth growth vector on the discoverability side – media coverage. It could be written about in magazines and newspapers or shown in TV news and current affairs programming. But even on the rare occasion when this happened, it was of little utility to the multitudes of computer users who lacked the wherewithal to access a BBS or attend a software show.

To really reach the computer-using masses, shareware needed a new form of distribution – a stopgap, interim measure that could enable widespread access to shareware while the technology and penetration of the nascent Internet caught up.

That new form would rather fittingly be a twist on an old form: mail-order catalogues.

Many computer users groups around the United States had begun to amass large libraries of shareware programs that members could access. But the effort involved in updating and organising these libraries soon outstripped their meagre funding, so some groups started charging a fee for access.

In 1984, an enterprising soul by the name of Richard Petersen saw an opportunity to take this further – to reach that wider population that either weren't able or didn't know how to acquire shareware. He and a few other computer club members thought they could form a business that scaled up the volunteer-based computer club shareware distribution networks. Thanks to their memberships, they already had access to hundreds of shareware programs. Why not sell them nationwide?

They founded a company called PC-SIG (the PC Software Interest Group) to do just that, with an initial collection of 300 disks – most containing multiple programs by a single author or clustered around a theme. For $6 a disk, plus shipping and handling fees, PC-SIG would mail (unregistered) shareware programs to anyone in the United States. Shareware distribution had gone national.

To promote his service, Petersen took out ads in *PC Magazine*, and in May 1985 he self-published a 340-page catalogue called *The PC-SIG Library* that people could get for $8.95 in a bookstore. The catalogue included short descriptions of each program and it separated them into categories for easier discoverability.

Some months later, in January 1986, PC-SIG added a second volume, titled *The Supplement to the PC-SIG Library: Disks 301 to 454: More Public Domain and User-Supported Software for the IBM PC and Compatibles*, then a second edition of the original catalogue that combined the two together. Around the same time, PC-SIG also started publishing *Shareware Magazine*, with new issues released every other month. Its purpose was to guide readers through the world of DOS shareware and to add more context to the PC-SIG catalogue. And once or twice a year, from 1989 until the company's sudden closure in 1993, they published new editions of *The PC-SIG Library* that updated the listings to the latest version – albeit retitled *The PC-SIG Encyclopedia of Shareware*.

PC-SIG was first to the mail-order shareware vendor party, but only just. Hot on its heels, *Softalk-PC* columnist Nelson Ford – the man who established 'shareware' as the standard term for software of this type – established the Public (software) Library, or PsL for short, after *Softalk-PC* ceased publication in late 1984.

PsL's distribution business took a different form to PC-SIG's. PsL was less discerning when it came to accepting programs into its catalogue, which quickly led to PsL having a much larger library than PC-SIG. But that larger library also made it infeasible to offer blanket nationwide coverage, so PsL became a champion of low-volume sales for smaller shareware authors. They soon also became a common source of shareware for other low-volume distributors like BBSs and regional shareware vendors. And like PC-SIG – and actually beginning slightly earlier, in late 1984 – PsL offered a subscription-based periodical, *PsL News*, that reviewed new shareware and freeware releases.

PsL wouldn't remain the number-two shareware vendor for long, though – it would quickly slide to third, courtesy of a man called Bob Ostrander. He'd been a computer programmer for 15 years come 1984, but not for much longer. Data-processing behemoth Ross Perot was taking over computer operations at his job at General Motors, and he refused to work for them. So he quit.

Shortly thereafter, Ostrander tagged along with a friend to a 'hamfest' – an amateur radio festival and swap meet. These hamfests could draw big crowds. One three-day event, he recalls, 'attracted well over 20,000 people'. And his friend loved them.

To give himself something to do as he tagged along to more hamfests, Ostrander started taking his computer with him. He had some shareware programs he'd acquired through his local computer club, and he put them together onto ten disks that he catalogued on a single sheet of paper. If people wanted a disk, he'd copy it and sell it to them right there and then for $5.

Quickly his catalogue expanded to 40 disks, and soon he moved beyond hamfests to also selling at electronics festivals and fairs. One day, he recalls, he took two trunks filled with around 2,000 disks to a two-day computer festival in San Francisco. He sold two-thirds of them on the first day, then his wife and a friend from their neighbourhood stayed up all night making more disks and flew in from Massachusetts to bolster his stock for day two.

Before long he had a thriving shareware distribution business called Public Brand Software, co-owned with his hamfest buddy Don Schlensker, and that neighbourhood friend Terry Ramstetter. They had 16 employees (later rising to 21) and – after they first outgrew his house and then a rented space – their own building.

They did a mix of mail-order and festival sales, earning millions in revenue. The biggest sellers were well-known productivity applications like PC-Talk, PC-Write and PC-File, but family-friendly and educational games were popular too.

At the beginning they'd sourced programs from local computer groups, but 'after a while people came to us', says Ostrander. Every day they'd hear from a few new shareware authors who hoped to see their work included in the Public Brand Software catalogue.

But just asking wasn't a sure-fire way to get included. Public Brand Software's reviewers would evaluate every program received according to a form Ostrander wrote. At the end of their evaluation, they'd give it a rating out of four – plus a 'trophy' if they thought it was better than anything available commercially.

'They handed that to me, and every three months I'd come out with a new catalogue and merge in what was useful,' Ostrander explains. 'Get rid of what wasn't selling. I had sales numbers, of course, and basically sat around my house for two weeks coming up with a new catalogue.'

By the end of 1988 they were selling over half a million disks a year and had cracked the top 100 fastest-growing, privately held companies in the United States. They'd built up a rivalry with the other big distributor PC-SIG along the way, but for Ostrander, at least, the goal was not to squash the competition – it was to bring people together. 'There was plenty of market share to go around,' he says. The bigger shareware could get, the better it would be for business.

To help facilitate this growth and bring the community closer together, and to fill the gap between COMDEX (Computer Dealers' Exhibition) trade shows, Ostrander started the Summer Shareware Seminars. 'Three days of fun and shareware' he promised attendees, who flocked to Indianapolis from all around the world in their hundreds – 300 at the first event, then slightly more in later years.

'It didn't grow and it didn't need to,' Ostrander jokes, 'because people were falling out as fast as they were coming in.' But it was there, for those with the drive and the business acumen, to make connections and secure deals.

'That's what you're here for,' Ostrander would tell them. 'Get somebody to do something with your stuff that makes you money. Organise. If you've got a grading software for elementary schools and somebody else has something that teaches the alphabet, go together.'

Shareware wasn't a zero-sum game, and Ostrander's attitude was that anything that could benefit a shareware-focused business was worth trying. He followed this philosophy with his own company. Nationwide shareware distribution was a profitable enterprise, but he had a catalogue with international appeal. Ostrander and his team had painstakingly created their catalogue by hand, taking care to personally review every program they distributed, and that was value that several overseas vendors thought worth paying for. They asked for permission to license the Public Brand Software catalogue for use in their country. (Ostrander said yes.)

Crossing borders

Of those overseas vendors, the biggest and most successful was called Atlantic Coast. It had been founded as Used Computer Sales by an entrepreneur called Steve Lee in 1984 as a new endeavour to rescue him from his work at a rural petrol station, following the collapse of his small trucking business.

In the beginning it was, as the original name suggested, a second-hand computer retailer. But after a while Lee learned about public-domain software, and then through a public-domain distributor he found out about the emerging shareware scene in

the US. Lee looked upon this shareware thing as a revelation – commercial-quality software sold via donation (incentivised or not), as opposed to the low-quality fare that he'd seen for computers running the CP/M operating system prior to that.

He bought a copy of Jim Knopf's PC-File (sold through Knopf's company Buttonware), then wrote to Knopf asking if he could resell it in the UK market. Knopf responded enthusiastically, suggesting Lee also sell Buttonware's other programs, PC-Calc and PC-Type. 'We took £36,000 in year one and £112,000 in year two,' Lee later wrote.

Clearly he was onto something special, so Lee renamed his company Shareware Marketing and arranged UK reselling rights for several other US-based shareware authors.

'Somehow or other, I got invited to shareware conferences in America,' Lee recalls. 'And at one of them, I met a guy called Bob Ostrander.'

For 'next to nothing' (around $500 plus discounted updates), Ostrander agreed to license Public Brand Software's catalogue to Lee – who dropped the 'Marketing' from his company name to become Shareware Ltd, then Shareware plc, before ultimately renaming it Atlantic Coast plc to better reflect its US sourcing of software and to avoid being permanently pigeon-holed into shareware.

As with the US-based vendors, Atlantic Coast would sell primarily through a mail-order catalogue (in their case, a licensed copy of the one Public Brand Software produced). But Lee also arranged for them to sell to UK-based CompuServe users through the SWREG system, and to pick up additional income through providing software for Future Publishing's *PC Plus* magazine coverdisks. And he made deals with some of the more popular shareware authors (such as WinZip author Nico Mak) to be their sole agent in the UK.

For around a year he even had a magazine of his own – a monthly publication called *PC Shareware Magazine* that he bought in 1991 from 'a couple of blokes in Bradford' who had not realised how hard the magazine business was. Lee thought that with his huge audience Atlantic Coast could make it a successful venture. But he too learned the hard way that magazines 'are a black hole' and sold it on to a friend who relaunched it in October 1992 with a new editor called Robin Nixon. 'Sadly the [new owner] was mainly a design studio,' recalls Nixon, 'and it had no resources to sell advertising, et cetera, so the money coming in wasn't sufficient to maintain publication.' The magazine shuttered for the third and final time after just six more issues.

Atlantic Coast was scarred from the magazine venture, absorbing around £400,000 in losses but still managing to turn a modest profit for the year. Lee took it as a wake-up call and recognised that the market for mail-order shareware disk vendors had by this point started to decline – mainly due to the rapid growth of Internet-based distribution. He diversified his business to get into disk duplication, retail software logistics (as a middleman in the distribution chain), and eventually – several years later – launched a web-based successor to SWREG (for which he'd purchased the rights from AOL after AOL bought CompuServe in 1998) called Atlantic Coast Soft Shop, making Lee one of the earliest online payment vendors for shareware authors and software publishers.

Fish disks

Even with the scale at which these big shareware vendors operated, there was ample room for smaller players to come in and try to own a space in the shareware world. All you needed to be a disk vendor was a floppy drive, a few shareware programs, and some blank disks. Almost as soon as PC-SIG and PsL had proven there was a market for mail-order shareware catalogues, dozens of small local and regional competitors had sprung up. And there were more vendors every year, all hoping to cash in on this burgeoning shareware scene via the path of least resistance.

As with shareware itself, most failed to turn a worthwhile profit and closed soon after, but some succeeded – at least for a while.

Perhaps the best-known of these was Amiga vendor Fred Fish. Fish was 33 years old when he bought himself a launch-model Amiga, an A1000, and immediately became besotted with it. This was late 1985, just a short time after the system's public launch, and Fish found a dearth of available software. But he did get his hands on a C compiler, and as a seasoned programmer himself he figured the best thing to do would be to write his own software.

Quickly, he ported over some public domain and shareware programs that he'd been using on his UNIX system. And as he did this, he also started to collect Amiga programs he found online (mainly on Usenet). Then he decided to put copies of all his programs on disks and give them away.

He took them with him to an Amiga users group meeting in Palo Alto. 'After the meeting I announced I had these disks,' he later recalled in an interview with *Amazing Computing*, 'and told everyone they could copy them if they wanted. Well, they went nuts!'

Everybody wanted a copy, it seemed, so he kept bringing his disks with him every time he attended a meeting. When he decided to formalise his operation in January 1986, with postal distribution to people all around the world at a cost of $10 per disk, he was up to four disks, but quickly it would climb to ten, then twenty, and on up to almost 400 by the end of 1990 and a whopping 1,000 disks – collectively amounting to several thousand programs – just before he shifted focus to CD-ROM distribution in 1994.

Most programs included on the disks were completely free, and many came with source code, but some (over 500) were shareware. Similarly, most programs were small utilities or productivity tools, but nearly 400 were games – a mix of puzzle games, unlicensed arcade conversions, strategy games, board games, text adventures, a handful of commercial game demos, and so on.

To give you a few examples: Jim Boyd's 1987 shareware title *Pacman 87*, included on disk 192, took arcade hit *Pac-Man* and twisted it into something much more devious, with extra hazards such as fire pits, flame throwers, and wall-mounted blades to avoid; platformer *Peter's Quest: For the Love of Daphne* by David Meny (disk 224) took its cue from Nintendo hit *Super Mario Bros* in its 20-level sojourn to save Peter's girlfriend Daphne; and one of the earliest games included, *Sword of Fallen Angel* (disk 32), was a shareware text adventure written in BASIC in 1986 about 'a

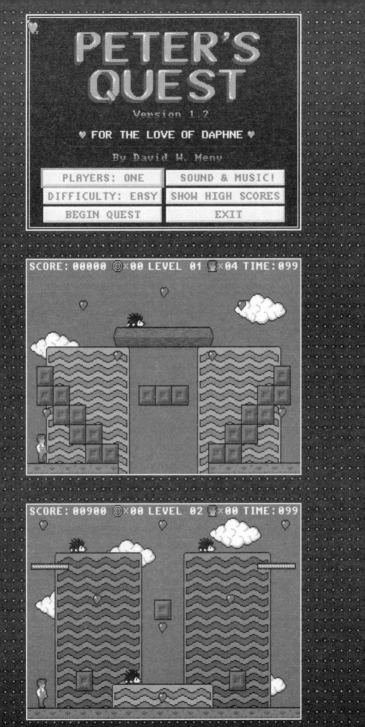

man with a great destiny [who] struggles between life and death to destroy the evil one.'

Fish called his library the AmigaLib Disks, but most Amiga users knew it as the Fred Fish Disks. And unlike big PC vendors, such as PC-SIG and Public Brand Software, Fish had no intention of running it like a business. The fee was to cover his time and materials, nothing more.

Direct subscriptions generally hovered between 50 and 100 people and groups, but the Fish Disks had a total reach encompassing nearly the entire global Amiga userbase. Fish himself estimated in 1992 that there were probably between 50,000 and 100,000 copies of each of his disks in circulation – some copies made with his explicit permission, but most not. And while there were times when he came close to quitting, disheartened by a declining direct subscription base, he always chose to continue – always driven by a desire to help his beloved Amiga community. As he told German publication *Amiga Magazin* in 1990, 'My aim is to spread the library as widely as possible, not to restrict it.'

Not all disk vendors were as civic-minded. Many operated with little concern for the hard work of either the developers who made the software or people like Fred Fish who compiled them into collections, and often programs would be redistributed in commercial collections both without permission and without any explanation that one or more of the programs included were shareware.

This was no mere annoyance to shareware authors, either, who would then receive angry support queries asking why this game someone just paid $5 for was incomplete or time-limited (or whatever else the original creator might have done to incentivise people to register).

Educomp

Any vendor that had hopes of forming a lasting, sustainable business knew that being responsive to authors and upfront about how shareware worked was essential both to the future of their company and the future of the movement. But even then, some would find repeated tension with authors who wished to tightly control how (and by whom) their programs were distributed.

One such repeat offender was a Mac-focused company called Educomp (later renamed Educorp), which upset a segment of the Mac freeware and shareware community in 1985 when it launched the *Macintosh Public Domain Software Catalog*. Despite the presence of a statement in the catalogue advising users to send donations to authors whose shareware programs they enjoyed, one disgruntled author took his anger to technology news periodical *InfoWorld* – which quoted him and a few other programmers who complained not only that they had not given their permission to distribute their works but also that Educomp seemed to be profiting from the enterprise.

This would become a common pain point for the company as well as for every other disk vendor that included programs sought out by their staff, as opposed to those submitted directly by authors. One rant-heavy opinion piece published a few years later in the National Capital Macintosh Club Bulletin incredulously summed up the range of reactions to this business practice:

> It may not be illegal or technically 'wrong', but it's not the kind of thing I could do and still be able to sleep at night. However, developers have complained about Educorp and other profit-making institutions selling their shareware products. Frequently, the end-user feels he has 'paid' for the product after giving Educorp $7 for a floppy disk, or

$199 for a CD-ROM 'full' of 'product'. We feel the end-user is not likely to contribute after paying such 'distribution' fees...

Many authors no longer make an effort. Most probably feel they've been beaten. Others aren't EVEN AWARE Educorp is selling their software. More amazing, some know and apparently don't care! If there's money to be made from my work, I want to make it.

In Educomp/Educorp's case, whatever the business practices and philosophies of owner Vahe Guzel, their initial catalogue was rooted in pure enthusiasm and naivety on the part of catalogue author Rob Eberhardt.

Eberhardt had found his way into the business almost by accident. He was working at a computer store in San Diego in January 1984 when a local entrepreneur called Charlie Jackson walked in looking for help with starting up the San Diego Macintosh User Group (SDMUG). This was an exciting idea to Eberhardt, then not long out of high school, who had been in love with computers since a friend took him to the third West Coast Computer Faire in November 1978, aged 13. (The West Coast Computer Faire was the world's largest computer fair, likened by *Hackers* author and technology journalist Steven Levy to Woodstock for computer hobbyists.)

Eberhardt was one of 35 people who then crammed into Charlie Jackson's home office to talk about Apple's revolutionary new personal computer, with many of them seeing it in person for the first time. And in the months that followed he became deeply embedded in the world of Mac shareware and freeware applications, clip art, games, and utilities. The passion came through his personal interests, where he says he was fascinated by the idea that 'anyone can publish their own software without having to make a deal with a professional software publisher.'

But it also came through his job, which entailed teaching people about why they should buy a computer more than it did actually selling the machines.

He thought this growing knowledge of his would be valuable to other members of SDMUG, so he volunteered to give presentations showcasing the best from the online software world at their monthly meetings.

'And then at the end of the meeting,' he recalls, 'I sat at a table, as people were leaving, with copies of compilations on disks that we sold for – I don't know – six dollars or something like that, with a little sheet listing what was on there.' Disk contents were curated according to what he thought was high quality and collated together according to theme – a disk of games, for instance, or multiple programs from the same author, similar to what the professional disk vendors were doing. In parallel he also began to offer these disks for sale at the end of classes he ran at the computer store for new computer users.

After he'd been doing this for a while he was approached by Educomp founder Vahe Guzel, who planned to sell compilations like Eberhardt's on a commercial scale nationwide. Eberhardt agreed and began to do that work part-time on the side of his retail job.

They sold disks via mail order and on the show floor at Macworld Expo. 'It grew really quickly and started making tons of money,' recalls Eberhardt. Clip art, games, and fonts were especially popular. But it wasn't entirely well received, as evidenced by the angry response from some shareware authors.

'Sometimes it was a symbiotic relationship and sometimes it wasn't at all,' remembers Eberhardt. 'I know that what I told myself initially when I was 18 at the user group was using a modem and CompuServe is *really* hard and a lot of people can't do it, but they might want these programs. And more people having the programs means more potential money for the shareware

author. So probably they wouldn't mind this. But there was no formal communication at all, ever, in the early days.'

When the letters came in from authors who were furious at their work being sold without permission, Educomp hurried to establish policies and frameworks around the removal of their work. But Guzel decided against chasing down authors for permission.

After a couple of years, in what he recalls were complicated circumstances – including unexpected contract changes and a big crush he had on Guzel's daughter (with whom he shared an apartment) – Eberhardt resigned from Educomp. Then his father and his father's business partners offered to fund a start-up venture doing the same work – writing catalogues and selling mail-order shareware and public-domain compilations – on his own terms. He accepted and set up a business called Somak Software.

He was determined that Somak would be different. It'd have a premium feel, with nicer (two-colour!) catalogues and disk labels, higher disk prices, better curation, and more of a personality and editorial voice in the program descriptions (and more copyright infringement too, with things like page-high *Simpsons* graphics in the background, though that echoed the rampant disregard for copyright evident in much of the software they were distributing). And it would actually take into account the feelings of shareware authors – aiming to strike some sort of balance between seeking their consent and the needs of running a commercial business.

It sounded great and started out alright, but Somak struggled to reach the volume needed to pay for their high expenditure and they were burning through cash. Meanwhile Educomp had grown rapidly into a multimillion-dollar business through an expansion into the nascent CD-ROM distribution market – which allowed for hundreds of shareware programs to be collected onto one disc, instead of just a few per floppy.

Then, just when Somak seemed to be getting a handle on how to run its premium shareware catalogue business, Educomp sued for breach of contract. More weird sitcom-worthy complications followed, including an apparent mental breakdown on the day of a hearing by Somak's lawyer, with the ultimate outcome being the closure of Eberhardt's business.

He moved to New York to start his life over, while Educomp turned into Educorp and established itself as one of the leading CD-ROM distributors of shareware – along with Walnut Creek CDROM, Gigabyte, Softkey, and the big-three early disk vendors (PC-SIG, Public Brand Software, and PsL, of which only PsL stayed in operation beyond 1993).

All of these – and the rest of the shareware vendors – continued to navigate the uneasy terrain between their business of selling shareware and free software and the rights and interests of authors. Many had to periodically fend off or settle lawsuits, while some made deals to pay royalties to authors on every disk/ disc sold. But whatever their solution to the ethical and legal quandaries of commercial shareware distribution, most found a balance that allowed them to operate a (very) profitable business.

For the continued rise of shareware, this was critical. With a thriving ecosystem of shareware disk vendors to add to the many ways to get shareware online, the twin problems of discoverability and distribution were fully sorted.

But for shareware game developers – much more so than other kinds of shareware creators – one problem still remained: earning money.

EPISODE I: PLANET OF DEATH

ENTERING ORBIT AROUND THE PLANET
TAMBI, CAPTAIN COMIC, GALACTIC
HERO, PREPARES FOR HIS IMPOSSIBLE
MISSION: TO RECOVER TREASURES
STOLEN FROM THE PLANET OMSOC.

ARMED WITH ONLY HIS COURAGE, HE
ENTERS THE TELEPORT CHAMBER...

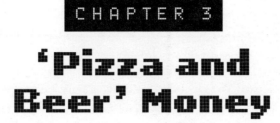

CHAPTER 3

'Pizza and Beer' Money

Nobody pays for shareware. Even at the height of Bob Wallace, Andrew Fluegelman, and Jim Knopf's shareware success, this was commonly accepted wisdom. Indeed, in a June 1986 *San Francisco Examiner* column, technology journalist John Dvorak named Knopf as 'one of the few programmers who actually make money by marketing so-called shareware or user-supported software.'

Shareware worked great for its inventors, whose work was trumpeted in magazines and newspapers around the world as the vanguard of a brave new world of software distribution – and who could earn tens or hundreds of thousands of dollars a month despite low install-to-registration rates. It also worked great for its distributors – companies like Public Brand Software and Atlantic Coast – that mailed shareware-filled floppies around the world, earning their fee irrespective of whether a program was subsequently registered by its user. But everyone else struggled.

Four months after Dvorak's article, *Washington Post* journalists T. R. Reid and Michael Schrage drew more attention to the problem. 'The sweet dream of shareware isn't working in this hard, cold world,' they wrote. 'It's not that people don't like to use shareware; it's just that they don't like to pay, even when bound by word of honour.'

Reid and Schrage also cited a McGraw Hill survey of shareware authors that put a finer point on it. The average rate of return on shareware, the survey found, was just five paying customers for every 2,500 who tried the program.

For those few who thrived off the model, shareware was clearly the wave of the future. 'Eventually, we are going to bury the mainstream [of software sales],' PC-SIG's marketing director told the Associated Press in 1986. Similarly, Atlantic Coast operated under the tagline that 'one day all software will be sold this way'.

But the tragedy of shareware was that for all that it did to democratise the world of software distribution, the chances of even a high-quality shareware program becoming financially successful were slim at best.

Online message boards filled up with conversations and cautionary tales about shareware's apparent inefficacy as a business model.

'All shareware does is give people the idea that it's all right not to pay for software; that you ought to pay only if you feel like it – if you're a wimp, or weird, or something,' complained one author of a shareware utility that, despite distribution through PC-SIG and other disk vendors around the world, had just two registered users.

A 'Shareware Marketing Concepts' document circulated by PC-Write author Bob Wallace explained that 'shareware is just "word of disk"' and to succeed with the model a program must be both valuable to its users and 'alive' (which is to say that it evolves over time, with regular bug fixes and new updates). But struggling authors and cynical computer users cried foul. 'Shareware doesn't work' and 'shareware is dying', they screamed in unison, pointing as proof not only to the hundreds of failed shareware programs but also to the fact that a few of shareware's big success stories – like PC Outline, PC-File, and Red Ryder – had turned (or were in the process of turning) commercial.

More moderate voices spoke to the root causes of the problem. There's too much 'garbage' being marketed as shareware, one person wrote. 'Someone puts in a weekend hack and decides to upload it and maybe make a buck. It's ugly, it's trivial, it's buggy. Maybe it'll crash your hard disk.' This scares people off trying new shareware programs, they argued, adding also that too many shareware authors had failed to follow through on promises of upgrades and support. And the result, they said, is that 'if you publish shareware, you can't win. Even if you have a killer product, you don't get paid for it.'

There were outliers, of course – a smattering of big hits like PC-Write and PC-Talk that made millions of dollars in revenue, and perhaps dozens of other programs that could support small companies of one or a few full-time employees. But even apparently successful shareware authors often struggled to earn anywhere close to enough money to cover their time and expenses.

Shareware game authors had it worse than most. Few of them had any chance of meeting Bob Wallace's shareware value proposition. Their programs were mere entertainment, to be toyed with and then cast aside – their value derived in full before a payment could be made.

No matter how great the popularity of a shareware game, or how brilliant its design, there was little incentive to register it.

Consider early Mac game *Scarab of Ra* (1987). It began as a learning exercise for Rick Holzgrafe, weeks into a new job as an engineer at Apple Computer, when he sought permission from his boss to make a game to help him understand the intricacies of Mac software development.

Over a period of several months, Holzgrafe evolved his game from a first-person maze into something much more substantial, with up to 200 randomly generated mazes that together formed a massive dungeon beneath the Great Pyramid of Ra. Intended as a non-violent, first-person take on the influential mainframe game *Rogue* (1980), the goal was to find three treasures while exploring this dungeon. Players had to avoid (or trick) animal threats such as monkeys and a lioness, solve puzzles, and try to stay alive. To accomplish these feats, they had only their wits, the occasional hint scrawled on a wall, some items (like food or lantern oil) left on the ground, and an auto-generated map that filled in as they moved – which at the time was a rare feature even in commercial games.

Holzgrafe got approval from Apple management to self-publish *Scarab of Ra* as shareware, then he uploaded it to a BBS and let fate take its course. It was as pure a shareware model as you could get – he enforced no limitations or restrictions and explicitly encouraged people to copy and share the game, but requested a $10 donation if you liked it.

The game rapidly spread around the tight-knit Mac community and even caught the attention of several magazines – including the typically game-shy *Macworld*, which included *Scarab of Ra* in its yearly best-of awards. But for all of the plaudits and accolades, and a likely installed base approaching six figures, Holzgrafe rarely received more than one or two payments a week. In the lifetime of the program, which included a few minor updates as well as one major update that expanded the game's maximum dungeon depth, he received between 450 and 500 registrations – approximately $4,500–$5,000 – for something that took the equivalent of several months of full-time work to create.

Other Mac-based shareware authors faced similar problems, such as *The Dungeon of Doom* (1985) creator John Raymonds and Kansas-based developer John Calhoun – whose paper-airplane puzzler *Glider* (1988), rollerball-style arena combat game *Pararena* (1990), and *Joust*-like game *Glypha* (1990) were among the most popular titles on the system. A few gained commercial publishing

deals off their shareware games – as indeed did Calhoun, with both *Glider* and *Pararena*, as well as Raymonds, and *Crystal Raider* (1985) author Patrick Buckland, whose obscure arcade-style action game was jazzed up and renamed *Crystal Quest* (1987) on the path to becoming one of the bestselling retail computer games of the era.

Many made enough money for their shareware game to serve as a summer job during college or to pay for the occasional 'pizza and beer' night. For the likes of Calhoun and his hero Duane Blehm, who'd made an immensely popular drop-a-man-from-a-helicopter-into-a-moving-haywagon shareware game called *StuntCopter* (1987), this was fine – they were having fun and their games inspired people. But exceptions to the 'pizza and beer' money rule were few and far between.

One pair of brothers even decided to make light of the low revenues shareware games generated. Computer science Ph.D. student Randy Wilson and his younger brother Brian had created space-themed action puzzler *Continuum* over a couple of years, beginning in 1984, and sold it to publisher Brøderbund, whereupon it was ported (badly) to Commodore 64 and released as *Magnetron* in 1987.

The brothers wanted their lovingly crafted Mac original out in the world, with its pixel-perfect collision detection, gravity-based movement, and easy-to-use level editor, but they were wary of publishing it commercially again. So when Brøderbund agreed to return the rights to them, they decided to self-publish the game. But not as shareware, because they believed that nobody paid for shareware. No, they thought, it'll be funny to sell this as 'beerware' – complete with a tongue-in-cheek copyright notice that requested players who enjoyed the game send Randy a case of fine beer or, failing that, alternative payments such as money, 'promises of firstborn, or foot rubs administered with suitably exotic oils'.

'We thought it was very clear that this was a joke,' Randy told me in an interview for *The Secret History of Mac Gaming*. 'We thought, sure, we might have a couple of friends bring over a six-pack of beer, but we ended up collecting about $5,000 worth of beer over the coming five or six years.'

Pass the hat

Over in the more populous world of IBM PC-compatible systems, shareware games were similarly situated as the realm of the hobbyist game makers.

One of the earliest titles was a 1985 *Donkey Kong*-style platform game called *Willy the Worm*, which swapped Mario (or Jumpman, as he was originally known) for a worm and Donkey Kong for a bell. Players could bounce on springs, collect presents, and climb ladders as they scrambled back and forth across each level.

Creator Alan Farmer had built this as a homage to a game called *Ladder* that he'd found on a CP/M 'luggable' (it folded into the shape of a large suitcase) computer his dad had brought home for a few days in 1982. Initially he'd written *Willy the Worm* for his own enjoyment on a RadioShack Color Computer, but he later decided to rewrite it for MS-DOS after he learned about the concept of shareware – though he didn't know it was called that, as the games he'd been downloading from a local BBS simply asked for donations and the only magazine article he'd seen about the idea was a 1984 *Rainbow* advertorial for a program called Spell 'n Fix II, which was marketed as 'pass-the-hat software'.

Willy the Worm's DOS version was hand-tuned to the clock speed of Farmer's IBM PCjr, making it run much too fast on anything more powerful – which any new IBM PC machine would have been in 1985. And it had simple, rudimentary graphics made from editing the PC's ASCII character set. But it spread like wildfire

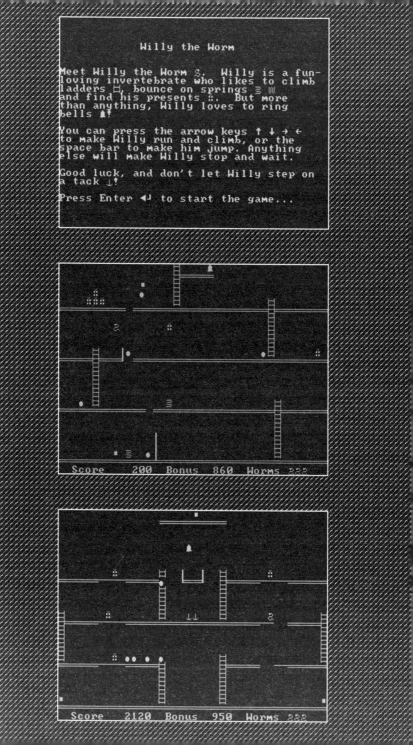

through the PC community, hopping from one bulletin board to the next – perhaps, Farmer reflects, because most boards required that you upload something before you could download something.

Farmer's request of a $10 donation from players who enjoyed the game translated into around $3,000 in earnings over the following several years, with cheques arriving from all around the US and Canada as well as from various European nations, Australia, South America, Tokyo, and even one from Botswana. It wasn't anywhere near enough to live off, but the income allowed Farmer to buy an IBM PC clone to take with him to college and it encouraged him to put out several other games – some sold as shareware, others published in *Big Blue Disk*, and one title presented as a sequel to *Willy the Worm*, but none gained much traction or notoriety. He soon shifted his attention to forging a career writing more practical kinds of software as a journeyman professional programmer hopping around different companies and software industries.

Around the same time that *Willy the Worm* fever captured the wider BBS userbase, a very different game called *CROBOTS* (pronounced See-Robots) was making the rounds among tech-heads.

CROBOTS was a programming game. Players would write simple C language code that instructed a virtual robot in how to seek out and destroy other robots in a textmode battlefield. Up to four robots could compete per match, each equipped with identical weapons, defences, and abilities – and either the same or different robot programs could be selected to guide their actions.

Creator Tom Poindexter had not initially intended to make a programming game at all. Rather, he explains, he wanted 'to learn more about compilers and the tools typically used in writing compilers' for the C programming language. (A compiler is a program that converts human-readable code into machine code instructions that a computer processor can understand.) And he was particularly focused on studying the Yacc (Yet Another Compiler-Compiler) grammar for C that was posted in Usenet group net.sources in January 1985.

He had started by inserting printf() statements everywhere in the C Yacc grammar, to 'print' to the screen what information was available and to help him visualise how code in C gets parsed by a compiler. But then he had a revelation: 'I could probably write a clone of the Apple II *RobotWar* game (of which I was a big fan), but using a "real language"', he recalls.

He had no concrete plans, nor any certainty that he'd succeed in this endeavour, but he soon figured out a core design for his game. He'd write a virtual machine to run a player's code, he decided, and he could omit several common elements of C – such as strings, arrays, do-while loops, and pointers – from his implementation to simplify both the design and the complexity of his own code.

Then it was a whole lot of trial and error, as with developing any game, whereby he had to test, tweak, and refine different values and ideas for robot movement and missile damage and everything else. 'This took a lot of time and testing,' he recalls, 'before I was satisfied that I had a decent balance between attacking and evasion.'

When he was done, Poindexter uploaded it to a couple of DOS BBSs and to a free software archive called Simtel. Any players who booted the game up would be met by an introductory screen with the extended title *CROBOTS – fighting robots C compiler and virtual computer*, along with a minor twist on the usual shareware notice of the era. Like most shareware programs from the time, it declared people 'should' pay the author if they chose to keep the software, and it explicitly encouraged copying and distribution (provided it remained unchanged). But Poindexter also offered to send a copy of his source code to anyone who donated at least $20.

'I liked the idea of sharing the source code,' he explains, 'but I still wanted to retain the copyright.' And if he made some money along the way, all the better – that'd help recoup a portion of the money he'd spent on his PC.

CROBOTS quickly spread through the BBS community, picking up some buzz along the way. People were excited at the thought of a game that taught programming. A year or so later one fan ported it to Amiga, while many others would in the next several years make their own derivative versions from scratch, much like Poindexter had done in adapting *RobotWar*. Poindexter even made a bit of money along the way. 'I recall earning several hundred dollars the first two years,' he says, adding that he tripled his takings in 1987 when Japanese magazine *ASCII* commissioned him to write three articles about the game that they would translate for their readers. (There was one general article on its form and function, another on its compiler and virtual machine, and a third on its physics and design.)

Another early test case for original shareware game publishing was Robert Sanborn's detective puzzler *The Sam Spade Game*, which was first released in December 1985. Players took the role of a private detective travelling around town trying to solve a case. 'It could be a housewife looking for her two-timing husband or "Three-fingered" Louie looking for his missing bag man,' the introduction teased. 'You don't really care because you're in this dirty business only for the cash.'

The flow of the game basically went as follows: get a case, with an advance to cover expenses and a deadline by which it must be solved, then select places around town to travel to (via one of a few different modes of transport, each with different time and monetary cost). In each visit to a location players could search for clues and talk to whoever was around, bribing them if necessary, in an effort to solve the mystery before time ran out.

There was just one case included in the initial shareware

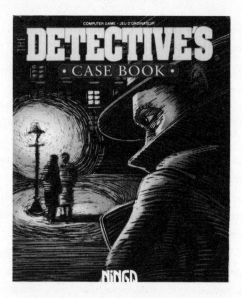

release: a stockbroker's business partner, Charlie, is dead and police ruled it a suicide, but his friends think otherwise, and some key stock certificates are missing. Who killed Charlie and where are the certificates?

Sanborn asked for payment of $10 if you enjoyed it or $25 for a pack of bonus content – namely ten (actually over a dozen) more case files, the game manual, and the latest update. He recalls that a few hundred people contacted him over the following several years. Many sent money. Depending on the person replying, he adds, he even sent the case files to some who didn't.

He was also contacted by several different disk vendors and shareware distributors to ask for permission to redistribute his game in their catalogues, but rarely did he ever learn of their sales – and so he had little knowledge of the total number of unregistered users. (That said, though, his records show that one distributor, Ninja Software, sold over 2,000 copies under the alternative title *Detective's Case Book* before they removed the game from their catalogue in 1992.)

Tommy's toy chest

One early developer got around the low profitability of shareware games by focusing instead on volume. T. L. Winslow, who operated under the name Tommy's Toys, was perhaps the most prolific shareware author of all time – outdoing even the top shareware publishing companies on rate of output.

Winslow had graduated with an electrical engineering degree in 1976 and moved into creating embedded systems – first for aerospace technology company McDonnell Douglas Astronautics and then on US Air Force systems for TRW. But after several years in the field he wanted out.

'I realised I didn't want to spend my career working for somebody else eighty hours a week to produce some state-of-the-art project that became obsolete in five years,' he says. Worse, he noticed that the older engineers tended to be either 'miserable overworked losers' or soulless management husks who'd become obsolete in their original careers.

'So when the IBM PC came out, I, along with thousands of others, saw a big opportunity to become an entrepreneur.' The only trouble was he couldn't find an investor willing to support his ideas and talents (which came with a penchant for grandiosity, as he was truly 'the World's Greatest Programmer'). Shareware, however, offered an alternative route.

Winslow decided he'd make simple, little games in a variant of BASIC called QuickBASIC, which allowed him to work much faster than the more powerful C programming language, and which included convenient features like built-in sound effects and easy programming of function-key toggles.

He was an 'obsessively private' person who didn't want his real name known, so he invented a persona called Tommy – an alien whose spaceship had crashed somewhere in downtown Denver (near where Winslow lived), and who now lived with his crew in some anonymous human's basement. With the US Government denying the existence of extra-terrestrial beings, Tommy had no choice but to enter a field in which he could remain incognito: software toys.

Thus began a nearly 13-year obsession, from early 1985 to late 1997, in which Winslow – always working alone – would publish over 200 games. 'I was never a good businessman,' he recalls, 'but always had my nose in code and spent 10–12 hours a day at the computer.' Sometimes he'd lose track of time and forget to eat or shower, and when shaving became an unnecessary nuisance he grew a beard.

His Tommy's Toys programs were an assortment of word, card, mind, and action puzzle games. One, *Tommy's Towers*, took chess and scaled it up from an 8x8 board with 16 pieces on each side to 20x50 with 300 pieces each. In addition to the usual six-piece types there were numerous others with similar movement rules, but then also there were special pieces like bridges – which could only be crossed in the direction they were laid; and cannons – which fired through hills (another special piece type).

Another, *Tommy's Old Maid*, was a straightforward computer rendition of the children's card game Old Maid. Similarly, *Tommy's Hanoi*, *Tommy's Monopoly*, *Tommy's Euchre*, *Tommy's Gin Rummy*, and various others were all based on their real-world equivalents, while *Tommy's Ant Farm* involved controlling an ant as it sneaks past soldier ants and the queen from a rival colony to steal their eggs.

Winslow could crank these games out in as little as a few days, if he was particularly inspired, with ideas popping into his mind at all different times and added to a list that peaked at 500 concepts. 'I never knew which toy I would program next,' he recalls. 'It would just come to me when the time came.'

Money trickled in as he went along – never anything close to enough to get rich, but enough that he could support himself

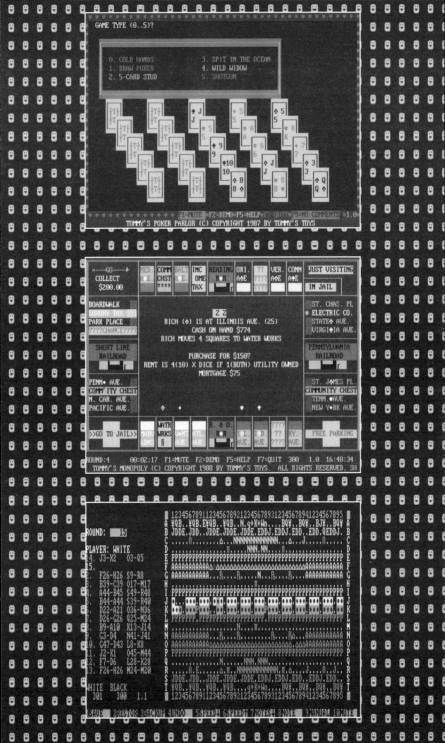

entirely from this Tommy's Toys enterprise. His approach differed from the shareware norm, though. He hated paperwork, so he avoided asking for registrations and instead nagged freeloaders with a start-up delay countdown unless they sent him $6 for one game, $5 per game for at least three games, or $50 for a pack of fifteen games.

> The big goal was to sell toy chests with the entire line for $360 in a floppy disk chest with my logo on the lid. I'd include all kinds of free bonuses like packs of cards, dice, dominoes, and anything I could get from local toy stores on sale, and usually threw in a paperback copy of *According to Hoyle*. I always had a standing offer to get a free toy for reporting a bug in any toy, and purposely left a big bug in my solitaire game so that I could try to hook them on buying more toys.

To what extent it worked isn't clear, but Winslow's prolific output meant that he needed no job other than Tommy's Toys through the entire life of the product line – which he stopped developing in 1998 and finally retired after the September 11, 2001 terrorist attacks on the World Trade Center, whereupon he turned to writing history articles instead.

Dream games

Less prolific shareware game makers in the 1980s struggled to earn anything more than a hobbyist income from the craft, however. Even Michael Denio, creator of the widely played, highly influential *Super Mario*-style platformer *The Adventures of Captain Comic* (1988), never came close to earning enough money to quit his job as an engineer at Texas Instruments.

Captain Comic was a complete version of a prototype game called *The Adventures of Captain Pixel of the Galactic Security Patrol in 34010 AD*, which Denio had programmed in 1987 for a TMS34010 'Flippy' graphics card (with graphics by Anthony R. Henderson). After completing the prototype, Denio had wondered whether it would be possible to create a high-quality arcade-style game like *Captain Pixel* using just a standard IBM PC with its built-in EGA card, and furthermore whether it would be possible to make any money from doing so.

Captain Comic conquered the technical challenge with aplomb, presenting a bright and colourful scrolling world with a large, double-height, sprite-animated character who could leap between platforms, run across the screen, shoot at enemies, gather items and power-ups, and more. Controlling the titular hero Captain Comic, players had to recover three treasures from the planet Omsoc (Cosmo backwards) that were stolen and hidden on the remote world of Tambi (a reference to the IBM AT, the IBM PC model introduced alongside the EGA card in 1984).

The world was non-linear and large (for the time), with multiple viable routes to completion and graphics that changed as the player moved into different areas. It wasn't a match for the very best platformers of the day, but it rivalled all the rest – with just one key difference: unlike those other games, which (apart from 1986 Mac game *Dark Castle*) benefitted from specialised graphics processors and dedicated video game hardware, *it worked on a PC*. And it was notably also the first DOS shareware game to have large, animated sprites (which similarly were common in commercial games and had been established earlier on the Mac shareware side by *Cap'n Magneto*).

For these reasons, it was a revelation – a monumental, platform-defining moment with far-reaching implications. Its reach extended so far that technology journalist and historian

Benj Edwards would rank it the 12th-greatest shareware game of all time in a 2012 *PC World* article. Here, for the very first time, was a DOS game that looked like something made for the Nintendo Entertainment System.

And it was free – or close to it, with only a note in the readme file 'comic.doc' declaring it as shareware and noting that 'if you enjoy playing *Captain Comic*, you are encouraged to register yourself as a user with a $10 to $20 contribution'. (Registered players received Denio's home phone number and the promise of being 'first in line' for any new *Comic* adventures, neither of which served as much incentive to the masses of people who played the game without paying for it.)

'I was totally unprepared for its popularity,' Denio admits, confessing that he made 'very little money' from the game, its NES port, and its 1990 DOS sequel (a groundbreaking commercial effort that included a hub world, eight-directional scrolling, and a raft of other innovations), 'but it fulfilled a childhood dream to write a video game.'

Dreams fulfilled was indeed a common reason for making a shareware game. And for one game, 1989 Mac point-and-click mystery-adventure *Caper in the Castro*, quite possibly the first gay-and-lesbian-themed computer game ever made, it was a dream fulfilled for the community that played and supported the game. An article published in the LGBTIQ-focused *Washington Blade* newspaper soon after its release enthusiastically pondered the wider ramifications of the game. The author wrote of hopes that it would lead to others creating whole genres of games that reflected women's values, and to 'consciousness-raising role-playing games like "Teen Pregnancy" or "Patriarchy", where each player is required to alternate between characters of different genders and sexual orientations.'

It was a historical milestone for the games industry – a game about a lesbian detective searching for her missing drag-queen

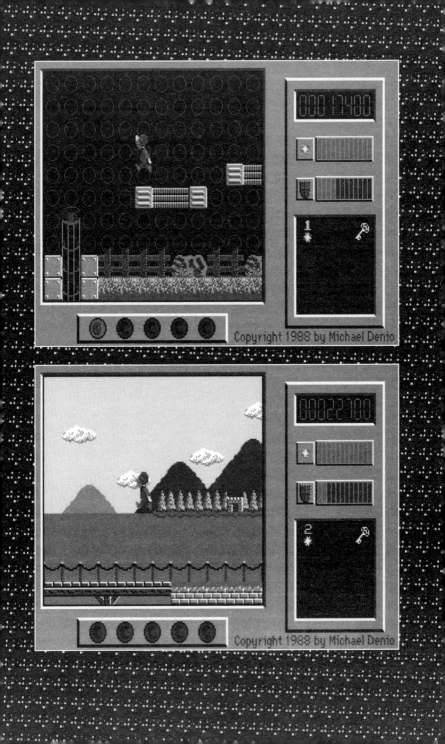

Copyright 1988 by Michael Denio

Copyright 1988 by Michael Denio

friend, created by non-binary transgender person C. M. Ralph (who at the time identified as a lesbian woman). It had references to the 1980s AIDS epidemic, and to the LGBTIQ communities of Southern California – where Ralph had lived prior to making the game – and San Francisco – where Ralph lived while creating the game.

Ralph worked at the time as a precision mechanical inspector for a medical device manufacturer in Silicon Valley, and in their spare time, like many other technologists of the era, they liked to explore the wonders of personal computing. This had manifested in learning and experimenting with Apple's HyperCard, a database-driven software authoring tool that used the metaphor of stacks of cards. A card could contain buttons, formatted text, graphics, animations, checkboxes, and a variety of other kinds of interactive and non-interactive content, and objects could be assigned 'hyperlinks' – much like the links on a present-day web page – to other objects or cards.

People made all sorts of things with HyperCard, which could be used to build functioning software without typing a single line of code. (For those who needed it, HyperCard also offered advanced functionality via a scripting language that used a sentence-like natural-language syntax.) There were recipe managers, company and household budgets, digital catalogues, interactive tutorials, and much more. Many people even figured out how to make HyperCard games, some of which ended up being published commercially. (One HyperCard game, *Myst*, would become the bestselling computer game of the 1990s.)

Ralph joined the ranks of the HyperCard game makers who liked to push the limits of the software's capabilities. They'd work on it during weekends and evenings after work, improvising characters, dialogue, in-jokes, and plotlines as they went. After a year, it was done.

Ralph released *Caper in the Castro* as 'charityware', which had been emerging among civic-minded authors as an alternative to the traditional shareware model. Instead of paying a fee to the creator, players would be encouraged to donate to a particular charity – 'any AIDS charity of your choice', in the case of *Caper*. (There was also a one-time variant of this charityware model called 'ReliefWare', which Apple IIGS developer Ken Franklin later used to raise $6,000 for homeless relief in Clarkesville, Tennessee, whereby the money was collected by the author and *then* donated.)

Caper in the Castro was shared widely within the American LGBTIQ community, spreading primarily via BBSs, but also through computer users groups around the US. At one point someone took a copy of the game with them on a business trip to London, where it began a second viral spread – this time around the UK and Europe.

Like all shareware, its exact reach is impossible to measure, and its distribution as charityware makes it hard to even estimate such numbers, but Ralph and a friend later guessed, from looking at BBS download statistics, that it may have received as many as a quarter of a million downloads over a five-year period.

Whichever way you look at it, though, *Caper in the Castro* was a resounding success. It helped drive the emergence of new kinds of games, made by a wider range of developers, and it reached an audience that wasn't just underserved by games but unrecognised by the medium as a whole.

But for those trying to make a business in shareware games, rather than pursuing social impact or personal development goals, the standard model just didn't seem to be viable. Shareware would have to change before shareware games could meet their full potential.

```
                    *** *** ***
-----------------   *  * **   *      -----------------
| THE ASSASSINS PRESENT |  ****  ***   *      | PD GAMES  VOLUME 01 |
-----------------   *  *   * *       -----------------
                    *  **  * *
                    *  * *** ***
```

ONCE AGAIN WE PRESENT TO YOU ANOTHER GREAT COLLECTION OF SOME OF THE BEST
GAMES AVAILABLE FROM WITHIN THE PUBLIC DOMAIN/SHAREWARE MARKET. WE HOPE
YOU ENJOY THE GAMES ON THIS DISK, AND WHERE POSSIBLE, WE HAVE TRIED TO
INCLUDE ALL THE DOC'S FILES OR INSTRUCTIONS ETC. ALL WE ASK IS THAT YOU
FOLLOW ANY REQUESTS OF THE WRITERS OF ALL THE PROGRAMS ON THIS DISK AND
                SUPPORT ANY SHAREWARE TITLES...ENJOY.

```
**************************************************************
*    The complete ASSASSINS games collection are available   *
*     FROM OUR OWN DISTRIBUTER AT THE FOLLOWING ADDRESS       *
*                                                             *
*                         STU.                                *
*                   32 RIPLEY AVENUE                          *
*                    NORTH SHIELDS                            *
*                    TYNE & WEAR                              *
*                      NE29 7SA                               *
*                                                             *
*   ALSO ASK ABOUT THE SPECIAL RE-PACKED A1200 COMPILATIONS   *
**************************************************************
```

Please note that some of the games on this pack may not be A1200
Compatible. To ensure that the packs you want are compatible for
this machine ask about the ASI NEW WAVE PACKS on which there are
only A1200 compatible games...

CHAPTER 4

Licenceware

Shareware in its early years struggled to gain a foothold in the UK, and doubly so for games. The reason was in part an economic one, driven by the UK's 1980s recession. But it was also a logistical issue, as most shareware authors were in the US and international payments were complicated.

Most of all it was a culture gap. The American and British personal computer markets had a very different character – and very different machines – at the time of shareware's invention. By 1984, the dominant systems in the US were the IBM PC, Commodore 64, Apple II, and Atari 800, with the IBM PC, Mac, and Amiga (together with a fast-declining Apple II) leading the market by the close of the decade. But in the UK it was the Sinclair ZX81 and ZX Spectrum, Acorn's BBC Micro, and the Commodore 64 that led the charge, with the Amiga, Atari ST, and Amstrad CPC surging in the latter half of the 1980s and the PC only racing ahead in the 90s.

These machines had different demographics. The UK's first mass-market machine, the ZX81, was a fraction of the cost of even the budget-oriented Commodore 64 (often called the C64), and as such it was bought by people across a broad spectrum of the British public – from wealthy upmarket customers down to the working-class masses. The ZX81 and its bestselling ZX Spectrum successor were seen as learning tools – a chance for even the most novice of computer users to tinker and play and acquaint themselves with the emerging technology revolution.

The Commodore 64 and its predecessor the VIC-20 had a similar learning-oriented placement in the US market, but the lower cost of Sinclair's systems meant they met a wider demographic and had reduced capabilities compared with Commodore's systems. As such, their use was even more deeply rooted in do-it-yourself computing – in typing programs directly out of magazines and tinkering with BASIC to learn programming – and in sharing.

A British commercial games scene quickly built up, with games typically sold for just a few pounds each, driven by hobbyist adults and teenagers in their bedrooms – many of whom self-published on self-duplicated tapes and floppies that they sold via mail order and at microfairs (regional computer fairs). This scene gradually splintered into budget games, which followed much the same formula (but later increased in price to £5–£15), and 'full-price' games that cost upwards of several pounds on cassette or something in the region of £15–£25 (later more like £25–£35) on disk. In parallel there also emerged a public-domain software scene – where everyday punters lacking the confidence or wherewithal to go commercial would share their work via small software libraries, excited just to have other people enjoy it, on the proviso that *nobody* turned a profit from the exchange.

When shareware took off Stateside, it was viewed in the UK as a curiosity: scoffed at as a strange, impractical, doomed-to-fail effort to tap into a collective goodwill that didn't exist. The whole motivation to pay for a program, the reasoning went, was to get a copy of it – and even then most people would circumvent the whole 'paying' thing and instead pirate it via a friend of a friend of a friend who'd received a complimentary copy. Why pay for something you can get for free?

Part of the problem, also, was the *act* of payment. If the majority of high-quality shareware was made outside of the UK, and only a fraction of it ever got picked up by local distributors (who could act as middlemen for registrations), then it fell to the individual to figure out how to pay their shareware fee. This was no simple feat for a program from overseas, both then in the 1980s and extending well into the 1990s. *ST Review* contributor Nial Grimes would sum up the sentiment well in a March 1994 opinion piece:

> The simple fact is, the hassle involved in registering shareware is frightening beyond belief. To buy a commercial package, you simply pick up the phone, say the magic 'VISA' word and relax, safe in the knowledge that your software will arrive two days later. What about popular German shareware? Perhaps exchange some currency, put the cash in an envelope and hope that you get something back within six months?

It hardly seemed worth the bother. And without mindshare for the concept, or a proven precedent for it working outside the US, most UK-based developers didn't see the point in trying. (It probably didn't help, either, that shareware was primarily a PC and Mac thing, and PCs weren't the leading home computer in the UK until well into the 1990s.)

Those few British game developers who *did* try shareware in these early years brought in little more than a slow trickle of registrations. Take, for instance, Nick Harper's 1989 Atari ST puzzle-platformer *Ozone*. It had the look, feel, and sound of a commercial game, and indeed it very nearly was one – until the publishers he'd submitted it to realised it was made with STOS BASIC. (Sidenote, to emphasise how ridiculous this anti-STOS attitude was: Harper later entered the industry as a designer at

Psygnosis, then went on to work in creative/design director roles on multiple Codemasters and Ubisoft games.)

Even a glowing review and coverdisk inclusion in *ST Format* three years later failed to give the game any meaningful sales momentum. Harper later told *Atari Legend* that he earned maybe £250 for the game in its lifetime, despite the likelihood that tens of thousands of people had installed it on their machines.

Word quickly got around among programmers that shareware games didn't sell, so most non-professional developers in the UK and Europe instead tried to make their mark via the public-domain (PD) and demoscene talent pipeline. This was a thriving hotbed of talent, filled with a mix of new-to-programming amateurs, gifted hobbyists, best-in-class hackers, and wannabe-pros all coalesced into one. So strong was its reputation as a talent incubator that it became the standard route to professional game development.

An emerging programmer, artist, or composer (or a cross-disciplinary team) would release technically brilliant small-scale projects in the hopes that they'd get noticed and hired to work for established software houses. And to support this ecosystem there were dozens of public-domain software vendors and libraries that would collect these programs and collate them onto disk collections that they'd then sell at, or close to, cost. (The Fred Fish Disks covered in Chapter 2 was one such library.)

Some PD outfits grew rapidly, and one of the best-known was called 17-Bit Software (with the motto 'That bit better than the rest'). They'd started out in 1987 as an entrepreneurial endeavour by Michael Robinson, the owner of a (then) small chain of computer retail shops called Microbyte, with help from one of his shop managers, Martyn Brown. Robinson figured that he could use the software label to recruit talented young developers and sell their games through Microbyte stores, and Brown was a big Amiga fan – so they set their focus there.

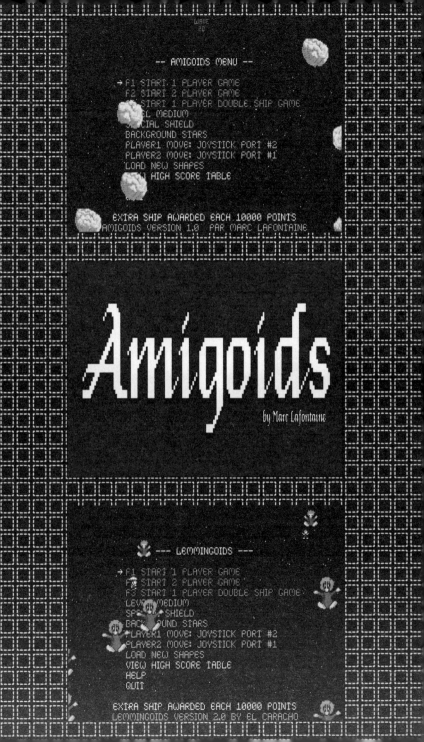

WAVE
20

-- AMIGOIDS MENU --

→ F1 START 1 PLAYER GAME
  F2 START 2 PLAYER GAME
     START 1 PLAYER DOUBLE SHIP GAME
  EL MEDIUM
  IAL SHIELD
  BACKGROUND STARS
  PLAYER1 MOVE: JOYSTICK PORT #2
  PLAYER2 MOVE: JOYSTICK PORT #1
  LOAD NEW SHAPES
  W HIGH SCORE TABLE

  EXTRA SHIP AWARDED EACH 10000 POINTS
AMIGOIDS VERSION 1.0 PAR MARC LAFONTAINE

Amigoids

by Marc Lafontaine

--- LEMMINGOIDS ---

→ F1 START 1 PLAYER GAME
  F2 START 2 PLAYER GAME
  F3 START 1 PLAYER DOUBLE SHIP GAME
  LEVEL MEDIUM
  SPE   SHIELD
  BACK OUND STARS
  PLAYER1 MOVE: JOYSTICK PORT #2
  PLAYER2 MOVE: JOYSTICK PORT #1
  LOAD NEW SHAPES
  VIEW HIGH SCORE TABLE
  HELP
  QUIT

  EXTRA SHIP AWARDED EACH 10000 POINTS
LEMMINGOIDS VERSION 2.0 BY EL CARACHO

Like most PD groups, they took ads in magazines both to encourage submissions from emerging programmers and to sell disks directly to readers. They'd also regularly send free disks to magazine editors in the hopes of a review of one or more of their new programs in special two-to-four-page PD software sections. Most months they'd get at least one of their programs (usually a game, but sometimes a utility) reviewed, and in this way they steadily built up a reputation as one of the finest purveyors of PD software.

They were hardly the only company in PD games publishing with a reputation for quality, however. The most popular and highest-regarded PD group (from late 1991 onwards) was composed of four friends – named Arty Carhart, Bill Woodcock, Bryan King, and Stu Morton – who together called themselves The Assassins. Their disk compilations contained primarily the work of other people, often plucked from magazine coverdisks, although occasionally they had something original to show off. And their platform of choice was the Amiga, although the group had formed when King and Carhart met through mutual friends in the Commodore 64 scene. (The other two joined a little later through correspondence within the Amiga scene.)

They'd bonded over a shared disappointment with the quality of PD disks on the market – not so much through subpar games and utilities, but rather because the prices seemed too high for the content being delivered. They wanted disks filled to capacity, and they believed everything on there should be of outstanding quality. And they were determined to meet these goals. Every. Single. Time.

Sometimes that meant two games, sometimes six, but usually somewhere in between, and always it meant a custom menu screen with background music and a cropped screenshot of each game in the compilation.

Their first disk contained five programs: artillery game *Tanx* offered randomly generated landscapes and required that players consider wind speeds as well as gravity in calculating the power and trajectory of their shots; while *Amigoids* riffed on *Asteroids*; *Rollerpede* adapted *Centipede*; *Cave Runner* cloned *Boulderdash*; and *Avatris* made a three-player game out of *Tetris*. Magazine *CU Amiga* gave it five stars and labelled it both 'one of the best game collections currently available' and an 'immensely playable' collection that 'could easily hold its own against full-priced software'. *Amiga Action* agreed, calling it a 'wicked selection'.

Quickly The Assassins forged a reputation for pulling together the best in PD games (plus the occasional shareware gem, like Othello clone *Flip-It*). Amiga magazines set aside space in their PD reviews section nearly every month to cover the latest Assassins release. Even when the disks were deemed to fall short, reviewers often recommended Assassins releases – such as in the case of volume 22 from mid-1992, which included four games, two of which *The One Amiga* rated mediocre. However, the disk also included a third they thought decent, and one, *Wizzy's Quest*, a platformer about a wizard's apprentice who must protect his absent-minded master, that was considered essential playing. 'Tarted up a bit this could easily pass for a full-price release,' said the review. 'Don't miss it.'

More remarkable than the fact that they consistently put out high-quality disks packed with games (of which at least one was superb) was that they did so for next to no money. Assassins disks bought direct from the team were sold barely above cost, and being PD software their income from other sources was non-existent. They weren't much concerned, though. 'Basically we're just a group of friends who enjoy what we do,' Woodcock told *Amiga Action* in 1994. 'We're not out to rip off the public by selling inferior merchandise at inflated prices. We see ourselves as more of a club.'

Shareware may have struggled to catch on in the Amiga and Atari ST scenes, but clearly the PD model suited Britons (and Europeans) well.

Yet a tension slowly began to build among PD software creators and publishers. Most PD game authors earned nothing from their work, while many PD libraries turned a tidy profit – selling at prices beyond the material cost of disk duplication, packaging, and postage. Running the libraries cost significant time, however, and defenders of this practice argued that it was therefore reasonable that their sales margins include a cut for the library staff. But then, critics of the practice would counter, the same goes for making PD software – which takes weeks or months of work on expensive hardware. And in any case, they'd point out, if one person is making money from PD games then it's only fair that *everyone* involved in their creation and distribution chain does.

Purists shot both sides down. PD software was fundamentally rooted in the hacker ethic. It was supposed to be free. Not *close* to free but *entirely* free. Their words fell on deaf ears. The cat was out of the proverbial bag. 'More and more these days,' a June 1991 *Amiga Computing* cover story noted with disdain, 'this principle seems to be lost.'

17-Bit's success was a fine example of the problem. In the early days, they had the same vibe of a bootstrapped, extemporaneous operation as everyone else. But quickly they ballooned in size and scale. By February 1988 they boasted a library of 40 disks. By June 1991 that had climbed to around 1,500 (of which two-thirds had been compiled in-house from developer submissions), with permanent office space for a full-time staff of five and a whopping 19,000 subscribers (which jumped to 22,000 within a few months). These numbers made many observers suspicious, thinking the team at 17-Bit must be getting rich off the scheme.

On the contrary, 17-Bit's Martyn Brown told *Amiga Computing*: the £1.50 they charged for most disk sales didn't generate much profit. Nearly half the sale price alone was accounted for by material costs, while the remaining 80p had to cover lighting, heating, phone, wages, advertising, and other day-to-day costs – to the extent where they had to sell 85,715 disks a year before they'd turn a profit.

But not all PD libraries operated on such tight margins. And year after year the number of PD libraries increased exponentially, with most drawn in by hopes of a quick and easy profit. The PD model wasn't broken, but it had a serious problem rotting away at its core.

Changing approach

A simple solution would have been to change the business model, but commercial sales models were the antithesis of PD ideals – which decreed that software should be free to acquire and distribute, or as close to it as possible – and nobody had any confidence in shareware.

In 1988, early in the emergence of this antithetical trend, one PD outfit had an idea for a new model that could retain much of the spirit of PD software while also allowing authors to make some token money for their efforts. They called it 'licenceware'.

It was the brainchild of the duo in charge of games-focused Atari ST PD group Budgie UK – Camy Maertens and Simon Rush. Their scheme entailed charging PD libraries a licence fee for every disk sold and controlling the means of distribution by allowing *only* those companies to sell the software. (In keeping with the tradition of PD software, buyers were at liberty to then pass the disk's contents on to a friend.)

Budgie would take a 15p–50p cut from each sale, depending on the contents of a disk, with disks typically priced around £3–£4. And a library had to pay out at least £15 per quarter – even if the earned royalties were less – or it would be removed from the scheme. Despite the strong language, Rush recalls that they never actually had the means to audit or verify the numbers a PD library sent them.

These payments would then be entirely dispersed to a game's author(s), despite the effort Maertens and Rush had to go through as middlemen.

Maertens and Rush even elected not to claim a share from sales of their own games. The royalties earned from each of their titles would instead be split among Budgie's other authors.

The rest of Budgie's contributors, meanwhile, had little chance of getting rich off the model. Indeed, typical author earnings in those early years of licenceware amounted to around £10 or £20 a month – hardly enough to live off, but enough that a hobbyist programmer could pay for a memory upgrade, a magazine subscription, or a nice night out. This would remain fairly consistent throughout the life of the company, with quarterly intake of £1,000–£1,700 across the Budgie UK catalogue of 130-plus titles come 1992.

Rush's *Football 88*, a soccer-management game, was the most popular title, from what they could tell. (Both Rush and Maertens later had stints as full-time developers of commercial soccer-management games, in separate companies, due to the letters of praise received for *Football 88*.) Other highly regarded licenceware games from Budgie include Paul Dowers's *International Cricket*, slot-machine game *Bandit* by Gary Wheaton and the Shapeshifters, platformer *Space Blob* by Robin Edwards, *Galaxian* variant *Annihilator* by Robert Leong, and a pair of original games from university student Andrew Oakley – who 'made a few quid every month for a few years' from his first title, *Ballpark*, which involved

FaST

The Fast ST Basic Users Group Presents:

FOOTBALL 88

Simon Rush. © 1988
LICENCEWARE   V1.01F

Program written using COMPUTER CONCEPTS FAST BASIC

FAST. 42 YORK ROAD, RAYLEIGH, ESSEX SS6 8SB.

Press Left Key On Mouse

Desk FILE STAFF GAMES PLAY OPTS

FOOTBALL 88

A NOTE FROM THE WRITER.
This is only a preview of what may be to come. If
you have any suggestions or critisms please write
to me at the address below.

SOME OF The final version plans are :-

1. Commentary on Match of the Day
2. Increase speed of play & use real names
3. Include scouts, trainees improvement schemes
4. Mid week games and All other cup competitions
5. Merge files for individual multi-playing
6. Free and Loan transfers
7. Pick any team you like
8. Make the Buy system fairer
9. Many more excellent play features

TIPS & INSTRUCTIONS see the READ_ME's

If you are interested in buying the full version
write now to add your support.

THIS IS A LICENSEWARE   PROGRAM
from : BUDGIE UK, 5 Minster Close, Rayleigh, Essex.

Press Left Key On Mouse

Desk FILE STAFF GAMES PLAY OPTS

LEAGUE TABLE DIVISION 4

Team	Pl	Home W	D	L	Away W	D	L	F	A	Pts
Torquay	2	2	0	0	0	0	0	6	0	6
Northampton	2	2	0	0	0	0	0	5	1	6
Preston	2	1	1	0	0	0	0	5	2	4
Hudersfld	2	1	0	0	0	1	0	4	2	4
Tranmere	2	0	0	0	1	1	0	3	1	4
Orient	2	1	0	0	0	1	0	3	1	4
Stockport	2	1	1	0	0	0	0	2	2	4
Crewe	2	1	1	0	0	0	0	2	2	4
Swansea	2	0	0	0	1	1	0	3	2	4
Rochdale	2	0	0	0	1	0	1	4	2	3
Southend	2	0	0	0	1	0	1	5	3	3
Scunthorpe	2	1	0	1	0	1	0	3	2	3
Peterboro	2	0	0	0	1	0	1	2	1	3
Hereford	2	0	0	0	1	0	1	2	3	3
Exeter	2	0	0	0	1	0	1	2	4	3
Cambridge	2	0	0	0	1	0	1	2	3	3
Wolves	2	0	1	1	0	0	0	2	2	1
Cardiff	2	0	1	1	0	0	0	1	2	1
Lincoln	2	0	1	0	0	0	1	2	4	1
Wrexham	2	0	0	0	0	1	1	2	3	1
Colchester	2	0	0	0	0	1	1	3	5	1
Burnley	2	0	0	1	0	1	0	1	1	1
Hartlepool	2	0	0	0	0	0	2	0	4	0
Halifax	2									

Press Left Key On Mouse

rolling a ball through a maze to a chequered end zone without getting eaten by a monster. He later had his moderately successful shareware ('well over a thousand pounds' in registrations) grid-escaping puzzler *Square Off* republished by Budgie with 50 extra levels and a level editor.

PD libraries had mixed reactions to the licenceware scheme. Some went along with it, like PD-Soft, Goodman PDL, and Softville PD, while others refused – complaining at the higher prices, extra logistical overhead, and especially its bastardisation of PD ideals. But British computer game magazines got behind the idea and gave licenceware games considerable coverage in their PD game sections.

Once the concept was proven, more licenceware groups sprang up – most notably Netherlands-based Amiga group United Graphic Artists (UGA), which pulled together some of the best talent in the Amiga scene across Europe and was world-renowned for offering commercial-grade collections of utilities; and (a little later, in 1992) Amiga games-focused group F1 Licenceware, which would remain active long after the Amiga was discontinued and quickly became the de-facto route to market for Amiga game programmers who couldn't or wouldn't get a commercial deal.

Many PD libraries started to publish their own licenceware products, such as the AMOS PD Library, while others continued to rant and rave. *CU Amiga* drew attention to the still-brewing controversy in their October 1992 issue, referencing the tired old arguments on each side and noting that the tide seemed to be turning in licenceware's favour – as even some PD libraries that had previously been complaining were now jumping on the licenceware bandwagon. Regardless, PD columnist Mat Broomfield promised that he'd continue reviewing licenceware products for as long as they remained priced 'significantly less' than traditional commercial software.

The Atari ST and Amiga establishment's begrudging acceptance of licenceware turned official in mid-1992 with the creation of the Central Licenceware Register (CLR for short). The CLR took care of the growing complexity of licenceware distribution. With several licenceware groups each on the Amiga and the Atari ST by that time, each setting their own prices and conditions of access, PD libraries had a lot to keep up with. But this CLR standardised the business. Now any library could offer licenceware products from any licenceware group (as long as they were signed up to the register) and everything was available under the same terms. Licenceware sold via the CLR had a fixed price of £3.50 for a one-disk program or £4.50 for a two-disk program, of which authors would receive £1 in royalties per sale.

Now only the 'PD should be free or sold at the cost of distribution' argument remained against licenceware. But in a world where both authors and PD library customers had made clear their fondness for the scheme, saying so was just screaming into the void.

While licenceware thrived on Amiga and Atari ST computers, it never caught on with other platforms. F1 Licenceware would briefly try in 1999, then abandon the idea due to lack of interest, while no one else really went for it.

But then they didn't need to, of course, because PC gamers had a shareware revolution of their own to celebrate, and it would prove much more influential and lucrative than anyone had imagined.

KINGDOM OF KROZ

A Scott Miller Production
_____

In your search for the priceless Amulet within the mystical Kingdom of Kroz
you have stumbled upon a secret passage leading into a strange land.   With
your worn lantern you journey forward void of fear,   sweat beading on your
forehead as you anticipate the great treasures. Undoubtedly, the Amulet is
guarded by unspeakable dangers. So armed only with a single whip and great
                 courage, you decide to journey onward...

       Use the cursor keys to move yourself (☻) through the kingdom.
         Use your whip (press W) to destroy all nearby creatures.
       You are on you own to discover what other mysteries await--some
                          helpful, others deadly...

              Would you like game instructions (Y/N)?

CHAPTER 5

The Apogee Model

Scott Miller had a problem. He wanted to take games seriously – to become a professional game developer – but the publishers he'd contacted weren't buying his stuff.

He had been immersed in computer games for years. He'd discovered the medium while living in Australia in the mid-1970s when his high school got a Wang 2200, one of the world's first all-in-one microcomputers. Bewitched by the magic he saw on the screen, he'd spent every moment he could learning how to make simple BASIC games rendered in ASCII graphics. He had painstakingly copied games from the pages of *Creative Computing* magazine, typing their code in line by line, until he knew how to create his own ideas from scratch, then he'd repeatedly sneaked back into school after hours to work on the machine uninterrupted.

'I was making my ideas sort of come to life,' he recalls. 'Creating my own digital worlds.' And it was his passion. But not his occupation.

In college (back in his native Texas, USA) at the beginning of the 1980s Miller had held a part-time job at a McDonald's-esque fast food restaurant called Water Burger, and he'd spent 'every spare penny' at the local arcades – playing *Space Invaders*, *Pac-Man*, *Asteroids*, *Donkey Kong*, *Defender*, and anything else he could get his hands on. He'd dropped out of college after his second year, whereupon games had become his entire life.

He would practise at the arcades on weekdays and compete in tournaments on weekends (some of which he won), and in 1982 he and his friend George Broussard had the idea to write a book – a strategy guide of sorts called *Shoot-Out: Zap the Video Games*. Both thought they would get rich off their royalties of $1 each per sale.

'I remember running the book's potential sales figures though my mind,' Miller later wrote. 'In each of the top 250 cities there must be at least an average of 10,000 game players, and if just 100 of them bought our book that would be 25,000 sales, plus in all the remaining cities we should count on at least 5 more books sold in each, which should add another 25,000 sales.'

In reality the book sold poorly, but it got Miller a new job – one that put his talents to better use. He was hired at the *Dallas Morning News*, the biggest newspaper in his home city, to write a weekly column about the world of video games. 'I was on everyone's list,' he said in a 2009 *Gamasutra* interview. If a new game came out, he'd know about it and he'd have a copy sent to him for review. Alongside that, he started to contribute freelance articles to various national magazines, such as *Compute!*. 'This was sort of my education,' he recalls, 'playing games, working in an arcade, writing about them.' He was thinking about them, deeply and critically – what works, what doesn't, and why. And making them on the side, too.

One day it occurred to him that he should be trying to become a professional game developer, so he started to send proposals and demos to publishers with ideas he thought they'd like. None took him on. He was a college dropout with no industry experience (other than writing *about* games, which counted for nothing), and the sorts of games he was making didn't appeal to them anyway. They wanted flashy graphics, cutting-edge technology – anything that would excite retail shoppers and magazine readers browsing for a cool, new game to buy. By contrast, Scott Miller was making a mix of ASCII-based action games and text adventures styled after the work of genre leader Infocom (creators of *Zork* and *A Mind Forever Voyaging*, among many other games).

Disheartened but not defeated, Miller sent his games to disk magazines like *I.B.Magezette* and *Big Blue Disk* – which actually did want ASCII-based games, because these worked on the widest range of computers and so wouldn't exclude any current or would-be subscribers. He could earn 'a couple hundred dollars' a game that way, often giving them six or twelve months' publishing exclusivity as part of the deal. He recalls one game he co-wrote with his friend Terry Nagy, a text adventure called *Supernova* (1986), made him around $1,000. It was decent money, but not enough to live off, and so when the rights reverted to him he looked at how else he could make money from the games.

Self-published retail seemed neither feasible nor practical, but shareware jumped out as an option. Lots of people on CompuServe and bulletin boards were publishing their games as shareware, so he decided to try that too, under the name Apogee Software Productions. But his shareware re-releases didn't yield any great gains either – they earned more than the disk magazines had paid, but not by much.

Unable to hold off any longer financially, Miller quit his job as a newspaper columnist (as well as his other job in the computer lab at the college he dropped out of) and took full-time work in tech support at a computer consulting company. He didn't give up his dream, however. Instead he started to look more seriously at self-publishing his work online. He hadn't earned much from his republishing-to-shareware experiments, but maybe it would work better for a new game that was purpose-built for shareware distribution?

Unsure, he did some research. 'A lot of people were making money in this market,' he recalls. 'But the common wisdom was that games weren't making any money in shareware.'

He did more research. Some shareware games were actually pretty good, he thought. Some even seemed close to commercial quality. Surely those authors must be making money?

'But when I contacted these authors, they said, yeah, we're not making any money,' Miller says. 'And so I was doing all this background work to figure out how I should release my stuff as shareware. And that's where I got the idea of, well, let's not release the whole game like everyone else is doing. Let's just release it as sort of a teaser.'

By breaking a game into three episodes and releasing one of them free, he reasoned, people would be enticed to pay for the other two. It was the best of both worlds. He could leverage shareware's virality *and* sell his games for a profit, relying not on honesty or altruism but simple supply and demand: he supplies an entertaining game, his players demand more content for said game. He called his concept 'the Apogee model', in a nod to his publishing label Apogee Software.

A brief aside here, for context: demos of commercial programs were still years away from becoming commonplace at this time, and they were almost unheard of as a marketing technique. Magazine coverdisks – those beloved bastions of the game demo – were just then emerging, but at that stage they mostly contained a mix of complete games and shareware utilities. It would be another few years before commercial publishers realised en masse that they could promote their games by sending in playable time- or content-limited demonstration builds. So, with no established precedent to point to and expand upon, this was a revolutionary concept that Scott Miller devised for selling his games. And it would have been a very risky one, too, if not for the fact that he had a well-paying job to support him should the experiment have failed.

Episodes of Kroz

Miller's first release under this new Apogee model would be a continuation of a series he'd already started. He'd sold *I.B.Magazette* two episodes of *Kroz* – *Caverns of Kroz* and *Dungeons of Kroz* – and now he decided that he would release the third one, *Kingdom of Kroz*, as shareware.

While the name came from reversing the spelling of text adventure *Zork*, *Kroz* took its initial inspiration from a now-forgotten action game called *Chase*. The central premise was to not get caught by the agent(s) chasing your character, and to do so you could move in such a way that their pursuit (always via the shortest possible route) would lead them onto one of the mines scattered around the level.

Having begun development by making a game similar to *Chase*, Miller then decided to expand it with ideas from the DOS port of 1980 ASCII-graphics, dungeon-crawling game *Rogue* (which is now better known through the 'roguelike' genre that spawned from its repeated imitation). He had poured many hours of his time into exploring the procedurally generated dungeons of *Rogue*, but he disliked its degree of randomness and its reliance upon luck to see players able to reach the end without dying for some stupid, unavoidable reason. He wanted his game to have the feel and depth of *Rogue* but to be more consistently winnable. It should blend the fast-paced action of the arcades with the thoughtful strategy and puzzle-solving of his favourite computer games.

In *Kingdom of Kroz*, the goal was to survive a journey through 25 underground chambers (plus 40 more in *Caverns of Kroz* and

30 in *Dungeons of Kroz*) in search of the Magical Amulet. Along the way, players would encounter large numbers of three different kinds of monsters – each of which would make a beeline towards them – and a variety of objects such as spells that would slow down monsters or teleport their character to a random position on the screen. They could also collect gems, which served as a kind of life force that would protect against monster attacks, and whips, which would destroy any monsters about to make their attack.

Each level was harder than the previous one, with more fiendish puzzles to solve or more unavoidable monsters to defeat, and some levels were even randomised like in *Rogue*. But where *Rogue* had allowed just one attempt at every playthrough, to prevent completion through memorisation, in the *Kroz* games the player could save at any time and reload if they died. Similarly, in *Rogue* the dangers of a level were entirely hidden at its commencement – as was the location even of its walls. But in *Kroz* a player could see the entire level and plot out a strategy before they began.

In a nod to his arcade roots, and in what was then a rare addition to a computer game, Miller also hid a secret mode in the game. If a player pressed the 'x' key before they left the title screen, they could start the game with extra gems and other supplies.

Like Miller's prior games, *Kroz* took its graphics from the standard IBM character set – comprised of all printable ASCII characters plus diacritics (accented letters), icons, line-drawing symbols, around a dozen characters from the Greek alphabet and several additional mathematical operators. The player's character was a smiley face, monsters were mostly Greek letters, and various blocks and other characters would represent different kinds of walls and objects.

Despite these rudimentary visuals, the game looked great. *Compute!* writer Orson Scott Card (author of sci-fi novel *Ender's*

Game) wrote in 1990 that 'you have to use your imagination a little more, but because Miller has been both clever and clear, you soon forget that you're looking at the standard character set.'

Would-be players could find *Kingdom of Kroz* on various BBS servers as well as on the CompuServe and America Online portals, or in the catalogues of various shareware disk vendors, which were encouraged to distribute the game and explicitly permitted to do so for their own profit. If a player finished the game or looked at the readme file they'd see a message that explained Miller's business model – complete with his mailing address where they could send their registration cheques. For $7.50, players could register the game – at which point they were able to buy additional episodes for $7.50 each. Alternatively, they could pay $20 in one go to register the game and buy both additional episodes as a trilogy set.

In addition to publishing the game as shareware, Miller submitted *Kingdom of Kroz* to the IBM PC category of Softdisk's CodeQuest '87, a national programming contest for Apple II, Commodore 64, and IBM PC compatibles. *Kroz* came second behind *Willy the Worm* creator Alan Farmer's The Compleat Filer, a file management program with user-friendly menus and a few advanced features. His prize was $500, a mention in *Big Blue Disk* #19, and inclusion of the game in *Big Blue Disk* #20 (June 1988) – which was perhaps more valuable than the money, as it put the game in the hands of thousands of potential customers for Miller's new Apogee model.

Much to his surprise, the Apogee model soon proved itself a smashing success. Miller estimates that he earned somewhere in the range of $80,000–$100,000 from *Kroz* sales. Most days he'd receive multiple orders, with a particularly large influx on Mondays.

While *Kroz* continued making waves around the DOS shareware circuit, Miller set to work expanding his catalogue.

He had his two old text adventures he could sell to these new fans who were pouring in, but he needed something else that followed his Apogee model. He thought trivia might do the trick, as it would be easy to make, it could be split neatly into multiple episodes, and it could run on any system that had DOS on it. 'I love the original *Star Trek*,' he explains, 'and at the time had seen each episode ten-plus times.' With the *Star Trek* films putting the franchise back in people's minds, he figured a *Trek*-themed trivia game had a good chance of success.

Rather than just three episodes, however, he made ten – each with 100 multiple-choice questions drawn from research through all the *Star Trek* literature he could get his hands on. For $4, players could register their copy of the shareware episode, *Trek Trivia – Volume 1*, with the promise of phone and written support, and they could buy additional volumes for $4 each (plus $2 per order 'to cover disks and postage') or order all ten for $30.

The whole set took him around two months of work to create, but over the next couple of years he estimates it earned him between $50,000 and $70,000. (Eventually it was removed from distribution because Paramount threatened legal action for unlicensed use of the *Star Trek* intellectual property.)

Miller had cracked the code to financial success in shareware game development, and it wasn't 'make better games'. It was 'give people a worthwhile incentive to pay when they already have the game'. Quality mattered, but it was the added incentive to pay that would drive higher revenues.

By 1990 he realised he was making so much money from running his shareware business that he didn't need his $30,000-a-year consulting job. His full-time occupation should be Apogee Software.

To support and grow his new livelihood, Miller needed to expand Apogee's catalogue at an even faster rate. This would entail a few things.

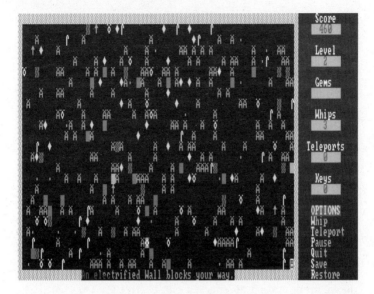

With the success of his *Kroz* trilogy, and the keenness of its fans for more levels to enjoy, it seemed natural to make another one. He released three more *Kroz* games, sold in the same format and packaged in the same core design, in June 1990: *Return to Kroz* (also published under the names *Shrine of Kroz* and *Castle of Kroz*), *Temple of Kroz* (also called *Valley of Kroz*), and *The Final Crusade of Kroz*. Together they comprised *The Super Kroz Trilogy*, and owners of the earlier games could purchase them as a set. But individually, in keeping with the Apogee model, only *Return to Kroz* was freely available.

The essence of the experience remained the same as the previous trilogy, except with 65 new levels for fans to enjoy (20 each for the first two episodes, plus 25 for the third).

And to help boost sales to his new customers, Miller also rewrote the original trilogy in a newer version of the Turbo Pascal programming language (5.0 rather than 3.0) to improve their performance and tune their design based on player feedback.

Once again Miller turned to disk magazines to boost his

distribution beyond the CompuServe and BBS circuit, and once again he found tremendous success – thousands of dollars a month and dozens of orders a week (50–60, typically, according to an October 1990 *Compute!* article written shortly after he'd given in to fan pressure and published a seventh and final *Kroz* game). But this alone wouldn't sustain Apogee long term, and he knew he was nearing the limits of his own abilities as a programmer. He needed to collaborate with other people.

Spreading the model

He started regularly dialling in to the virtual boards and identifying all the shareware authors who seemed like they had the talent to make a hit episodic game. Over the next few years, Miller would send letters to dozens of potential collaborators and pitch each of them on the idea of making a game that he'd market under the Apogee model.

Many took him up on the offer (and we'll get to some of them soon), but not all. *Captain Comic* creator Mike Denio was quick to turn him down, for instance. He preferred to do his own thing and stick with the security of his day job at Texas Instruments.

Likewise declining the offer was David Gray, whose adventure game *Hugo's House of Horrors* owed much to the existence of Denio's game.

'There weren't that many shareware games around at the time,' recalls Gray. 'And they were nearly all done using ASCII character graphics, not true graphics-card manipulation.' *Captain Comic*, with its big, fluid, animated, cartoony character sprites, had been a revelation to him.

Gray had been a programmer writing air traffic control software at the time, in 1988, and had just started a side business coding office apps – beginning with a touch-typing tutor program and an optical character-recognition utility. But he'd felt an itch to make games instead. He'd made computer games on scientific computers during his downtime at a previous job, so he knew he loved the process, and by luck he happened to meet a fellow called Nels Anderson at a party around this same time.

Anderson worked as a gynaecologist, but as a hobby he ran a BBS and made shareware DOS versions of games he'd enjoyed playing on other platforms. One, *EGA Trek* (1988), was an enhanced remake of the popular 1970s mainframe space strategy game *Trek*, with near-identical *Star Trek*-themed, sector-based combat and exploration but 16-colour EGA graphics to jazz things up. Another, *Mah Jongg* (1987), was a remake of Brodie Lockard's hit tile-matching game (*Mah-Jongg* on the PLATO system; *Shanghai* on personal computers). Both of Anderson's games were selling all around the world and making some decent money.

That was all the encouragement Gray needed. He decided he would make a game, 'and if it sold well,' he told himself, 'that would be a bonus.'

He turned to a Dover Publications book of monochrome-silhouette clip art for thematic inspiration. He decided to set his game in a haunted house after seeing a picture of one in the book, and he could draw on his love of the *Hammer House of Horror* British TV series and films to give it thematic colour. Next, he thought about the gameplay and quickly settled on something that imitated the design of Sierra On-Line's popular graphic-adventure game *Leisure Suit Larry in the Land of Lounge Lizards* (1987):

> [*Larry*] was exactly the kind of thing I wanted to do as it had large, cute characters that moved around, and the rudimentary artwork seemed like I could maybe attempt

something similar. The text parsing was right up my street; I knew I could do that. I hadn't played any other graphical adventure games at this point; it was my first introduction to the genre. I'd only played adventures using text before this: *Colossal Cave* and *Dungeon*.

His game would have static rooms that a player could walk their character around, typing simple verb-noun text commands like 'look at [object]' or 'talk to [object]' to interact with the scene, while a nameless narrator would respond wittily, seriously, or awkwardly – depending on the command – through comic-style text boxes that appeared on the screen.

His graphics and room designs mostly came from sketches on paper that he'd then recreate in a paint program, using the 'pattern fill' tool to apply homely-yet-spooky wallpaper. And to keep the design straightforward, he devised ways to block the player's progress through puzzles that required only a bit of lateral thinking combined with everyday objects one might find in the rooms.

Publishing under the name Gray Design Associates, Gray uploaded *Hugo's House of Horrors* to CompuServe and a few local BBSs on 1 January 1990. Players could enjoy the whole thing free of charge, but they were asked to pay $20 to register the game if they enjoyed it. In return, they'd receive a hint booklet, an auto-playing version of the game intended for young children to watch, and a free new game 'when available'. (The hint book was divided into three sections: the house floorplan, 'medium hints' such as 'you might want to concentrate on that pumpkin', and 'obvious hints' like 'say "look in the mirror"' when in the bathroom.)

In its first month, he received just $140, but every month it gained momentum. By the end of the year, he was getting $1,000 a month – and that ramped up considerably when disk vendors like PC-SIG, Public Brand Software, and The Software Labs added it to their catalogues in 1991. Gray wasn't much surprised. He'd suspected he had something special when an early demonstration with his wife at a local computer club got 'tons of interest' and great feedback, and he knew he was looking at a potential hit once he received a letter from Scott Miller in August 1990.

Hugo was 'an excellent game', Miller told him, but 'it does not fit the mold of a successful shareware game'. He suggested Gray talk to him before starting his next game, noting the possibility of helping the *Hugo* author achieve greater success. The pair spoke on the phone soon after. 'He asked me how *Hugo* was doing sales wise,' Gray recalls, 'and when I told him, he said it sounded like I didn't need any help and should probably carry on by myself, with his best wishes. So I did!'

Miller had enough going on to keep himself busy, in any case. He'd only months earlier found a young developer who'd made a cool shareware game that was similar to *Kroz*. It used the IBM character set to make up its graphics and it involved searching through a multi-level underground maze for three missing items, all while shooting any enemies that showed up and collecting whatever items might help the player in their quest. The developer, a Californian teenager called Todd Replogle, later told the *Santa Cruz Sentinel* that he'd spent four months making *Caves of Thor* in direct response to *Kroz*. 'I knew I could do a better job,' he said, 'so I made my own game.'

Impressed, Miller had convinced Replogle to repackage *Caves of Thor* as an Apogee Software product and make two paid sequels that they could advertise in it. But that was just the beginning. In 1990, Replogle returned with a new game called *Monuments of Mars*. It was a simple platform game, with rudimentary tile- and sprite-based graphics, inviting players to explore a series of mysterious structures on the Martian surface.

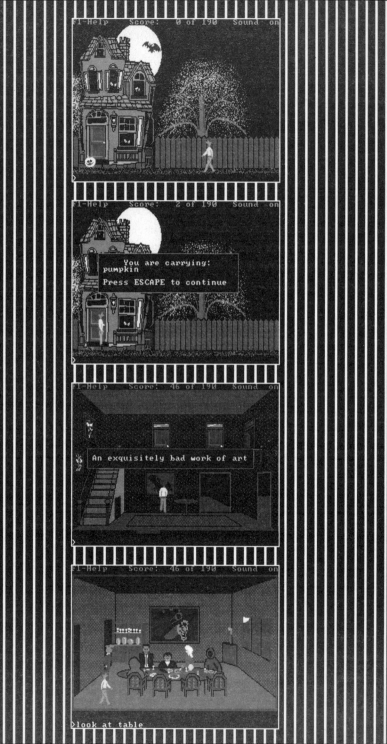

Each of its 20 levels entailed finding a way through a locked door or – in a few early levels – simply moving to the opposite side of the screen. To do so, players needed to enact a combination of jumping between platforms, shooting enemies and switches, dodging traps, collecting key cards, and pulling levers.

And in an unusual move for arcade-style games of the era, players had unlimited lives with which to complete the game. Rather than getting a 'Game Over' message and being forced to begin again from scratch, when the player's character died he would simply teleport back to the beginning of the level, its state reset to initial conditions, ready to try again.

Monuments turned out to be a hit. Replogle estimated that he had earned around $30,000–$40,000 from his cut of Apogee's shareware takings in his first year working with Miller. With *Monuments* and another game he made called *Dark Ages* (released February 1991), this would double. (Then it would double again every year until he left the industry in 1997, but that's jumping ahead a bit.)

In the meantime, Miller had brought on a business partner in the form of his friend George Broussard – the guy who co-authored the book about arcade games. Broussard had started selling shareware under the name Micro F/X soon after Miller, having seen how much money his friend was making from it. In 1988 he published two shareware trivia games according to Miller's Apogee model: the *Star Trek*-themed *Next Generation Trivia* (in three volumes) and general trivia game *Trivia Whiz* (in five volumes). Then he began work on a puzzle-platform game called *Pharaoh's Tomb*.

Pharaoh's Tomb followed archaeologist and adventurer Nevada Smith through a perilous Egyptian pyramid in search of the titular Pharaoh's Tomb. Its 80 screens (20 per episode) contained all manner of traps, moving platforms, and monsters ('no two levels will have the same animated creature patrolling it', an official description of the game stated), combining routinely to foil careless and careful players alike. And as with Replogle's *Monuments of Mars*, it used rudimentary sprite- and tile-based 16-colour CGA graphics to help it stand apart from the competition.

Broussard released the game somewhere around mid to late 1990, not realising until it was too late that he'd misspelled his own name as 'George Broussad' on the title screen. This mistake notwithstanding, the game made a minor stir in the shareware community and eventually even caught the attention of leading computer games magazine *Computer Gaming World*, which later declared *Pharaoh's Tomb* good enough to warrant a rare shareware review.

Reviewer Michael Lasky praised the game's flicker-free animation, customisable controls, exciting action, and thoughtful level design, noting that the $25 price tag for all four episodes together marked 'an outstanding value'.

Miller liked what Broussard was doing too, and he thought Apogee and Micro F/X were heading in a similar direction. (To the extent where he even allowed Broussard to create Amiga versions of *Trek Trivia* and *Zork* – the latter retitled *Rings of Zon*.) Better yet, he recognised that Broussard had talents he didn't. Miller was great at business and marketing, but he was a terrible artist and only a decent programmer. Broussard was talented both in art and code. It made sense that they should officially join forces under the Apogee banner. And in June 1991, a year after Miller had quit his job to pursue Apogee full-time, Broussard finally agreed.

Right in the nick of time, too, as the little company he was coming into had just entered a period of explosive growth – largely thanks to a group of friends who all worked at *Big Blue Disk* publisher Softdisk in the neighbouring state of Louisiana.

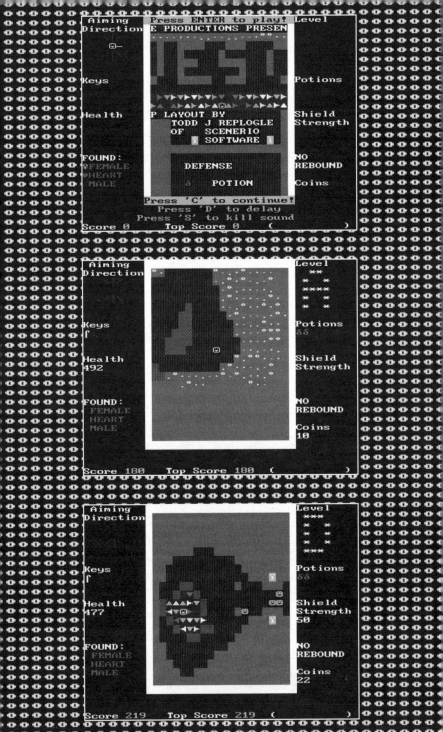

ID SOFTWARE

"We're In Demand!"

WE ARE A GROUP OF SOFTWARE ARTISTS
WHOSE GOAL IS TO BRING COMMERCIAL
QUALITY SOFTWARE TO THE PUBLIC
AT SHAREWARE PRICES.

OUR EFFORT IS ONLY POSSIBLE WITH
YOUR SUPPORT. WITHOUT IT, WE CANNOT
CONTINUE TO MAKE THIS FINE
SOFTWARE SO AFFORDABLE.

THANK YOU IN ADVANCE FOR YOUR
CONTRIBUTION TO THE FUTURE OF THE
GROWING SHAREWARE MARKET.

CHAPTER 6

Invasion of the Vorticons

Buoyed by the resounding success of Scott Miller's episodic business model, Apogee soon shifted its focus into publishing games that weren't developed by Miller himself.

He'd reached his limits as a programmer, both in terms of ability and rate of output. 'If I wanted to really be successful,' he told Benj Edwards in a 2009 *Gamasutra* interview, 'I realised that I shouldn't try to make the games myself anymore, 'cause I'm only one person, I can only do so much.'

Miller's greatest talents lay in marketing and business, and so now, after proving his Apogee model could work with other people's games (courtesy of Todd Replogle and George Broussard), he needed to put them to full use.

He paid particular attention to the shareware boards and disk magazines in his search for new talent. He'd contact anyone whose games he thought could work in an episodic format. Usually he'd explain how he was doing really well with his own stuff – making thousands of dollars a month and building up some brand recognition – and then he'd pitch them on the idea of working together.

The approach didn't always work, but it soon nabbed him Dave Sharpless (*Jumpman Lives!*, 1991), Frank Maddin (*Crystal Caves*, 1991; *Monster Bash*, 1993; *Realms of Chaos*, 1995; *Shadow*

Warrior, 1997), Jim Norwood (*Bio Menace*, 1993; *Shadow Warrior*, 1997), Karen Crowther (*Word Rescue* and *Math Rescue*, both 1992), and various others.

Contacting these people was generally easy. Most had email addresses on CompuServe, while the rest had their mailing address listed in their existing games. But one potential collaborator would prove more of a challenge.

That person was John Romero, a staff programmer at Softdisk, the company that ran *Big Blue Disk*, where some of Miller's games had been published before he went all-in on Apogee. Romero had been obsessed with game development since he got an Apple II in 1982, aged 15, and had seen around a dozen of his games published either in print magazines or diskmags by the time he entered the industry proper in 1987. He worked for a while at Origin Systems, the company famous for creating the *Ultima* RPG series, where he wrote tools for the Apple II version of *Space Rogue*, then left to join a start-up with his boss. When that new company didn't work out he'd phoned Jay Wilbur, the editor who'd published several of Romero's games in *Uptime* magazine, and asked for a job. Wilbur was in the midst of a job change of his own; he was about to move to *Uptime*'s main competitor, Softdisk, and suggested that Romero should join him there.

Romero started out in Softdisk's new Special Projects division making Apple II games, but after a while he began to worry that the Apple II was on the way out – that the PC was the future. Afraid of being left behind, he taught himself how to program the PC and started making DOS games. That went so well that he was shifted to the *Big Blue Disk* team, where, much to his chagrin, he had to make utilities as well as games.

Romero's *Big Blue Disk* games caught the attention of Scott Miller, who thought the young programmer had great potential to succeed in shareware. But Miller doubted he could approach Romero directly. Softdisk were acting as a go-between for mail addressed to their staff, and Miller figured they would probably be screening Romero's mail before forwarding it onto him.

Pitching Romero on working with Apogee would therefore need a craftier approach; Miller had to try to draw Romero into writing or calling him back.

So he decided to pose as a fan – or rather multiple fans – of Romero's games. He sent handwritten letters to Romero courtesy of Softdisk, each under a different pseudonym. 'I loved your game (*Pyramids of Egypt*), it is better than another pyramid type game that was in *Big Blue Disk* a few issues ago,' read one, attributed to Scott Mulliere, that asked about secret keys, high scores, and recommendations for similar games. It ended with a P.S. stating: 'I think I found a minor bug (undocumented feature?) in the game!' and a sign off of: 'Please call me collect if you want.'

Each letter varied in exact content, but they all took the same basic formula: *Your games are great, and I play them all the time, but I think I found a bug. Please contact me.*

Excited to have so many fans, Romero taped them all up on the wall. Then one day he read an article in *PC Games* magazine about Scott Miller and the great success he was having with shareware distribution of his *Kroz* games.

'And I'm just thinking, "well, this is text-based stuff",' Romero remembers. 'I'm not really that interested in text-based stuff, but let me just read about it. And when I got to the end of it I saw Apogee Software Productions, ASP, and the address for his company... And I'm like, wait a minute. *I know that address!* I've *seen* that before, you know?'

He looked over to his wall, and there it was: 'They all had his address on it.'

Fuming, Romero drafted an angry letter, then he came back the next day and rewrote it – reiterating his confusion and annoyance but this time noting his curiosity at the 'numerous approaches'. He sent both letters together, then Miller responded, this time as himself, with a typed proposal.

'Dear John,' he wrote, 'Enjoyed *Pyramids of Egypt*, it really demonstrates your talent as a game designer well. I would like to propose to you the idea of making a shareware game, similar to *Pyramids of Egypt*, but a different storyline may be necessary.'

Miller formally introduced himself and his company and explained that Apogee was the leading publisher of its kind. 'My most popular shareware game pulls in $1,500–$2,000 per week,' he added, 'and that amount continues to rise,' while the rest of their games weren't far behind.

Romero wasn't convinced. 'He didn't think that you really could make money in shareware,' Miller remembers.

'I didn't think that you'd make money on things that nobody has heard of,' Romero elaborates. 'And I never went online either. I didn't have a modem and I didn't download games and stuff.' Indeed, his only prior exposure to shareware was seeing a colleague at Softdisk playing *Captain Comic* for several weeks. But Romero had thought that game was free; he'd never even heard of shareware until he read the *PC Games* article about *Kroz*.

Miller pushed harder. He was sure Romero could succeed with the Apogee model. 'And I said, "Well, I'm working with a team here,"' Romero remembers – the others being John Carmack, Tom Hall, Lane Roathe, and Adrian Carmack (no relation to John) – '"and we are doing some really amazing stuff. Let me show you a demo." And we had just finished making the *Super Mario Bros 3* demo that we were sending to Nintendo.'

This demo had come from John Carmack's eagerness to bring smooth-scrolling animation to the PC – not the hackneyed, chunky form that a few others had figured out, and that *Captain Comic* had perfected (by scrolling small groups of pixels a tile at a time), but rather the smooth, rolling landscapes of games like *Super Mario Bros*.

By making a custom screen buffer that was wider and taller than the screen and then redrawing only the pixels on the screen that changed colour between frames, in a process he called 'adaptive tile refresh', Carmack discovered he could drastically speed up the scrolling effect. He'd shown it to Tom Hall, who immediately recognised an exciting application for the technology: they could recreate *Super Mario Bros 3* on a PC. Hall and Carmack had then stayed up all night doing exactly that, with the original game booted up on a TV in the office as a reference point and the character Dangerous Dave (who they'd made for a previous Softdisk release) standing in for Mario in a rough approximation of the first level's design. They called it *Dangerous Dave in Copyright Infringement.*

The next day Romero saw it and immediately realised the potential implications of getting approval from Nintendo to complete the game: this could be their ticket to stardom – to fame and riches and a studio of their own. The whole team all pitched in over a weekend of intense effort to finish off the demo. They made a near-exact replica of World 1-1 of Nintendo's beloved bestseller, then they threw in a few custom levels of their own to show off their creative talents. Once they'd finished they put their team name 'Ideas From The Deep' underneath Nintendo's logo and their friend Jay Wilbur penned a letter pitching the Japanese company's American branch on an official PC port.

They sent it off to Nintendo, hopes high that they'd get a deal to publish *Super Mario Bros 3* for PC, then a few weeks later received a brief reply. They'd done well, it stated, but Nintendo wasn't interested in the PC games market.

When Scott Miller came calling with an offer to publish his work, Romero realised they had another potential avenue for using Carmack's new tech to chase fame and glory. Or at least a way to make history and own it at the same time.

So I sent that [demo] to Scott. And he was like, oh my God. He was just, you know, *ruined* basically. He could not understand. The PC has never done this before. So he was like, 'Please make a game. It has to be a trilogy. It has to be three pieces. And I'll give you an advance.'

The Ideas From The Deep team liked the sound of that. This was a new and weird business model that Miller wanted them to jump on, but so too was the model used at Softdisk where they worked. 'Usually people went to a software store and they would buy a game for 40 bucks and it was retail and that's how it worked,' recalls Romero. But Softdisk published software in subscription-based disk magazines like *Big Blue Disk* – the division Romero worked in. They charged $80 a year to send people a collection of programs (usually one or two games plus a few utilities) every month. 'And it had 50,000 subscribers, so that is $4 million dollars a year just for that one product,' he says.

With Miller so confident in their success he'd put down an advance, it made sense, then, that they should give his Apogee model a chance – it wasn't really any weirder than Softdisk's model, after all.

So with a $2,000 advance in hand – drawn from the mere $5,000 Apogee had in its company account at the time – the trio of John Carmack, Tom Hall, and John Romero chatted about what they could make. 'And John [Carmack] said, "How about a game about a genius kid who saves the universe behind his parents' back?"' Romero remembers. 'And Tom's like, "Oh my God, what a great idea! I'll be right back." And Tom runs into his office and he writes up the [story].'

Fifteen minutes later Hall returned with a single typed sheet and read it out in his best impression of 1930s/40s/50s radio announcer Walter Winchell. Hall said the game would star eight-year-old genius Billy Blaze, who had built an interstellar

spaceship in his backyard from old cans and plastic tubing. When his parents went out, he'd donned his brother's football helmet and transformed into defender of justice Commander Keen, and in this episode he'd be marooned on the mountains of Mars by aliens from the planet Vorticon VI, who had stolen his ship and left pieces of it around the galaxy. Billy needed to recover the pieces, repel the would-be invaders, and get back to Earth before his parents came home.

That was perfect, the trio decided. Carmack, who rarely showed his emotions, enjoyed it so much he both laughed and applauded. They put Hall's story treatment in a letter and sent it off to Scott Miller, who immediately greenlit the concept. Then they set to work building their *Commander Keen* trilogy.

Each had a distinct role to play: Carmack built the engine while Romero made the tools and Hall did the base game design; Romero and Hall together designed the levels; and Hall also drew the graphics (though artist Adrian Carmack later took over large parts of the graphics workload – albeit reluctantly, as he found the game 'too kiddie' for his tastes).

Every Friday evening they'd load up their office computers into their cars and drive out to a four-bedroom lake house that Carmack, Jay Wilbur, Lane Roathe, and Softdisk programmer Jason Blochowiak were renting. They drank copious amounts of caffeinated soda and gorged themselves on a steady diet of pizza, bought out of the $100 'pizza bonus' Scott Miller sent over every week to keep them going.

The game itself reflected this diet of excess junk food. Players could earn extra points for collecting pizza slices, lollipops, and soda cans, while the graphics made liberal use of EGA mode's gaudy, iridescent 16-colour palette. Keen could run, jump, and pogo-hop around levels, bouncing off the goofy-looking enemies to stun them or alternatively shooting them into oblivion with a ray-gun blast. There were typical platforming hazards like spikes and traps and ledges to climb atop or leap across, but also cryptic puzzles and elements of non-linearity. Where *Mario* platformers required the player to always be moving forwards, *Commander Keen* would at times require players to backtrack and find coloured keycards to unlock new areas.

They finished development in early December, two and a half months after they'd begun, slapped an 'ID Software' logo on the game (the 'ID' short for 'In Demand'), sent floppies with each of the three episodes off to Scott Miller, then went back to work – knowing they'd receive their first royalty cheque in a month but otherwise unsure what lay ahead.

On 14 December 1990, Scott Miller uploaded the first *Keen* episode, *Marooned on Mars*, to Software Creations BBS and Apogee's other key distribution platforms. The whole trilogy would set players back $30, with a bonus hint sheet and 'cheat mode' password thrown in to sweeten the deal. Orders could be placed either via the mail or by calling a 1-800 number Miller had set up.

Within days he was inundated with orders. BBSs around the world lit up with callers eager to download this hot, new shareware game that some were declaring was better than a Nintendo game. In the first month *Commander Keen* was available, it brought in $30,000 in revenue – quadruple their usual earnings across *all* of Apogee's games. Demand was so strong that Miller had to recruit his mum to answer phones and to hire someone full-time just to help take orders.

On 15 January the ID Software boys received a $10,500 royalty cheque from Apogee. They were stunned – if this kept up it would be more than enough to live off. 'And it was just the beginning,' says Romero. 'So when we saw that we're like, "We're quitting our jobs now."'

That was easier said than done. Softdisk had launched a new disk magazine called *Gamer's Edge* just five months earlier, with Romero at the helm, *at Romero's behest*, that was supposed to publish a new game from Romero and his team every two months. Now they were planning to leave after making just two games and a demo disk.

To square things up with their old boss, and to stave off a potential lawsuit for making *Keen* on company computers, they made a deal: they could leave and do their own thing, but they'd have to write a new game every two months for Softdisk for one year. (Plus *Gamer's Edge* could hire a new internal team that would have access to their engine and tile editor.) Six games to buy their freedom, and they could do whatever they wanted on the side of that.

They officially incorporated in February 1991 as id Software – the 'ID' dropped to lower case to signify the Freudian concept of impulse and desire – and set to work cranking out game after game for Softdisk, mostly using their ever-improving *Keen* engine, including a standalone *Keen* adventure called *Commander Keen: Keen Dreams*. As they did that, they also found the time to create a two-part *Keen* sequel for Apogee – with better graphics than the original and the ability to save anywhere – plus a second standalone *Keen* game, this time for retail market distribution by FormGen (thanks to a deal made by Canadian fan-turned-id-business-rep Mark Rein). And somehow, amidst everything else, they *also* began work on an all-new 3D game engine – one that would blow everything away, including *Commander Keen*.

Apogee meanwhile had big moves of its own. Up until this point they'd been operating out of Scott Miller's parents' house, with the post-*Keen* addition of sole employee Shawn Green coming by every day to join Miller's mum in answering phones. But now, with an easy $30,000-plus a month (peaking at more than double that) coming in just from *Commander Keen* orders, Miller realised they needed a proper dedicated office space. Somewhere with the room to fit desks for staff fielding tech-support queries and phone orders, plus space for storing inventory, duplicating disks, and shipping orders.

The bigger space would allow for a revolving cast of around a dozen office helpers who'd take on much of the laborious support and shipping work so that Miller and Broussard could focus on business and production. For most games they'd serve as producers, usually with one or the other taking the lead so that they could split the load between them. This meant giving feedback on development builds, sharing ideas for potential improvements and pushing developers to embrace Apogee's golden rules of game design: that every game be fun, fair, and innovative; that every game have a way to save and restore player progress; and, wherever possible, that games ditch the entrenched concept of limited lives – which Miller saw as an outdated holdover from the arcades, ill-suited to a world where games can have save and restore options.

Sometimes Miller and Broussard would be more deeply involved in the development process, as was the case with *Duke Nukem* – one game among many in what was turning out to be Apogee's year of the platformer.

In January they had Todd Replogle's *Dark Ages*, followed by the short-lived *Jumpman Lives!* from Dave Sharpless in June (which was pulled from distribution a few months later after a copyright claim by *Jumpman* publisher Epyx), then *Duke Nukem* in July, George Broussard's *Arctic Adventure* and Frank Maddin's *Crystal Caves* in October, and finally *Commander Keen*'s two-part sequel in December. Only Keith Schuler's puzzle-adventure *Paganitzu* in October would buck the platforming trend.

While the *Keen* sequel served as another big money-spinner, it was *Duke Nukem* that bore the greater importance for the fast-growing company. This one was homegrown, conceived several months earlier by Scott Miller and Todd Replogle – and with

character art redrawn by George Broussard late in development, just before he came on as a business partner.

Replogle wrote the code, with some help from John Carmack – who provided hand-tuned Assembly code for a few time-critical parts of the game engine – and John Romero – who had taught Replogle the previous year how to use an EGA/ VGA graphics programming technique called latch mode, which vastly sped up the scrolling in his previous game *Dark Ages* by reading and writing pixel data in four-byte chunks.

Meanwhile Miller created sound effects and designed the levels for episode one, eventual *Bio Menace* author Jim Norwood drew the background graphics, and Replogle's friend Allen Blum came in to handle all the levels in episodes two and three. Blum also drew most of the foreground graphics (aside from a few bits they ripped from other DOS games), drawing art on his Amiga that they then copied over to the PC.

The game itself was pitched as a 'spectacular' action-packed arcade-adventure game, with 'vivid EGA graphics' and arcade sound effects, 'that compares to the Sega Genesis home systems' and is 'far superior to games typically seen on the Nintendo home system'. Like *Keen*, it had four-way scrolling and fast, colourful animation, but *Duke*'s tone leaned much more into the blockbuster action films of the 1980s – with a burly, muscle-clad hero, a smack-talking mad-scientist villain, and a darker, grittier palette.

Your Computer contributor Eric Holroyd called it 'another nice one from Apogee', praising it as a no-nonsense shoot-'em-up that 'plays very well'. German magazine *PC Games* agreed, praising its technical achievements – especially the large levels and 48 frames-per-second refresh rate.

Apogee fans were impressed, too. *Commander Keen* had led the Shareware Top Ten sales charts since its release, but *Duke Nukem* soon leaped to the top – where the two games would swap back and forth for another year. It was Apogee's new bestseller, but also shareware's new bestseller – not only in games but across all categories – for both 1991 and 1992. Even a name change to *Duke Nukum* couldn't slow it down. (The name change happened in the version 2.0 update because Apogee got worried about copyright infringement after learning about a character in the *Captain Planet* cartoon series called Duke Nukem. They were later informed that copyright protection on the cartoon character's name didn't apply to video games, so the original name would be reinstated from *Duke Nukem II* onwards.)

Two chart-toppers meant huge financial windfalls for Apogee. For the entirety of 1991, their turnover hit $2.2 million (though not $22 million, as was mistakenly printed in British newspaper the *Guardian* in March 1992), making it one of the biggest shareware success stories up to that time. But Apogee's success wasn't uniformly embraced by the shareware industry.

Unconventional

Early in Apogee's life Miller had joined the Association of Shareware Professionals (ASP), the shareware industry trade organisation founded in 1987 during a 'Meeting of Shareware Professionals' hosted by Nelson Ford, the magazine columnist and Public (software) Library owner who had standardised the 'shareware' name.

The ASP served simultaneously as industry advocate, watchdog, and gatekeeper – meaning they'd fight attempts to trademark the word 'shareware' or to pass laws that would be detrimental to shareware authors, but also rein in unscrupulous vendors and combat 'crippleware' (shareware that was so limited in functionality pre-registration that it barely worked at all), and they'd only accept members that met certain criteria for 'good' shareware.

With all the most-recognised shareware authors as members, its name carried weight. Being an ASP member not only gave an author access to a variety of helpful tools and best practices but also it granted access to a community of their peers and, critically, it made potential customers more willing to part with their money – safe in the knowledge that if something went wrong they could turn to the ASP Ombudsman for help in resolving a dispute.

But some ASP members rallied against Miller's Apogee model. 'They had a rule that basically said that when you give

away shareware, you need to give away the whole thing,' Miller recalls. 'And that generally worked, it seemed, for business or utility-type software.' But games were different, and Miller thought he'd found the perfect middle ground with his episodic model – whereby customers were effectively paying for sequels. Others disagreed. They argued he was breaking the rules.

> I tried to make all these arguments, like no one feels like they're being ripped off by the way we do things, so you've got this arbitrary rule that doesn't work in the real world. And people love what we're doing. I mean, look how much money we're making. We're making more than anyone else in your group. So clearly it's a system that works. You guys need to adjust to the times. I was trying to make that argument for many months and they finally just kicked me out because things got very heated and so on. And so me and a few other people said, well, fine, we'll create our own group that allows for this to happen.

Miller joined forces with a number of other people who were unhappy with the politics of the ASP and together they formed the Shareware Trade Association and Resources (STAR) in September 1992. STAR would serve the same core purpose as the ASP – to inform and educate people about shareware – except it would make no attempts to regulate shareware marketing methods or the actions of its members.

The standoff between Miller and the ASP wouldn't last, however, and Miller rejoined the organisation when they modified their rules to allow for some limitations – such as time-limiting (e.g. a 30-day trial) or premium episodes (à la the Apogee model) – as long as people had a chance to fully try a shareware program before paying.

These changes had been long brewing as trends outside of the ASP. Apogee had shown the world that games could succeed in shareware; they just needed to give customers a selfish reason to pay. And increasing numbers of shareware authors were trying to put that lesson into action.

One such author, Peter Steffen, had first learned about shareware from magazine advertisements in 1990 and subsequently bought multiple Apogee titles before he started work on his own game, *Crime Fighter*, in 1991.

He drew on memories of the 1986 German-language Commodore 64 game *Mafia*, which cast up to four players as wannabe mobsters in 1920s Chicago who take turns committing ever more serious crimes en route to the top of the underworld. It had a map that players walked around on, entering different kinds of buildings to activate various mini-games and choice-based menus that, depending on the player's decision, would lead to either an increased points tally or a shoot-out (with either the good guys or a rival group of bad guys).

Crime Fighter took that concept and game structure and transplanted it to a nameless 'near-future' German city. It had recreated versions of some of *Mafia*'s mini-games (such as a safe-cracking game that uses sound to tell players when they've found the next number), but also had several of its own – including various escape-the-police mazes to run through and a *Sokoban*-style time-limited challenge of pushing as many boxes into marked spaces as possible.

Steffen sent it off to around 20 shareware disk vendors in May 1993, with a requested payment of 25 DM to buy the full version (with game saves and a higher maximum points target). It didn't make him rich, by any means, but it was popular in the German shareware scene. 'I even received kid drawings with scenes from the game,' he recalls, 'and some fans also came to visit me at home.'

He would later (in 1997) update the game with his friend Hartwig Holtkamp, together designing a new city map with LEGO blocks. The new version would also feature an English translation for international audiences, as well as a registration-code system to take away the need to ship out floppy disks to customers. But while it too was widely played, it sold just a fraction of the first release – a mere 500 registrations, compared to 2,700 for the German-only original.

Rather more successful, Steve Moraff's one-man company MoraffWare carved out a strong niche with colourful, quirky, exacting, and slow-paced episodic games. It started with *Moraff's Revenge*, a roguelike dungeon game published in 1988. Just as early shareware shoot-'em-up *Flightmare* had presented the player simultaneously with both top-down and side-on perspectives, *Moraff's Revenge* split the screen into two distinct viewpoints. On the left was an overhead map view that would start blank but fill out as the player explored the maze-like dungeon. Then on the right were four boxes encircling an illustration of whatever shared the player's current position on the map. Each box showed a first-person view pointing in the corresponding cardinal direction – one looked ahead, another behind, and the other two to the sides.

Drawing inspiration not only from the likes of *Rogue* but also from the rich legacy of early computer RPGs like *Wizardry*, *Moraff's Revenge* had players first select a character class and then proceed with a simple action-loop: enter the dungeon, explore its passageways and kill any monsters encountered along the way (to gain experience points and wealth), return to the town to heal and buy equipment (and maybe to level up the character's stats too), then go back to the dungeon to head deeper down and repeat the cycle.

'Like life itself,' Moraff wrote in his synopsis, 'this game has no single simple objective.' Indeed, like most roguelikes, it had a MacGuffin (an object useful to the plot but nothing else) in the form of a special artefact – in this case the fountain of youth, located on level 70 – but the real reason to descend into the dungeon each time was individual. Here was a game with a fluid, self-directed objective. It may be to reach a particular level of the dungeon and return alive, or to take out revenge on all wraiths after one 'drains' the player-character's level.

Moraff was unaware of Scott Miller's Apogee model, and initially also of the term shareware, but he published his game under the same logic – give a significant chunk away as a standalone product and upsell players on a full version with more levels. He called the shareware release the 'Beginner's Version' and locked it to 17 dungeon levels and 17 experience levels. To gain more experience, and to unlock all 70 levels, players could order the 'Advanced Version' for $10. And to help sell players on its apparent brilliance, he boasted – in one help screen full of multicoloured text – that it was 'probably the most sophisticated game of it's [sic] type' thanks to 'many advanced features that the Apple computers do not have' and eight years of work that started on an early microcomputer called the NCR 7200.

Whether impressed or bemused by the ostentatious sales pitch, the shareware community loved it – but not right away. At first *Moraff's Revenge* struggled to get noticed, but it became a consistent bestseller when it got picked up for distribution in the PC-SIG catalogue and was subsequently a favourite entertainment choice from many other shareware sources for a few years. Its full version also got picked up by *Big Blue Disk* for its May 1989 mail-out.

Around the same time as *Revenge* hit *Big Blue Disk*'s subscribers, Moraff followed up with his second game, *Moraff's Pinball*, a colourful pinball game with rudimentary graphics but built-in support for 640 by 480-pixel VGA mode. This one came in a 'try out' version that limited players to just one ball per game unless they paid the $10 registration fee.

Then in 1990 he returned to the free 'Beginner's Version' and paid 'Advanced Version' model with *Moraff's Entrap* – which instructed players in one of its start-up screens to 'please copy this game for all your friends and all your aquaintences [*sic*]'.

The goal in *Moraff's Entrap* was to reach the other end of a long, suspended playfield as efficiently as possible (more moves meant fewer points). To complicate matters, this playfield was filled with robots that spent their every turn making a beeline for the player. To add strategy to the experience, and as a protective measure, players could dig holes in the playfield to block these robots – albeit at the cost of a few turns.

Entrap was where Moraff really found his style. It was colourful, dense, punishing, sloppy yet precise, and bewilderingly idiosyncratic – right down to the extensive self-aggrandising and aggressive huckstering in an 'Important People and Friends' menu that (perhaps semi-jokingly?) targeted agents, movie producers, record executives, book publishers, and book authors with 'a broad range of well thought-out, but flexible concepts' he'd devised that he promised would later receive 'free advertizing [*sic*]' in Moraffware's games. These included, for instance, a concept pitch for Moraff's World, the Movie, 'an adventure and romance story set in a world of wizards, warriors, and gods' that he believed could work with either a low or a high budget, as well as a description of a 'fictional-reality band' that specialised in catchy tunes but had yet to record a demo tape.

Nobody in the world made games like Steve Moraff because nobody thought quite like Steve Moraff, a 27-year-old programmer with an exacting approach to his work. But in the world of shareware it was a boon – not a curse – to be unorthodox. Moraff's games were memorable and instantly recognisable. That made them easy to spot in the endless churn of new shareware releases that clogged up online listings – even as he leaped at whim between different genres. He had RPGs, platformers, ball-and-paddle-style games, card games, board games, puzzle games, and more, each clearly, *obviously*, a Moraff joint even if you somehow failed to notice the 'Moraff's' prefix in the title.

And right through until the mid-1990s, when he shifted his attention solely to card-and-board-game-loving casual gamers, he held significant mindshare in the shareware market. (And even after he made that shift that lost him mindshare, he would remain a professional – and successful – shareware games author for the best part of a decade.)

Alternative models

Steve Moraff wasn't the only 1980s shareware author to invent his own version of the Apogee model.

Nels Anderson – the gynaecologist whose successes with 1980s shareware titles *EGA Trek* and *Mah Jongg* had inspired David Gray to enter the shareware arena – remained active through this era, too, and in 1990 he caught on to the effectiveness of holding part of the game back for registered users only.

Anderson's cryptogram game *Cipher* (1990 on DOS, 1991 on Windows) asked players to decode a cipher to reveal a famous quote, with just 32 of its 200 quotes available in the unregistered shareware release. Similarly, duck-shoot game *Shooting Gallery* (1990) and memory game *Tile Match* (1992) both held back content from the free version – though the simple nature of these games meant that registered players only gained more secondary content (extra sound effects and more tile sets, respectively).

Not everyone publishing notable new shareware games at the time was looking to Apogee for influence, however.

Some, like Carol Standley's *King's Quest*-style graphic adventure *MythMaster: A Vagabond's Adventure* (1991), looked instead to the examples set within their genre – in the case of *MythMaster*, that meant offering players a free hint book, phone support, and a cheap copy of the next game by the author, similar to the model used for David Gray's *Hugo* games.

Meanwhile, games released in the traditional fully functioning, non-episodic 'pay if you like it' shareware model still remained common. One notable example was Richard Olsen's *BassTour*, a popular fishing simulation that was first released in 1988 with a $10 registration fee. It followed the same model for years afterwards – though just one year in Olsen introduced an extra revenue stream in the form of add-on packs, for $10 a disk, of extra lakes to fish in. Even in 1992, when Olsen finally incorporated one of these add-on packs into the game's registered version, the base game remained completely free.

The most famous such title from the era was Wendell Hicken's *Scorched Earth* (1991–5), a colourful artillery game where between two and ten tanks try to obliterate each other with an arsenal of ridiculous tools of mass destruction on a two-dimensional side-view playfield.

There were the 'standard weapons', which included regular missiles as well as tracers – for easier targeting of a rival – and a selection of different kinds of bombs: nukes, toxic 'funky' bombs, napalm, and so on. Then there were the 'Earth-destroying weapons' that could be used to level a mountain, dig a tank out of an early grave, or perhaps escape an enemy's sights; the 'Earth-producing weapons' that would create terrain or bury a rival; and finally the 'energy weapons' that would radiate a blast out from a tank – provided a player had the batteries to power it.

The game also included a raft of defensive and guidance systems, the option to move a tank around (pending available fuel and navigable terrain), and a rudimentary economy (most

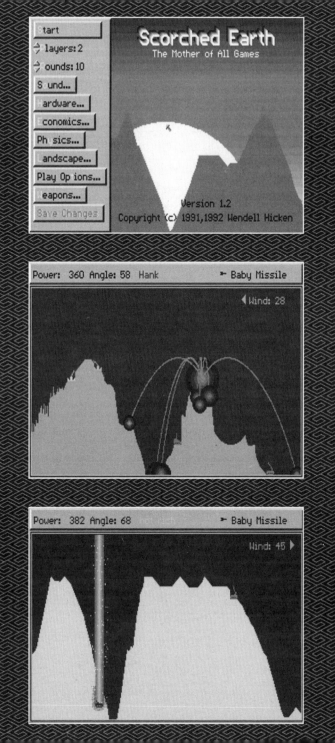

equipment cost money, which accrued interest if unspent, and players could also sell items they didn't want). Plus, for humour, tanks could deliver taunts when attacking or state final words when they died, with their lines plucked randomly from two player-configurable talk files.

And, as if that wasn't enough features already, *Scorched Earth* could be played as a real-time free-for-all or as a choice of two different turn-based modes – synchronous (all players aim their weapons, then the round executes) or sequential (turns happen one after another).

Hicken had started developing the game in 1990, squeezed in between computer science studies at Caltech and sessions of *Sonic the Hedgehog* and *Contra* on his Sega Genesis. It was a hobby project, initially aimed more at putting his new computer through its paces than creating anything meaningful.

He based his first version on an old BASIC game he'd copied out of a magazine years earlier, with player input limited to defining the power and angle of each shot, but where that one was single player – the goal being to hit the target in as few attempts as possible – he made it competitive multiplayer. Two tanks in a fight to the death.

Hicken's demo build was soon installed in the college dorm computer labs, along with a sheet of paper for people to write down their suggestions and ideas. In the months that followed, *Scorched Earth* would go through intensive revision and expansion, adding more players as well as layer upon layer of strategy and in-game destructiveness, which culminated in the arrival of an unexpected cheque for $10 from someone in Washington (evidently it had spread to other colleges interstate) sometime between March and July of 1991.

Hicken had not planned to publish the game outside of his circle of friends. But with this unsolicited payment he decided to upload a version to CompuServe under a traditional shareware model. For their $10 registration fee, players would receive nothing more than a code to remove the nag messages. ('Scorch is not crippleware,' Hicken wrote in the game's detailed 50-page manual. 'Each and every copy is a fully functioning game.')

Scorched Earth was an instant sensation, copied gleefully across the BBS and college FTP scenes as well as throughout whisper networks of high-school and college students around the world. *Computer Gaming World* even got in on the action with a review praising its simple addictiveness.

It wasn't making much money – Hicken later quipped in an *Ars Technica* interview that 'it was enough to keep the Ramen coming while the school bills piled up' – but it was making waves. Thousands of threads sprang up on Usenet, CompuServe, and AOL message boards, with people trading tips, sharing stories, asking where to find a copy, and enthusiastically making their own versions of the game for other systems or with 3D graphics. He was inundated with ideas (lasers, night sky, weather, joystick support, supply-and-demand equipment pricing, teams!) and bug reports that he then did his best to implement across multiple updated releases. And even when the new releases dried up after version 1.5 came out in 1995, the discussions still raged on.

Hicken hadn't reinvented computer game distribution or marketing, nor had he got rich from his game, but with a legacy hanging over the artillery genre – later dominated by the *Worms* franchise that shared its zest for comically-over-the-top destruction – and a collective memory stretching across millions of fans, he'd inadvertently made one of the most influential shareware games of all time.

Little did he know that a very different kind of shareware experience – released just weeks before *Scorched Earth*'s pre-shareware build reached Washington – was poised to have an even bigger accidental influence on the medium.

CHAPTER 7

Epic MegaGames

When Tim Sweeney was 11 years old, he fell in love with computers. It was 1981, and he lived on the outskirts of Potomac, Maryland, but was visiting his oldest brother in California. Young Tim had never seen an IBM PC before, but now he'd never forget it.

He was besotted with the machine for a week, during which time his brother taught him the basics of programming, but then he had to go back to Potomac, where he had no computer. His new passion was put on pause. Lucky for him, though, it wouldn't be much of a wait as that same brother bought their dad an Apple II a few months later.

The younger Sweeney spent the next several years quietly mastering the machine, making all sorts of little games (starting, suitably, with his own version of *Pong*) and downloading programming guides from BBSs. Then he graduated high school and went to the University of Maryland to study mechanical engineering. His father bought him a 286-class PC, but by this point it was two generations behind the new 486 processor line, and therefore a low-end model.

Sweeney immediately set to work recreating the programming and editing environment that he'd built for himself on his Apple II, starting with the text editor. But before he could move on to the rest of the tools – before he'd even finished the text editor – he got sidetracked. He'd just implemented the text cursor controls, which would allow a user to press the arrow keys to select where on the screen their new text would appear. And he was testing it – idly moving it around, enjoying the novelty of seeing that cursor fly across the screen. Then he had an idea.

He fashioned a level of sorts out of text, with the cursor turned into a smiley face and cast as the player – lost in a barren world where empty spaces were navigable and ASCII characters impeded movement. Then he made it so that different characters had different functions. Some became monsters and animals, others walls. Or gems or keys or magic scrolls.

He could type it all out, designing the level with the text editor, then hit the 'run' button to start playing. 'And that was WAY more fun than writing a text editor,' Sweeney later said in an interview with the *Interactive Fantasies* website. 'So I started building levels and extending the editor as I thought of new features.'

After a few months he had the makings of a proper game, so he began inviting people from his neighbourhood – kids, mostly, but also teenagers and young adults – over to play. Then he'd watch them and observe how they played, what they liked, what they didn't like – how much they enjoyed it.

Slowly the game coalesced into something more complete, with ideas drawn from these playtests as well as his own imagination and his experiences with other games like *NetHack* (a popular roguelike) and *Kroz* – both of which he first played during this development period. Along the way he got the idea to publish it as shareware.

That seemed to be going pretty well for Scott Miller, who didn't just have great games at Apogee; he also seemed to have everything figured out. His marketing was so professional, so polished – and his episodic business model so impressive – that Sweeney wrote him a letter to ask for advice. Even the reply was polished, he noticed.

To compete, and to succeed, Sweeney knew he had to do the same. So he took his time to polish his own game, and to present it professionally. He already had a business name. He'd started a small computer consultancy called Potomac Computer Systems on the side of his studies, hoping to find something more profitable than mowing lawns for $20 an hour, but it hadn't gone anywhere. He still had the company letterhead and business cards, so he figured he may as well use it.

Sweeney also noticed that a large number of shareware authors were coming up with game names – or filenames for their games – that started with the letter 'a' or a number or special character. It was a predecessor to search-engine optimisation – a way to ensure they'd be first in the list of files available for download on a BBS, because usually these were sorted alphabetically. It caused a huge clutter of junk to pile up at the top of most repositories, so he figured he'd do the opposite. He named his game *ZZT* so that it would appear at the bottom of all the lists.

After nine months or so of spare-time development, Sweeney published *ZZT* on 15 January 1991. He followed the Apogee model. Episode one, *Town of ZZT*, was free to re-distribute and share, but if you paid the $12.95 registration fee you'd get a personalised copy with a second game world, *Caves of ZZT*, also included, plus a subscription to the *ZZT* newsletter. Two additional worlds were available for $6 each (or $10 for both), and players could use the built-in 'Board Editor' to build their own worlds – or to add more levels (called 'boards' in-game) to existing worlds – even if they hadn't registered.

Almost immediately he began receiving orders in the mail. Not many – just three or four a day – but enough to live off. A short time later – perhaps as little as a few weeks – he pushed out an updated version that announced a 'Best of *ZZT*' contest. Entrants had until 1 December to submit their own *ZZT* worlds for consideration, with the winners promised a cut of the royalties for the resulting *Best of ZZT* game release.

Entries were initially slow to roll in, but Sweeney received 'well over' 200 fan-made worlds (and perhaps as many as 1,000) by the contest's close date – so many, and of such a high standard, that he decided to expand the prizes. The six grand prize winners would be siphoned off into a new release called *ZZT's Revenge*, with boosted royalties, while a further twenty-four community-created boards would be compiled into a two-world *Best of ZZT* collection.

Much to Sweeney's surprise, a whole community had formed around the game. People wrote in sharing maps and stories. Some started to trade their custom worlds and board-editing tips online. And a few began working with him directly. One, Allen Pilgrim, had built a world called Fantasy in June 1991 and submitted it to the Best of *ZZT* contest. 'Tim called me and said that it was by far the best game they had received,' Pilgrim later recalled in an interview, and so the two began to collaborate.

Pilgrim was put to work helping with world design on a *ZZT* follow-up called *Super ZZT* – which was essentially the same game, except now boards could be several times larger in each direction and the game scrolled vertically or horizontally as players moved. He would end up contributing the world Monster Zoo, which Sweeney liked so much he made it the shareware episode for the game. And while he worked on that, Sweeney cooked up another idea. He thought that Pilgrim could make a space shooter in the vein of arcade hits *Galaxian* and *Galaga*, and sent some materials through to help him learn C. That game would eventually turn into *Kiloblaster*, released around a year later.

In the meantime, Sweeney decided a name change was in order for Potomac Computer Systems. He wanted to build a real company, and for that he felt he needed a serious name – a name that sounded like a big games company – to conceal the fact that he was just a 21-year-old college student (and soon-to-be college dropout) working alternately out of a dorm and his parents' house. But also a name that would stand up well against Apogee – a name that oozed quality. After a bout of brainstorming he settled on something he thought sounded impressive: Epic MegaGames.

He devised a tagline, too: 'The New Name in Computer Entertainment', and made it official on 15 October alongside the release of *Super ZZT* – by which time *ZZT* had received around 600 registrations. He also created several documents laying out his vision for the company, along with his operating strategies. These he sent out to all current and potential collaborators so that everyone knew where the company was headed and how they fit into the picture.

Epic MegaGames would offer a standard royalty rate of 40 per cent to a game's authors, with an estimated 40 per cent needed to cover expenses (disk duplication, postage, phone bills, advertising, disk mail-outs to hundreds of shareware vendors and so on) and the remaining 20 per cent to serve as profit for the company. This was testament to the greater efficiency of shareware, Sweeney told his authors, as standard royalty rates on commercial releases at the time amounted to just 5 per cent – even with the higher sale price. Shareware was better for both authors and customers, he insisted. 'Everybody wins with shareware.'

True to his assertion, he had plans for Epic and its fans and authors to all win. Writing in the first Epic Insider Newsletter to his fast-growing ensemble of game authors and contributors, including 'a team of eight brilliant graphics wizards from Holland' that he'd found and recruited online, Sweeney said the goal for 1992 would be to get three games in the Shareware Top Ten – to out-compete Apogee and outdo leading independents like David Gray (*Hugo's House of Horrors*). To do that he argued that they needed to place both authors – 'The key to success is promoting our *authors* more than just our name' – and customers – their 'first and foremost priority' – on a pedestal. Alongside this, they had to make the best games. They needed to have cutting-edge graphics and sound that matched or exceeded the standards set on the Sega Genesis and just-released Super Nintendo.

And in a show of how far he was already thinking into the future, Sweeney predicted that they'd have multiple full-time staffers within a year, 'once the next generation of games debut and the royalties start flowing.'

He had good reason to be optimistic. That Dutch team of graphics wizards, together known as Ultra Force, was one of the leading demoscene groups in the world, capable of incredible feats of real-time graphics and sound programming that blew everything else out of the water – commercial or shareware. They'd just built their famous VectorDemo, the first real-time 3D graphics demonstration software for IBM PC compatibles, which was shared around the world and displayed at computer trade shows to showcase what the machines were capable of. And they were interested in working with Epic.

Better yet, Tim Sweeney himself was well underway with creating a 256-colour Nintendo-style action-platformer that he was sure would leave *Commander Keen* and *Duke Nukem* in the dust, and he had another of his Best of *ZZT* contest winners, Beth Daggert, in the early stages of development on a breakthrough fantasy RPG that would combine the role-playing aspects of genre stalwart *Ultima* with the graphics and action of *Duke Nukem* – whereby traditional RPG traits would not be a weighted random element in combat but rather an actual skill bonus such as faster shooting or higher jumping.

Epic had already rocketed its way into second place in the shareware games business. Now, Sweeney was sure, they'd be toe-to-toe for first.

Try, try again

With a second major player on the shareware scene using the Apogee model, and numerous others beginning to adopt the concept for their own games, the old style of shareware had gone out of vogue. People had long joked that nobody paid for shareware, but here, clearly, was evidence that plenty of people did. They just needed a push – a tangible, enticing reward, preferably in the form of more of something they already loved.

Many authors began to enforce the 30-day restrictions they'd put in their shareware notice (typically written in some variant of 'if you use this software for more than 30 days, you must register it'), writing code to check at start-up how many days had passed since it was first launched on the computer. A user would be locked out if they ran over. Others looked to the precedents set by successful shareware programs. Most tried multiple things, and kept the ideas that worked.

Take the example of box-pushing puzzle game *Crates* (1991), by Mark Batchelor. The original shareware release (self-identified as a demo) had five levels – each of which involved moving a character around to push boxes onto marked squares, taking care not to get them stuck in a corner along the way (because they couldn't be pulled back out). Registering for $15 would get players 50 new levels, a level editor, a save game option, sound and playing-speed toggles, and the latest version of the game plus one free upgrade.

Come *Crates* update V.150, released a year after the original demo, Batchelor changed his tune. The *Crates* shareware edition now included all the features of the main game, except for the level editor (now listed as an inaccessible menu option) and the 50 extra levels of the full version – meaning players of the free version could now save, turn the sound off, and adjust the playing speed, for an experience exactly like the registered game.

When it came time to release his second game, falling-block puzzler *Jelly Bean Factory*, in 1993, Batchelor would follow the same format: the shareware release was a full-featured game, but only for one level – then it put up a notice saying you had to register to play any further.

Likewise, Carr Software made its shareware debut in 1990 with just one playable mission out of the full game's eight, in the remarkable textmode multidirectional shoot-'em-up *Hover Craft*, which asked players to destroy several missile launchers without being struck by any of their missiles or running into any of the fortifications that protected them – and while managing separate sets of keyboard controls for guiding craft movement and shooting direction.

It was based on a commercial game that Richard Carr had written several years earlier for the Atari 8-bit home computer – before Atari crashed and forced him to return to non-games programming for a few years. When Carr saw shareware towards the end of the decade he decided to get back into games again, so he made *Hover Craft*, which soon changed name to *Islands of Danger* for reasons he doesn't recall.

Its fast action and scrolling combined with the perils of navigating sweeping mountain ranges, narrow passageways, dense forests (which slowed the craft down), and wide-open fields and waterways made for an intense, exciting experience that wowed players. But it gained little traction and Carr doesn't believe it ever made him much money across either of these initial releases or its later re-release as *Rescue* in 1994 – with an added 'learning mode' for beginners and the option of random missile-launcher placement.

Carr's second shareware game *Capture the Flag*, by contrast, earned rave reviews and tens of thousands of dollars.

His concept this time drew from a childhood experience, around 'late elementary or early junior high', when his dad took him to join his older brother on a Boy Scouts overnight trip. 'And out in the high desert, they were playing a game called Capture the Flag,' Carr recalls. 'And they were having a blast.'

The experience stayed with him, so after *Islands of Danger* he combined it with the turn-based mechanics he'd seen in *Sid Meier's Civilization* and Avalon Hill's military board games and asked his dad to draw graphics for him. Nearly three years and an estimated 2,600 hours of development time later, *Capture the Flag* was done.

The game worked as follows: two players (or one player and the computer) were each granted control of a team, their goal being to infiltrate the other team's territory and capture their flag. Players took turns to move all of their team members, assigning commands until no movement points remained. Characters could run, walk, crawl, or stand, their visibility and their field of vision both affected by their stance as well as their terrain, and their effectiveness in each stance evaluated against their innate attributes (vision, agility, movement, and stealth). If 'captured' by the other team, rendered in a little animated scuffle, a character would be sent to 'prison' to wait until either the end of the game or a set number of turns elapsed. The majority of the map would be blacked out initially, with terrain revealed as the player explored the wilderness – which was a beautiful blend of grass, trees, rocks, roads, rivers, fences, and fields.

From these simple rules and mechanics emerged dozens of viable strategies and a raft of tactical options worthy of any great wargame – except with none of the military history or violence.

Critics adored the game's non-violent strategy and playful reproduction of a childhood pastime. The Associated Press called its programming 'top of the line, with thoughtful help and dialogue boxes and widely varied terrain', while *Computer Games Strategy Plus* noted it would 'fill many a lunch hour' and *Computer*

Gaming World described it as 'an enjoyable diversion worthy of consideration' – with added praise for its multi-generational appeal and commercial-quality presentation. *Computer Player* went even further, suggesting it was 'strategy in the purest sense', with a remarkable and original design and slick interface that made it 'a shareware gaming experience not to be missed'.

Shareware vendors rallied behind it, too. Public Brand Software and PsL gave it awards and prime catalogue placement while AOL marked it a Top Pick after it surpassed 25,000 downloads through the service.

Its mega-success was not reflected in shareware registrations, however, which Carr says were 'almost enough to live off of' for a year or two. He'd tried to adopt the emerging wisdom of selling people on access to extra content, with the registered version allowing for any combination of eight distinct game types (such as traditional, multiple captures, and visible flags) rather than just one, plus 30 scenarios, 30 maps, a map builder, and several other additional features. But it didn't work. *Capture the Flag*'s registration rate was appallingly low. 'I don't know whether I gave away too much of the game,' ponders Carr, who suspects maybe the problem was the type of game it was.

'With Apogee, you were left hanging there,' he says, in reference to their episodic model. 'And with *Capture the Flag*, no, you can play a complete game... What you miss now is more of a variety, different maps. And you can have larger teams, et cetera. But apparently not enough of a draw for someone to send in a cheque.'

Another developer that struggled to figure out how to market a shareware strategy wargame was Casey Butler (publishing under the name Viable Software Alternatives), who had first released his *Risk*-like world-domination strategy game *World Empire* in December 1991 with a request to 'send a contribution' if players enjoyed the game.

By March he was ready to try a new approach, dropping a new version through a small publisher called Ultimate Software that overhauled the message. Now players were asked to send $25 if they'd enjoyed the game for either thirty days or five plays. In return they were promised not a vague 'disk full of neat stuff' as a reward – as with the original release – but rather technical support and a deluxe version of *World Empire* that allowed for up to three computer-controlled opponents (rather than just one) in solo play.

This worked well enough that Butler was able to further expand the game. *World Empire II* (1992–3) switched from DOS to Windows, added an alternative start condition – all nations conquered versus all nations neutral – and increased the possible player count. Plus it introduced three new ideologies, which functioned in the game as a kind of religion – nations that shared the same ideology would be easier to conquer and retain than those that followed a different one.

This sequel got a favourable write-up in the book *Windows Shareware 500*. *World Empire II* was one of 'the best' shareware Windows programs available at the time, the book declared, with special praise for its immense detail and propensity to surprise players with sudden revolts. A third entry published in 1994 did even better, thanks to a glowing review and Best Shareware Strategy Game Award from *Computer Gaming World* in 1995.

Dongleware

But when it came to designating a 'best of' label to shareware games from the era, many puzzle fans could look no further than German title *Oxyd*. It was an updated version of an earlier Atari ST game by developer Meinolf Amekudzi (né Schneider) called *Esprit* (1989), which followed the principle that players should learn how to play a game *by playing it*.

GENERAL RICH:
YOU ARE THE HEROIC LEADER OF THE
WORLD POPULIST MOVEMENT. YOU ARE
CURRENTLY BASED IN MADAGASCAR.

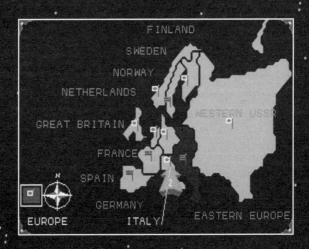

FINLAND

SWEDEN

NORWAY

NETHERLANDS

GREAT BRITAIN

WESTERN USSR

FRANCE

SPAIN

N

GERMANY

EUROPE   ITALY   EASTERN EUROPE

For *Oxyd*'s design, Amekudzi devised a series of virtual 'landscapes' in which the player explored the interactivity of different game elements through a mouse-controlled, momentum-directed ball. 'Most landscapes are about touching stones one after the other,' he explains, 'which then display a pattern. If the same patterns are revealed one after the other, these stones remain open, [and] a landscape is solved when all stones are opened.'

Many stones are blocked or hidden by other objects in the environment, and so the challenge is, as Amekudzi explains, 'to find out how to get to the individual stones with the ball'.

To sweeten the experience, and to make the most of the Atari ST's high-resolution monochrome display mode, Amekudzi layered in a number of cutting-edge technical features. The whole game ran in perfect synchronisation with the 72-hertz CRT computer monitors of the day, for one thing, which meant it had smooth, fast animation as well as an unusually high degree of responsiveness to player input. But also it had six-channel high-bitrate sound at a then-high sampling rate of 20kHz (CD quality is 44.1kHz, but most computer games at the time were 11kHz or less).

ST-Magazin called *Oxyd* 'revolutionary', and it was – though not for its slick, well-designed puzzling, which required both patience and intelligence (as well as a steady hand) to solve. The cleverest thing about *Oxyd* was actually its business model.

Amekudzi had noticed how shareware was brilliant as a distribution method – between BBSs, shareware disk vendors, word-of-mouth sharing, and magazine coverdisks, shareware software could rapidly reach hundreds of thousands of people. But it was rarely successful financially. 'On the other hand,' he explains, 'a pure purchase software requires adequate financial resources for advertising and commercial sales.'

Many shareware authors had come to this same realisation before him, but Amekudzi's solution was new. He decided to repurpose the idea of a software dongle – a physical copy-protection device that had to be plugged in for an application to run. In his case, the dongle would be a book.

After the tenth landscape, players would, at every level, encounter a stone that could not be removed without typing a specific three-character code – a magic spell, as it were. And to get these codes (along with various hints and strategies), players needed to buy the *Oxyd Book* – which contained a multi-page table listing the codes, and which was printed in a variety of combinations of non-repro blue ink with several other shades of blue to prevent photocopying. Amekudzi called his model 'dongleware', and as luck would have it the move turned out to be cheaper for him too, as book sales in Germany were taxed at a lower rate than software.

He initially released *Oxyd* for Atari ST in 1990. An updated version with colour graphics followed in 1991, which in 1992 then got translated into English and French and cross-compiled (as they ran on the same processor type) for Mac, Amiga, and the NeXTcube – the second computer model from NeXT, which Steve Jobs founded after he was forced out of Apple in 1985. A DOS port followed that same year.

Its reception was almost uniformly positive. Fans wrote in from all around the world to tell Amekudzi how much they loved the game, while critics gushed over its addictive puzzles. Mac magazines *Macworld* and *Macwelt* gave it awards ('Best Brain Game' of the year and 'Game of the Month', respectively), while US-based Amiga magazine *Amazing Computing* wrote '*Oxyd* should please even the most jaded of Amiga gamers' and its British contemporary *Amiga World* called it 'an exquisite puzzle game of a sort we don't see very often'. *ST-Magazin* and *Amiga Power* gave it glowing reviews, too, and years later *Inside Mac Games* would rate *Oxyd* one of the ten best shareware games of all time.

For all the love, however, *Oxyd*'s financial success was rather more limited. 'Around 12,000 books of all [dongleware] games were sold worldwide,' Amekudzi remembers, combining the sales for both the original German Atari ST release with the multi-platform international version and the sequel *Per.Oxyd*. A commercial version called *Oxyd Magnum* was sold through retail channels at much higher volume, but Amekudzi says its profits were low due to the trading margins.

> I was able to make a living from the sales, but then there was no finances left for new developments. On the other hand, there were a lot of fans of my games and due to the idealistic success there were many freelance offers. Ultimately, I lived off the resulting fame, in which I received lucrative contracts from the industry.

Inventive as it was, Amekudzi's dongleware model of shareware proved logistically challenging. Books were expensive to produce, and to ship, and while the games could include a language toggle, to switch between English, French, and German, there needed to be a separate book created for each language and then distributed locally in each territory. As such, dongleware was widely celebrated but rarely imitated. More often, shareware authors focused instead on a wide array of variants of the tried and true: if you send in money, you receive more content to add to your game.

Refinement

One-man company Everett Kaser Software made a point of adapting – and experimenting with – other people's innovations in the shareware business models. Kaser was inspired to enter the shareware business by Nels Anderson's *Mah Jongg*, which he felt could benefit from alternative tile layout and graphics options. So he made his own tile-matching game called *Solitile* (1989 to present) and put it out under a traditional shareware model: if you like it, send $10 to support the author, $15 to have the latest version mailed to you on a floppy disk, or $35 to get the game's source code (for private use only).

With the version 3.0 release in September 1991, Kaser introduced $5 'Accessory Disks' that included additional tile sets, tile layouts, background images, and music files. (Then six years later, with his first Windows release, he would merge these into the registration price, which was increased to $24.)

In the meantime, encouraged by the minor, good-but-not-enough-to-quit-his-day-job success of *Solitile*, he expanded his games catalogue with a kind of *Pac-Man* meets *Robotron* arcade-style maze shoot-'em-up called *Snarf*, first published in 1988 as freeware, then remade in October 1990 as shareware. Players could press the arrow keys to control their character's movement and tap the W, A, S, and D keys to fire at enemies – who would try to dodge shots – in any of four directions, all while navigating a maze. And as if that wasn't already hard enough to manage, they also needed to collect treasure to increase their score, grab keys that unlocked doors, and avoid running out of 'tags' (health points).

Kaser set a registration fee for *Snarf* of $15, with the added incentive that registered players would receive 'at LEAST 20 levels' – the exact number being dependent on how many he'd finished creating when he received an order (which 12 months on had climbed to 39). Registered users could also submit their own levels, created with the built-in level editor, and if Kaser accepted three levels from the same person they'd receive one free update (otherwise updates cost $5).

After *Snarf*, Kaser wasn't sure what to do for his next project. *Snarf* registrations were far less than *Solitile*, so he knew it wouldn't

SHAREWARE HEROES

be another action game. He later said in an interview with RGB Classic Games that he then asked himself 'What actually made *Solitile* SO much fun to play?' It was simultaneously complex, simple, and highly interactive, he decided, and he had struck a fine balance between these three elements. The challenge was how to capture that magic in another puzzle game.

Then he remembered a famous logic puzzle he'd been given in a high-school geometry class: Who Drinks Water and Who Owns the Zebra? (also known as the Zebra Puzzle or Einstein's Riddle). It included a set of fifteen statements, such as 'There are five houses', 'The green house is immediately to the right of the ivory house', and 'Milk is drunk in the middle house', and then asked that titular question. Puzzle solvers needed sound reasoning and deductive logic to determine the answer.

With *Sherlock* (1991 to present), Kaser combined that puzzle format with pictographs and the popular number-placement puzzle game *Sudoku*. This time registration would grant players an alternative set of pictographs, but otherwise everyone had the same game. And once again he shifted the model over time. At release the shareware version had all 65,536 puzzles from the registered version, while version 2.0 – released in July 1993 – would reduce the puzzle count of the shareware edition down to 200, and version 2.07 – released three years later – would cut it to just 100.

The tinkering worked. Both *Solitile* and *Sherlock* had sold well from the beginning, but over time registrations grew. And even as Kaser shifted to Windows and added more games to his catalogue, each building on the lessons of past releases, they would remain his bestsellers. (So successful were they that in 1997 he cited them as the reason he could finally quit his day job and turn to shareware full time.)

But for now, shareware was still a business in flux. New ideas were coming and going constantly, with hundreds or even thousands of variants of each money-making concept. Only a few people had figured out what would make money, and how to package games for maximum success, and even they only really knew how to succeed within a tiny subset of what *could* work in shareware.

Word was spreading fast of Apogee and Epic's big profits with episodic shareware, but it wasn't driving copycats so much as encouraging more new entrants to the field – each with their own quirky, individualistic interpretation of what *might* succeed. Just as Tim Sweeney's infectious enthusiasm for the future was no anomaly, this was indeed an exciting time to be in shareware.

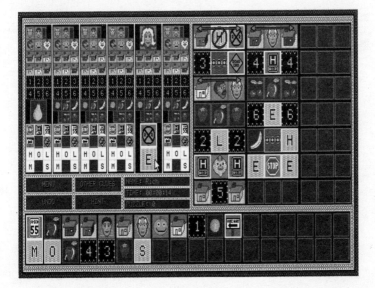

CHAPTER 8

Experimental, Experiential Weirdness

By the early 1990s, the computer games industry at large had lost much of its freewheeling spirit. It was a professional space, filled with established companies and genres, big-name designers, and the kind of money that makes people less creative with their ideas. It wasn't a stale industry, by any means – new genres and design innovations were still emerging every year. But the sense that they were at the vanguard of a revolution had begun to give way to an attitude more of evolution: take an existing concept and tweak it. Extend it. Combine it with something else.

The time had passed where major publishers would greenlight weird concepts like Denton Designs' *Frankie Goes to Hollywood* (1985; an avant-garde game named after a British band and set in a mundane, generic Merseyside neighbourhood) or David Crane's *Little Computer People* (1985; interact with a virtual man who lives in a house inside the computer). Partly it was a growing understanding of what does well at retail and what doesn't; partly it was a shift in the power structures from creatives to businesspeople; and partly it was the kind of risk aversion that comes when development teams and budgets grow exponentially, while sales fail to keep up. The end result was the same – weird games were hard to sell, even if they were good.

But over in the alternative dimension that was shareware, weird was half the point. A successful shareware game needed to stand out, and to stand out meant either being brilliant-yet-conventional or good-yet-unconventional. Weird, in other words, was a badge of honour in the shareware scene. It was not only part of the origin story of shareware's fast-growing titans – Apogee, id, and Epic – but also integral to the popularity of numerous shareware games, including *Continuum, Caper in the Castro, Moraff's Revenge, Flightmare,* and *Hugo's House of Horrors,* among others.

Case in point: *F. Godmom* by John Blackwell (publishing as Soggybread Software, a name he took from a quote he'd read of a Bible verse that he thought sounded like a good metaphor for shareware). Blackwell had designed the game after falling in love with the 1987 NES version of hit 1983 Apple II game *Lode Runner,* a puzzle-platformer in which the player had to collect all the gold on every level and then escape the pursuant guards through a ladder at the top. The player could also dig temporary holes in the platforms to escape through or to briefly trap a guard, buying more time for an escape or safe passage to a nearby ladder.

'I didn't want to just remake *Lode Runner,* though,' Blackwell recalls. There were already clones aplenty of it. Rather, he wanted to create a game *like Lode Runner.* Something similar, yet different:

> I had this picture in my head of a character running straight at an enemy, casting a spell to turn them into a ladder, climbing that ladder to safety, and then being safely away when the spell wears off the bewildered enemy. Taking the elements of a character who can cast spells to transform

things, but only for a limited time, led me to think of the fairy godmothers in the Cinderella story. DOS file names were limited to eight characters, though, so I had to shorten the name to *F.Godmom* (fgodmom.exe).

His concept involved playing a fairy godmother who needs to collect magic coins while avoiding evil crabs and searching for a key to reveal a level's exit in order to bring her one step closer to rescuing her friends. To help her in her quest, players could wield her magic wand in much the same way as a paint program's copy and paste commands. The wand could transform any object in the environment into another (a crab becomes a ladder, for instance, or perhaps a ladder becomes a wall), provided they first gather a 'wand pattern' by touching the wand to the desired object.

Blackwell was in college studying computer science at the time. He'd stay up until 4 a.m. working on his game each day, sleep until noon, then get up, go to his day's classes, and do his lab work. After nine months of this, he had a complete game – though he's the first to admit it wasn't very good. 'One of my issues was that I was working alone,' he says. 'My artistic skills range from very limited to non-existent. I was also still a novice programmer.'

Despite its technical and graphical shortcomings, he decided to publish his game as shareware. 'As a person who didn't (and doesn't) like trying to sell people things, it seemed like the lightest-touch sales model of all,' he explains. This way he could avoid the big pitch; you'd get the game free, then either you'd pay because you liked it or you wouldn't pay at all.

My assumption was that most people would be like me, cheap, and I expected to get mostly $5 registrations with a few people paying $10 and infrequently $20. I was quite surprised when the vast majority of registrations were $10 and $20, with an almost exact 50/50 split between the two highest tiers.

F.Godmom didn't make Blackwell much money – he estimates that he received 'maybe a couple thousand registrations' across the multi-year life of the game, which would receive its final update (to version 5.0) in 1996. But it soon caught the eye of Tom Hall, who shared the game within the office at id and then sent Blackwell a letter to say what a cool game he thought it was. Not only that, Hall also passed along sample code from John Carmack for faster keyboard input handling and gave Blackwell a tip about how to change the fairy's skin colour from yellow to pink. Better yet for Blackwell, id's resident artist Adrian Carmack redrew the game's graphics, unasked and unprompted, to polish up its presentation, and Hall slipped a mention of *F.Godmom* into id's next game (a not-so-little thing called *Wolfenstein 3D*, coming up in the next chapter).

No less unusual than *F.Godmom*, Christian Boutin's *Tournament of Zulala* (1991) put a fantasy twist on the then-emerging fighting game genre. It involved one-on-one duels and tournaments between an odd assortment of characters: a human, a four-legged 'land octopus', an ostrich, a dog, a half-human and half-spider creature called a 'drider', an eye, a zombie, and a cyclops, all rendered in hand-drawn CGA-coloured graphics. And to explain the strangeness, it had a fittingly elaborate set-up that established a great city called Zulala as a kind of early-sixteenth-century Constantinople – a vast, cultured, awe-inspiring, and chaotic city with the magnetism to draw competitors from far and wide for 'the greatest tournament of all'.

Boutin even incorporated his shareware model into the game's story. Anyone could access the tournament mode, but to do so required that players first accomplish an 'errand' for the guards at the gates of town. Fail to complete the errand – or get it wrong – and the player would be barred from tournament entry. And only registered players would be given the information – a list of drinking preferences for the characters – needed to get it right.

The offbeat quirkiness of their presentation and thematics aside, *Tournament of Zulala* and *F.Godmom* weren't all that weird – they were still conventional genre pieces beneath the surface. Not so for Robert Carr's surrealistic Mac games *Mormonoids from the Deep* (1988), *Mac Spudd!* (1990), and *MacJesus: Your Personal Savior on a Floppy Disk* (1991).

The first two leveraged the first-person-perspective graphics-and-text adventure game engine World Builder. Rather than offering a typical fantasy adventure, however, they sent players on weaponised vehicular quests to escape the fictional town of Mormonville (in the case of *Mormonoids*) or to haul potatoes across post-apocalyptic Idaho (in *Mac Spudd!*), along the way grappling with the likes of giant mutant bunnies, menacing helicopters, and Bible-toting missionaries. The third game, meanwhile, involved interacting with a sassy, smack-talking, blasphemous, nicotine-addicted depiction of Jesus Christ for off-colour life advice – or a spot of intentionally offensive cartoony pin-the-nail-on-the-saviour playfulness. (Clicking nearly anywhere on the screen would trigger some kind of animation involving the game's always-visible, hand-drawn Jesus face – usually in the form of some minor torture.)

Llama time

But weird as games like this were, with people like Jeff Minter just coming into the shareware scene, things were only going to get weirder.

Minter had made his name in the UK games industry during the 1980s bedroom coder boom as a creator of offbeat arcade-style games for retail or mail-order distribution on Commodore and Sinclair home computers. He'd dropped out of university to work as a programmer for software company DK'Tronics, for which he wrote several popular ZX81 games, but left due to a dispute over unpaid royalties. Then when a serious illness left him bedridden, mere weeks into a renewed attempt at further education, he'd turned again to games as a way to pass the time.

Soon after, in 1982, he started his own independent publishing label, Llamasoft. His first Llamasoft game was *Andes Attack*, a Commodore VIC-20 clone of horizontally scrolling kill-the-aliens-and-rescue-the-humans shooter *Defender*, except with the humans swapped for llamas. It wasn't anything special, other than the amusing idea that aliens would come to Earth specifically to ransack our llama population, but he sold all the copies he'd made during the first morning of a computer show. Then soon after he was offered a US distribution deal for a cartridge version.

And so began a new workflow for the sheep-, camel-, and llama-obsessed programmer. He'd make 'beastie'-filled arcade-style games, often with help on graphics or coding conversions to other platforms, then he'd sell them in the UK through computer shows and direct deals with local and international distributors – self-published.

One of his biggest successes from the era would prove to be 1983 Commodore 64 and Atari 8-bit game *Attack of the Mutant Camels*, which was inspired by a review he'd read of a licensed-game tie-in to *Star Wars* film *The Empire Strikes Back*. The review had described the game's AT-AT vehicles as 'giant mechanical camels', which Minter thought was delightful – so he made his own version where players would fight against a horde of giant mutant camels.

In an era of gradual consolidation and grouping of games programmers, plucked from their bedrooms and recruited en masse into software houses, Minter was a rare stalwart of the bedroom coder ethos – whereby experimentation, fun, and innovation trumped commercial considerations. He was also a rockstar of the 1980s UK software scene – a long-haired, unorthodox, often controversial programming genius whom the magazines loved to cover and whose fans adored him.

But come 1991, after contributing to the ill-fated and ultimately cancelled Konix console, Minter found himself unable to find a distributor for his latest game *Llamatron*. It was a multidirectional shoot-'em-up, inspired by arcade hit *Robotron*, whereby players would control a llama that had been equipped with a powerful laser weapon. The llama could move in any direction, and likewise the laser could fire in any direction – each independent of the other. The goal was to kill all the on-screen alien mutants while collecting any power-ups or friendly creatures that appeared. And in a typically Minter quirk, those nasty mutants could take various unusual guises – including Coca-Cola cans, hamburgers, skulls, kitchen utensils, exploding hedgehogs, Mandelbrot sets, and even a huge toilet that fired rolls of toilet paper at the player.

It was utterly nonsensical and absurd, but it displayed Minter's full mastery of the shoot-'em-up genre. And it even had digitised sound. Yet Minter had a problem.

'To publish a game effectively is no longer really practical for a small outfit like ourselves,' he wrote in his newsletter, disillusioned and downbeat. 'The simple act of putting out good games at a good price isn't enough to ensure that distributors will buy your games. You need to spend thousands on advertising alone to launch a game properly.'

The changing games market had finally caught up with him, and he was beginning to work with publishers on a 'game-by-game basis'. But he hated that publishers seemed to only want 'conventional stuff or licences'. There had to be another way – and of course there was.

Shareware had never taken off in the UK, and it had scarcely worked at all for UK-made games, but Minter's only other options for publishing *Llamatron* were to go through a budget enterprise – for a low-cost, no-thrills retail release that might net him several thousand pounds in royalties – or to roll with the hobbyists in the licenceware space. He didn't much like those ideas.

He did, however, love the concept of shareware. He considered it 'a near-perfect means of software distribution' – provided, that is, all parties were honest. Minter adored the idea that, rather than having to pay for advertising, flashy packaging, or disk duplication, a shareware author could simply start the chain of distribution and then let their fans do the rest. And he thought the long tail and editorial freedom of shareware was a godsend. 'You can be as weird as you like,' he wrote in his newsletter. 'Good software will tend to do well and survive, spreading out into the datasphere; bad stuff just won't get spread, and will fail.'

But ideal though it was, Minter doubted there were enough honest customers to support shareware games publishing in its purest form. So, hoping to be proven wrong, he decided to try an experiment: he'd publish *Llamatron* as shareware – unlimited, complete, and unencumbered – and as an incentive to pay the £5 fee he'd send anyone who registered the game a copy of *Andes Attack*, which he'd rewritten for Atari ST, along with a copy of his newsletter.

The magazines loved it. *ST Action* called *Llamatron* 'the best blastathon that the ST has and will likely ever see', while *Computer & Video Games* described it as 'one of the best things Minter's done in ages' and *Amiga Format* complained that the

Amiga conversion he released a few months later was so good they found it 'difficult to describe just how good *Llamatron* really is'. *Amiga Computing* loved it so much they put it on their coverdisk – netting Minter free distribution to thousands more potential customers.

All that press goodwill no doubt helped Minter as he became the first British game developer to have a shareware hit. By March 1992, roughly a year after *Llamatron*'s Atari ST release, Minter had already received 800 registrations (for a total of £4,000 revenue). Over the life of the game, which he later also ported to DOS, he would receive significantly more – thousands more, many of whom shared their stories along with their payment.

Llamatron's success spurred on a spate of other British shareware hopefuls in the Atari ST and Amiga realms. Most of these stuck with the usual PD formula of redoing a popular arcade game, as was accomplished particularly well on Atari ST shareware by Sinister Developments – which released well-received, unofficial conversions of arcade hits *Asteroids, Galaxian, Space Invaders,* and *Centipede.*

One of the most original shareware games of the era combined the familiarity of Sierra On-Line's bestselling graphic adventure *Quest* games (*King's Quest, Space Quest, Leisure Suit Larry,* etc.) with the unusual subject matter of an old man in a wheelchair. Ian Scott's *Grandad and The Quest for The Holey Vest* (1992) followed the trials and tribulations of a forgetful and grumpy 'old geezer' who had misplaced his favourite vest and wanted to find it.

Scott developed the game after deciding that Sierra's games were overly frustrating and 'far too pedantic' for his tastes. 'I just thought I could do it better,' he recalls. He'd been dabbling in programming and game development for around a decade at that point, starting in BASIC on a Sinclair ZX80 and the BBC

Micro machines at his school in the early 1980s and then moving into the more advanced (though slow) STOS BASIC when he got an Atari ST. On that machine he remembers making a few small games just for his family to play, including a hangman-type game and an adaptation of the TV gameshow *Countdown*, before secretly developing a program to predict betting pool results – badly, it turned out.

Grandad was a first attempt at making something more substantial, and it starred an old man in a wheelchair as a workaround for the Atari ST's memory restrictions. When coding in STOS, he found there wasn't enough memory available to both display the room and an animated main character. 'So I thought about how I could have someone moving around whilst being still,' he says. 'A wheelchair seemed the obvious solution.' Then couple that with an older, bearded version of himself and *bam* – he had his leading man, a cynical old guy who loves to crack wise at both his neighbours and the player controlling him.

The game's central premise was that old Grandad is a forgetful fellow who always puts his things in strange places and then can't remember where he left them. 'Waking up this morning he finds himself in his Entrance Hall (you see what I mean?) and discovers there is a bit of a nip in the air,' the introductory text stated. 'He decides that he'll need to put on his string vest but can't quite remember where it is...'

Thus begins an absurd odyssey through Grandad's weird home and equally weird mind, taking care to recharge his wheelchair before the battery runs out, briefly engaging in repartee with a neighbourhood boy, and collecting an assortment of keys to open doors to strange rooms that on close inspection reveal more odd clues that eventually lead to the discovery of accidental torture of Grandad's nurse, an underground labyrinth, and – eventually – Grandad's vest.

Scott decided to release *Grandad* as shareware in a nod to top coder Jeff Minter, whose own foray into shareware had seemed to accentuate his 'street cred' with Atari ST fans already in awe of Minter's ability to code entire games in Assembly. But rather than follow in Minter's footsteps by selling the game under the traditional shareware licence of 'if you like the game, please send me £5', Scott opted to incentivise players by requiring a registration code to continue past a certain point – the entrance to a maze-like underground tunnel section, a little over a third of the way through the game. (He also declared his game 'guaranteed llama free' at the end of its shareware notice.)

In exchange for their £5 registration fee, Scott would send players the code to enter into the tunnel door's security pad.

It worked a treat. *Grandad* registrations came swarming in after a glowing review in *ST Format* magazine, ultimately earning Scott more than £10,000. Occasionally he'd receive an angry letter from a disgruntled parent who was upset at the game's crude humour being unsuitable for children, but *Grandad* was a hit.

It was only natural, then, to make a sequel: *Grandad II: In Search of Sandwiches*. This time the cranky old man ventured far beyond his house, seated in his motorised tricycle, searching for his misplaced sandwiches in the local park and the adjoining Funland complex. It had better graphics, more animation, sampled sound, and much more polish, and it was – reviewers, Scott, and your humble *Shareware Heroes* author all agreed – a better game than the first one. But it never caught on.

Perhaps the extra year put it too late in the Atari ST's life to attract a large audience (the Atari computer line was discontinued in late 1993, amidst declining sales and shifting focus internally at Atari). Or it could have been the higher price tag (£8 to register, rather than the original's £5), or reduced novelty or less press coverage. Or, Scott suggests, 'I think I was just getting a bit too big for my boots.'

Whatever the reason, *Grandad II* faded into obscurity, and Scott's attempts to catch up to the emerging 3D revolution in games also failed (through a combination of poor reviews for his *Glass Buttock of Tharg* game and slow progress in learning C++). So after roughly two years, three published games, and nearly £20,000 in shareware registrations, Scott bowed out of the games business – never to return.

This kind of transience was commonplace in the shareware games scene. Developers would often make just one or two games and disappear – their fire for game-making burnt out through changing passions or priorities or technology, or perhaps from the discouragement of a shareware release left unnoticed and unregistered by an increasingly jaded audience that felt it had seen several-too-many unremarkable rehashes of the same few ideas. Or, in rarer cases, they'd disappear from the shareware scene because they had bigger things brewing in the commercial space.

MicroMan

Consider Brian Goble, a programmer whose brief foray into shareware as a mid-90s side project played a critical role in the rise of a now-major game company called Monolith Productions.

Goble had come to computer games in the 1980s through arcades and a seventh-grade computer class where he and his classmates would type in BASIC code to make simple ASCII-graphics games for Commodore PET. A few years later he'd got his own computer, an Atari 800, and when he wasn't playing pirated games he was making his own. He loved text-based adventures like *Zork*, so he developed his own adventure-creation system.

'And it would say like, "Enter the description for room number one? What are the exits?"' recalls Goble. 'And it was kind of a simple grid-based system. But you could make a text adventure out of it.'

He sent a copy of the program to *Antic* magazine, whose editors wrote back to say that they were going to publish it in an upcoming book of games (which was later cancelled). As one of the authors, he would receive a small share of the sales revenue. Goble couldn't believe it. 'I'm 15, right, and I'm just flipping out,' he recalls. 'This is the coolest thing ever to me. And plus I was like, "Wait, you can make money making [games]?"'

He was hooked on the idea, so when he moved on to IBM PCs a couple of years later he remade his text-adventure creation program. Then he made another version that could be used to create graphical adventures. Soon after, during his first year of college, he met Garth Hitchens, who did contract game development. To help spread the load, Hitchens asked Goble to do half of a new project to port an Apple II game called *Pharaoh's Revenge* to DOS. It would need Assembly language to run smoothly, but Hitchens promised to teach Goble everything he needed to know.

That led to Goble doing more contract work with Hitchens, then to him creating another game engine. He used this to make small action games that he sold to Softdisk magazines *Big Blue Disk* and *On Disk Monthly*. He'd earn 'a couple grand' for each one, and he even had one – 1989 game *Roboman* – published commercially by a small company called XOR Corporation.

When Windows 3.0 came out in mid-1990, Goble got a part-time job at the University of Washington technical communications department. They were all Mac people, but they'd received a grant (to make traffic software) that was partially funded by Microsoft – so they needed a PC guy, and they needed that PC guy to learn Windows programming.

After a while, Goble realised he had learned enough to make a cool Windows 3.0 game. There were scant few Windows games at that point – essentially just some simulations and solitaire card games plus the *Microsoft Entertainment Pack.* And none of the fast-action or sprite-animated graphics that were the standard on DOS. But Goble knew it was possible, so he decided to prove it.

He began to rewrite his game engine using Windows 3.0 software libraries, calling it Windows Animation Package, or WAP for short. And to test it out as he went along, he ripped the graphics from a DOS game of his called *Alien Planet* – which included a pixel-perfect walking animation that he'd painstakingly crafted with help from a book on animation.

There was just one problem. DOS games ran at a resolution of 320 by 240 pixels (or at 320 by 200, stretched so the pixels are taller than they are wide). Windows ran at 640 by 480 – twice as big in each direction. 'So all my art looked tiny,' Goble recalls.

Rather than redraw his sprites to fit the higher resolution, he decided to embrace the small size. The main character would be a tiny human shrunken down in a lab experiment gone wrong and left to fend for himself in a hostile and suddenly unfamiliar world – visually styled to look like an enlarged microchip – where he's smaller than nearly everything he encounters. Goble called it *MicroMan.*

The game itself took its cue from Mike Denio's *Captain Comic.* MicroMan could run, jump, shoot, and climb ladders, and during the course of his adventure he'd encounter robots, floor and wall guns, teleporters, power-ups, and platforms that would move or fade in and out of existence.

Goble uploaded his *MicroMan* demo game to Usenet as part of a post about Windows Animation Package in January 1993. WAP 'brings the quality of a DOS-based game to the Windows [3.1] environment', the post explained, and *MicroMan* was a free demonstration of its capabilities and potential.

It was proof that Windows could pull off flicker-free

animation, and other developers were fascinated. Many responded, asking to see the source code, so Goble wrote up documentation and made WAP available as a package people could license for their own games. 'But then of course nobody wanted it,' he laughs. A few made 'somewhat serious' enquiries, but nobody signed up.

The reception for *MicroMan* itself was so strong that Goble also decided to expand his demo game into a fully fledged shareware release called *The Adventures of MicroMan*. 'Shareware was getting more popular,' he recalls, 'and I'm like, "Well, I'm just going to make a shareware game and kind of see what happens."'

In a nod to the Apogee model, he initially planned three chapters. The first adventure, *Crazy Computers*, would be free to download and share. Then *Adventure 2: Savage Stones* would be available only to people who registered. He also started development on the third adventure and planned to make a fourth after that, but neither of these eventuated.

He uploaded *Adventure 1* to a university FTP site in April and advertised it on Usenet, then marvelled as it spread around on its own. Windows users were thrilled to have a platformer to call their own, though many complained at how bitterly difficult the game was to complete. Goble would sometimes receive letters from people saying things such as 'I like to play this with my kids, but it's pretty challenging' or 'I don't like that the tank boss says "die" because I like to play with my kids.' Then he'd revise the game and put out a new version.

The game soon got picked up for wider distribution on shareware CD-ROM collections with generic names like Shareware Hits, 100 Action Arcade Games for Windows, 1000 DOS and Windows Games, or Exclusive WinGames, thereby massively widening its installed base of players. But Goble doesn't recall ever making anything more than 'pizza and beer'-type money from it.

He did eventually find value in his WAP engine, however. The original *MicroMan* demo landed him a job at Edmark making children's education software – where once again his Windows expertise made him hot property. Then he and his friends at Edmark got the idea to break off and form their own company (Monolith) to make their own games, and as they were making moves to do so they were tapped by Apogee to collaborate on what would be Apogee's first Windows 3.1 game. They built a prototype called Nuclear Nightmare, then scrapped it and started building a new version of *MicroMan* with professional art and sound when Microsoft and Apogee entered talks for having a game built in to Windows 95. But that too fell through when it became apparent there would only be around 150 KB of space for the game – far too little – on the Windows installation disks.

Then, *finally*, Windows Animation Package found use in another published game after Monolith got going – albeit in another rewrite of the engine, now called WAP32 and targeted at DirectX and Windows 95. 'And so we made three games at Monolith with it,' Goble says. 'Then when I left Monolith, I negotiated the rights to keep it. And then we made two dozen more games at HipSoft with it.'

Not bad for a little engine built essentially to prove a point – that Windows could do flicker-free animation. But then again that wasn't so unusual. Over at id Software the best new engine technology always started in much the same way.

Wolken

Programmed
by

KEN SILVERMAN

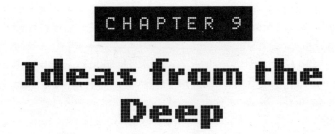

CHAPTER 9

Ideas from the Deep

After completing 11 games in just over 12 months and generating hundreds of thousands – if not millions – of dollars in gross revenue across four companies (Apogee, Softdisk, FormGen, and their own), the id Software crew had earned a break. But they had no intention of taking one. Instead, they wanted to invent a whole new kind of game.

As with *Commander Keen*, the driving force here was new technology – the relentless pursuit of new levels of immersion and immediacy. Three-dimensional graphics, or something that gave the illusion of them, combined with the smooth and fast action of id's 2D games. There was nothing inherently new about 3D in computer games – the idea had been around since the 1970s, with first-person-perspective games like *Maze*, *Spasim* (a contraction of 'space sim'), *dnd* (a first-person dungeon crawler), and *Airfight* (a flight combat simulator) giving the illusion of 3D in sharp wireframe graphics on mini-computers and the PLATO.

By 1991, the cutting-edge of 3D graphics in games had changed little. Those same four kinds of games had all improved their visual fidelity – they had texture and colour and real-time animation. But only flight simulators happened in true real time, and as such they were considered the pinnacle of games technology. They were popular, too. Barely a month passed by without at least one on the computer game bestsellers charts, and *Wing Commander*, a space-themed flight sim released months earlier to rave reviews, was at the cutting-edge of the genre. It had great atmosphere, stunning graphics, superb music, voiced dialogue, and hectic dogfights.

But Carmack thought it was weak. He didn't care about the cinematic stuff that the rest of the industry was gushing about. He wanted a 3D game with speed that rivalled arcade classics like *Defender* and *Asteroids*. And he didn't want to wait for computing power to catch up to the graphical fidelity pursued by games like *Wing Commander*. He wanted it now, even if that meant sacrificing visual detail. After some research, he had an idea for how to do it: raycasting.

The technique involved drawing lines and surfaces to the screen only if they'd be visible to the player in that frame, as though projecting them directly outwards from the player's eyes. By leaving floors and ceilings completely blank and using raycasting to fill in the walls and room contents, Carmack could drastically speed up performance. This was not a new idea; several others had done this before him – most notably in 3D maze game *WayOut* by Paul Allen Edelstein in 1982 on 8-bit computers and in the 1988 first-person action-adventure *The Colony* by Mac developer David Alan Smith. But these earlier efforts were hamstrung by a lack of computing power – made *possible*, not fast, by programming trickery. Carmack's timing was such that computers had just reached the point where they could handle the technique at the speed needed to make it convincing.

After six weeks of working on his new engine, Carmack took it to the rest of the team. They then developed *Hovertank*, a kind of indoor, fast-action, futuristic twist on *Battlezone*. While *Hovertank* went off to Softdisk to fulfil another game in the contract, Carmack continued improving his engine. *Hovertank*'s

speed was impressive, and its first-person perspective was cool, but it looked ugly and felt primitive, with big, garish blobs of solid colour everywhere. He needed to refine and extend his technology.

The answer came a few months later via a friend of Romero's – a former colleague from Origin, Paul Neurath, whose new company was developing a 3D first-person RPG called *Ultima*

Underworld with texture-mapped scenery. (Texture mapping involves painting images – or textures – onto the faces of 3D objects.) When Romero told Carmack, Carmack realised that he could put textures on the walls without compromising speed.

That led to *Catacomb 3-D*, a 3D sequel to an earlier id game called *Catacomb*. This time they did away with the futuristic tank conceit and instead made the player control a wizard searching a dungeon for an evil lich that had kidnapped his friend. The walls were textured as stones covered in green slime, and the player could see the wizard's hand outstretched in the lower centre of the screen, shooting fireballs – extending out as though it were the player's own.

When Scott Miller saw *Catacomb 3-D*, he knew he had to have a game like that for Apogee. For months he pressed the id boys to pitch him something similar. But when they finished the second *Keen* trilogy and finally had time to think about it, they came up with something better. They would do a 3D remake of 1981 stealth action-adventure game *Castle Wolfenstein*. Darting through labyrinths shooting Nazis, collecting treasure, searching for Hitler, exploring a contiguous space in real-time 3D – *it'll be incredible.*

Scott Miller agreed. He guaranteed them $100,000 and arranged for Apogee to make a game (titled *ScubaVenture*) for Softdisk in order to release them from their contract early. Then he offered them an unprecedented 50–50 royalty split, up from the 45 per cent he'd already boosted their *Commander Keen* royalties to post-release.

Before they dove into development, the id team decided to relocate to Texas to be closer to Apogee. They needed a place that could take five people, the fifth being artist Kevin Cloud, whom they'd just recruited from Softdisk. Romero remembers:

> So we went to all different kinds of [apartment] complexes
> and we finally settled on one called La Prada, which was

really nice. And it was Scott and George that drove us all over the place in their cars. George had an Acura, a red Acura NSX and Scott had a Nissan Turbo – a 360 Turbo. So they both had really nice cars (laughs). This is in March, late February of 1992, so they'd made money off of us already for at least a year at that point.

Once settled into their new place, they were back to work at the game. Then Scott Miller called and told them to forget about EGA graphics – just do the game in VGA. It would be a smaller market, but 'every single person who had VGA would absolutely have to own this game because they would want to show it off to all of their friends,' Miller told author David L. Craddock in an interview for *Rocket Jump*.

Soon after, they had another idea. *Catacomb 3-D*'s disembodied hand was a neat idea, but they thought it looked lame. And they didn't want to go to a third-person view, Romero explains, 'because we didn't want to waste CPU cycles by drawing a huge sprite over the back of the 3D render.' Instead, they realised, they could just draw a gun.

Meanwhile, as Hall and Romero relentlessly advocated the need for push-walls (walls that could be pushed in to reveal secrets), Adrian Carmack gleefully drew animations for the Nazi-killing carnage they would fill the game with, and composer Bobby Prince, who had also done the *Keen* sounds, brought the weapons to life (though the whole team chipped in on enemy shouts and death yells).

This would be the most in-the-moment game yet released, and anything extraneous to that vision had to go. Initial plans for elaborate design features like moving and searching dead bodies were stripped out in favour of pure id – violence, gore, aggression. To set the mood they added a voluntary rating of PC-13: Profound Carnage and a 'Death Cam' to replay boss kills at the end of each episode in slow motion. And to push back against retail partner FormGen's concerns that the game was too bloody, they dialled up the carnage to even more extreme levels. Blood and bits of flesh, extra Nazi screams, skeletons hanging from chains – anything that added shock value.

Scott Miller loved it. He approved the game, and the inventive difficulty-level descriptions that Hall typed up at the last minute – taunting players who wanted to play on easy mode with a portrait of protagonist B. J. Blazkowicz sucking a pacifier.

If all went well, they imagined, the six-episode *Wolfenstein 3D* release might earn twice as much as *Keen*. But – as before – their estimates were way off. A month on from its 5 May launch, id received a cheque for $100,000.

'It was very eye-opening for us and id Software,' remembers Miller, 'because no one expected the kind of revenues that that game pulled in. It was like 25 times more than any other game we'd ever released.'

Usenet, CompuServe, AOL, Prodigy, and the BBS scene had all gone wild with excitement. Nobody knew how to describe it – the nearest attempts to categorise were vague terms like '3D maze game' or '3D action game' – except to say it was intense, immersive, and brilliant.

Even the press got in on it.

Commander Keen (and *Duke Nukem* and *Jill of the Jungle* and every other popular shareware game) had barely registered a blip in the games and technology media. Only a handful of publications had covered them, and only briefly – with a few paragraphs or a half-page (or, rarely, full-page) review, usually in a shareware or public-domain section towards the back, far away from the other reviews. Games weren't taken seriously unless they were released commercially at retail. *Wolfenstein 3D* broke the mould. It was too good – too radically new – to ignore.

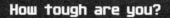

Computer Gaming World gave it a 1.5-page review treatment, with writer Chris Lombardi noting in awe how 'in *Wolfenstein 3D*, the player is "there" like no game I've ever played.' *Compute!* magazine deemed it the best arcade game of the year – 'a showcase of nearly flawless design and challenging gameplay' that managed to impress even more for its use of digitised sound than its remarkable graphical innovations. And *Electronic Games* remarked that the game not only offered a level of detail that 'almost approaches a kind of virtual reality' but also that it had shown that Apogee was 'ready to confront the Big Boys. [And] perhaps more significantly, it has shown that shareware is not just for the hobbyist anymore.'

This sense that the paradigm had shifted was not unique to magazine writers. In a February 1994 article for *PC Review*, journalist Dean Evans quipped that *Wolfenstein 3D* had 'done for shareware what Richard Branson has done for personal enterprise.'

Indeed, *Wolfenstein 3D* didn't just push shareware into the mainstream; it set new standards for what could potentially be achieved – and earned – with the model. It drew huge, new interest to the shareware space, both in terms of consumers looking at and being aware of shareware software, and businesses turning to shareware as a marketing and distribution tool. It set a new bar for quality in shareware, and it made Apogee and id rich.

The game had sold 150,000 copies by mid-1994, on the path to an estimated lifetime tally of 200,000 (plus around that many again for the FormGen-published retail episode). This was roughly triple the sales of Apogee's previous top-seller *Duke Nukem*, and it was steady money too – they averaged around $200,000 a month (so $100,000 each) in shareware takings for the game for a year and a half.

With a huge, new game came huge, new challenges in staying on top of the fan community that had built up around them. And one day Apogee fan and BBS aficionado Joe Siegler

Rob Eberhardt wearing his Educomp T-shirt, proud of his new car.

The Somak Software booth at Macworld Expo New York, 1989.

A retail release of the *Wolfenstein 3D* shareware version.

```
To: ALL                              Refer#: NONE
From: SCOTT MILLER                      Read: (N/A)
Subj: APOGEE NEEDS A TECHIE!          Status: PUBLIC MESSAGE
Conf: APG_BETA (65)                Read Type: GENERAL (-+)


Well, this seems like a good place to mention a job opening at Apogee.  We
are in need of a tech support/hints line person.  This is an easy job that
offers forty hours per week, lots of potential overtime if wanted, and
future advancement (in fact, we're promoting one of our tech support
people, which is why there's an opening).

Now, what you want, enjoy lots of Apogee [ ... ] free food and snacks
(plus in our office is a 25 cents Coke machine).  Over 18 other fun people
work in the office, mostly between 19 and 25 years of age.

We will pay for you to move down here and help you get set up.  We're looking
for a long term employee, obviously--at least interested in working here for
a few years (that's long term nowadays!).

Anyone interested?  Call Scott at (214) 240-0614, or leave a message
here (though it might take longer for me to reply).

Scott, Apogee
PgUp PgDn   F1-Help  S-Save  C-Clear  ESC-Exit   Queue 0
```

A printout of the 'help wanted' ad that led to Joe Siegler joining Apogee.

The 3D Realms crew watch a demo recording for *Duke Nukem 3D*.

Apogee's *Rise of the Triad* development team hard at work.

Scott Miller's mother, Pat, working at the Apogee offices in early 1993.

Apogee's Jason Reed sits atop 'Mt. Xenophage', *c.* 1996.

A snap of Scott Miller from the Apogee/3D Realms webcam.

© Joe Siegler

Duke Nukem II registered version box.

© Joe Siegler

Wolfenstein 3D registered version box.

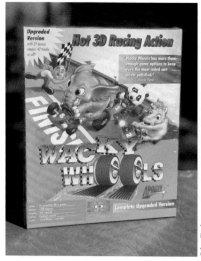

© Joe Siegler

Wacky Wheels 'Complete Upgraded Version'.

© Joe Siegler

Mystic Towers registered version box.

Australian edition of the *DOOM* registered version.

© Luke Jones

DOOM troubleshooting addendum.

© Luke Jones

© Joe Siegler

The *DOOM* registered version mail-order box and disks.

Various box and jewel case releases of *Halloween Harry/Alien Carnage*.

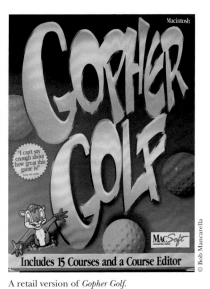

© Bob Mancarella

Includes 15 Courses and a Course Editor

A retail version of *Gopher Golf.*

© Bob Mancarella

The case for the registered version of *Goofy Golf.*

© Tom Warfield

A sampling of the many *Pretty Good Solitaire* releases over the years.

A *FreeCell Plus* full version floppy disk.

A *Pretty Good Solitaire 98* full version floppy disk.

The full registered version of *Crime Fighter* in 3.5" and 5.25" floppies.

The shareware concept defined in a German compilation CD.

The id Software crew celebrate their first Shareware Industry Awards win.

A *Quake* team photo from 1995.

Tom Hall working on *DOOM* levels.

MVP Software's 1996 Ziff-Davis Shareware Awards trophies.

Ian Lynch-Smith promoting Freeverse Software at Macworld Expo.

Glider developer John Calhoun working at his Macintosh Plus.

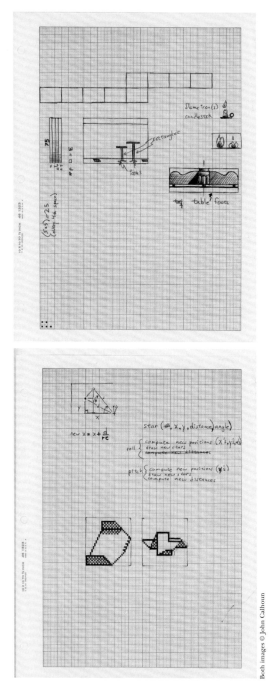

Design sketches from *Glider* by John Calhoun.

William Soleau's set of Soleau Software retail packages.

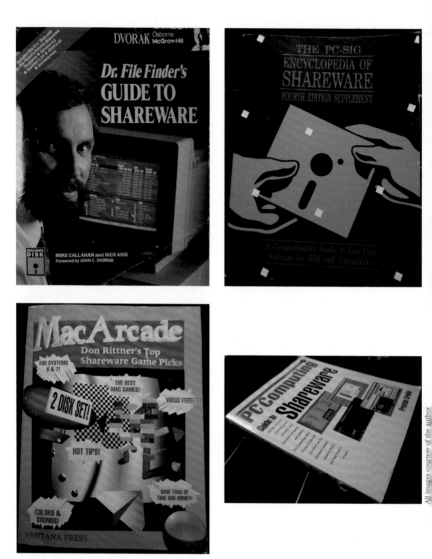

A selection of shareware-focused books owned by author Richard Moss.

– who ran a small board of his own – spotted something strange on the Software Creations BBS. 'I saw this thing that was calling itself version 1.3 of *Wolfenstein 3D*,' he says, 'and it was a "porn version" where they had naked women on the walls and things of that nature.'

That didn't sound legitimate to Siegler, so he wrote a message to Scott Miller drawing attention to the file. A day or two later, Miller replied that he was right – it shouldn't be there – and thanked him for pointing it out. Then not long after that – probably just weeks later – Miller got in touch again: 'Hey, would you like to be a beta tester?'

Siegler was granted access to a private area of Software Creations where beta testers could get pre-release versions of upcoming Apogee games, which at the time meant the opportunity to test out Allen Blum's vertically scrolling shooter *Major Stryker* and the educational game *Math Rescue* by Karen Crowther (who later did a second game with Apogee, *Word Rescue*, as well as a third shareware title, *Pickle Wars*, with MVP Software – covered in Chapter 12).

A few months later, Miller posted a message to the group asking if anyone was interested in moving to Dallas to join Apogee full-time as 'a tech support/hints line person'. It was to replace Shawn Green, as Green shifted into a dedicated role as Apogee's online representative – the voice of Apogee in services such as CompuServe, AOL, GEnie, Delphi, and Prodigy, and on BBSs and Usenet.

Siegler had been working as a computer repair technician at phone company Bell Atlantic, but it wasn't a 'career job' to him, and he loved the sound of Miller's sales pitch – free food, 'a 25 cents Coke machine', 18 other people aged in their early 20s, relocation help. Next thing he knew Siegler was packing up his life in Philadelphia and en route to casa de Apogee, 1,400 miles away, to do phone support for them.

By the time Siegler arrived, however, Shawn Green had left to join id, so he talked Miller and Broussard into letting him transition into that job once he'd settled in. It was an incredible time to join the company. The in-house team was still tiny, as most games were produced externally and so it was basically just a few core staff and then a whole lot of order fulfilment and support people. Yet *Duke Nukem* and *Commander Keen* were still raking in money, and now *Wolfenstein 3D* was comfortably outselling them. 'These were mega life-changing-income money games for the company,' remembers Siegler.

With fast money came fast cars, parties, poker nights, strippers showing up at the office on people's birthdays – the kinds of things you'd expect when a bunch of 20-something men get together to make and sell fast-action computer games for more money than they could conceive of. 'But it worked,' Siegler says, because everybody knew 'if you don't get your shit together and get products out that people care about, then you won't have fun anymore.'

Siegler's job was to wade through the negativity that came up online any time anything went even slightly wrong; to interact with fans so that they'd feel like Apogee was on their level; to make sure that Apogee *was* actually on their level; and to organise and upload Apogee game files online. 'When I first started, Apogee's distribution was all over the place,' he recalls. Games were compressed in different formats, with inconsistent file names, and readme and catalogue files weren't always included. Most didn't even have a file_id.diz file, which was standard in the shareware industry to keep file descriptions consistent across every BBS that held a copy of a program. Siegler standardised it all. He even instituted a policy whereby Apogee games would have a 1 at the start of the filename (e.g. '1bs30.zip' for *Blake Stone: Aliens of Gold* version 3.0) so that they'd appear first when listed alphabetically.

Siegler wasn't the only one working to improve Apogee's visibility in the BBS arena. Miller also hired Dennis Scarff, an early employee of the leading shareware catalogue/disk vendor Public Brand Software, to liaise with the BBSs and catalogues on Apogee's behalf – to pitch them on premium positioning of Apogee games and generally ensure they were helping to drive business to the company. And before either of them came on board, Miller made a deal with Software Creations BBS to serve as their Home BBS.

Software Creations had been around since December 1989, when it was founded by Dan Linton with one telephone line – enough to handle around 35 incoming calls a day – and a 209MB hard drive. Linton focused his BBS on the fast-growing world of shareware, and he quickly established his Massachusetts-based board as a leading source of shareware games. In less than a year it was up to four lines, then more than thirty by mid-1992 and later climbing above 100.

Linton leveraged his background in hardware design to build a technically superior BBS, and he freely shared that knowledge on his board – thereby turning it into a hub not only for people searching for the latest shareware programs but also for other BBS operators looking for tips and guidance on how to improve their systems. The board would later win the Readers' Choice award from *Boardwatch* magazine two years in a row, along with a Dvorak Award for Best BBS and Web Site in 1995.

As one of the biggest, most influential BBSs, Software Creations drew attention from the likes of Apogee and Epic as a BBS marketing base – with them making it one of the first places they'd upload new games and other files. And in late 1991 Scott Miller decided he should formalise the arrangement:

I had gone down to Boston where he lived several times. And he was really a very smart technical guy, and he had like

a T3 coming into his house. And he had a whole basement
that was just nothing but servers. And we were sending him
I think $30,000 a month just to pay bills, to keep expanding,
to keep the place up and running – just to give people a one-
stop sort of Internet store to get our games. And to make
sure that, you know, there was enough dial-in channels to
handle it all. And so on.

In much the same way that companies would soon have
homepages on the web, Apogee's Home BBS served as a single
destination to go for news, downloads (both new games and
updates), discussions, and informal help. 'It seemed like a smart
thing to do at the time,' Miller explains. 'We could control the
messaging. And people would go there and we would market our
other games for them to also try out.'

Apogee added the number to dial in to Software Creations to
all their games, telling players it was their 'round-the-clock source
for new Apogee shareware releases', while Software Creations,
for their part, doubled down on their branding as 'the home of
the authors' – leveraging the Apogee connection to entice other
shareware companies to make them their Home BBS too. Even
Apogee rivals Epic MegaGames got on there for a while (starting
in September 1992), though eventually, in 1994, Tim Sweeney
decided to make Epic's official Home BBS the rival board Exec-PC.

'That kind of started this feud,' remembers Glenn
Brengsinger, Dan Linton's second-in-command at Software
Creations. 'For many years their stuff was not allowed on Software
Creations.'

The feud even spilled over to Usenet, where representatives
of Apogee and Epic occasionally traded barbs and trash-talked
each other. But it rarely went deeper than a friendly rivalry,
either on the boards or in their games, as the two companies
battled for shareware supremacy.

Every year they'd meet at Public Brand Software founder Bob Ostrander's Summer Shareware Seminars in Indianapolis. It was the main event for shareware professionals, where 300–400 people across the industry – both games and software – converged from around the world for three days to share tips, make business dealings, and recognise the past year's standout software in the Shareware Industry Awards.

Apogee had the edge in these awards in the early years, thanks largely to id Software – which took home two awards for *Commander Keen* in 1992, with the team so excited at their first major award they all wore rented tuxedoes to the ceremony, and then won more awards for *Wolfenstein 3D*, *DOOM*, and *Quake* in the years that followed. (Apogee would also have winners in 1993 – with educational game *Math Rescue* – and 1995 – with first-person shooter *Rise of the Triad* – plus nominations for various other games.) But Epic would later claim multiple awards of their own, too.

Recruitment drive

Apogee and id weren't the only ones in shareware that benefitted from id's successes. *Wolfenstein 3D* had sent out a beacon – a virtual flare, perhaps – to ace programmers around the world. Shareware could be good. It could be *better than good.*

And with a master programmer at their helm in Tim Sweeney, Epic had a knack for recruiting top coding talent with an open mind to shareware. They'd already done that, to mixed success, with Allen Pilgrim (*Super ZZT*, *Kiloblaster*); Dutch demoscene programmer Arjan Brussee (who had yet to publish anything with Epic); and *Ancients 1: Death Watch* creator Mark Baldwin – a former space-shuttle engineer turned game designer. But now, buoyed by the reputational lift *Wolfenstein 3D* had granted shareware, Sweeney had a much easier pitch to bring in more top talent.

Case in point: Ste Cork, a journeyman programmer who'd made a name for himself in the UK's 8-bit computer scene as a ZX Spectrum specialist coder in the mid-1980s, and then had transitioned to writing PC conversions of Atari ST and Amiga games towards the end of the decade.

Before *Wolfenstein 3D*, Cork thought shareware was just for utilities and bad games 'that couldn't find "real" publishers'. He didn't want to be associated with what he'd seen. But *Wolfenstein 3D* broke the norm – or rather the myth – because it wasn't just commercial quality; it was *better* than most commercial games available at the time.

Cork didn't have anything on the level of id's hit shooter, but he'd been dabbling in something that re-used an engine he'd written for the DOS conversion of 1988 Atari ST vertically scrolling 2D shooter *Xenon*. 'By modern standard that would be horrendous abuse of company-sponsored code, but back then it was perfectly accepted and the bosses didn't mind at all,' says Cork. 'I'd already done something similar for a ZX Spectrum game I released called *Rescue*.'

Rescue had been a cult hit, despite having identical technical underpinnings to an earlier game called *Colony*, so there wasn't just precedent for re-using an engine made for a different company's game; there was also precedent for it succeeding.

For his *Xenon*-engine-recycling project, which he called *Overkill*, Cork wanted to make something along the lines of popular arcade games *Galaxian*, *Moon Cresta*, and *Phoenix*. 'I like vertical-scrolling shooters, or did back then anyway,' he explains. 'Up/down/left/right/fire, no complex plots to work out, and if some odd bits weren't quite as good as others they'd be scrolled off the screen shortly anyway.'

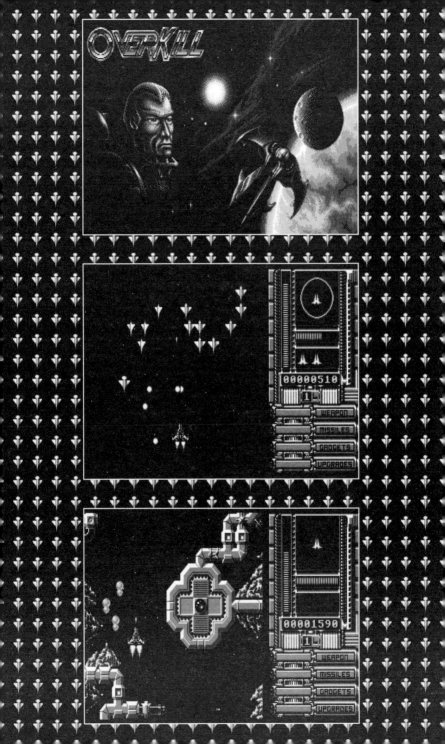

It was the perfect spare-time project. 'Any day I could come back and design/code/draw a few more screen inches of alien attacks and landscape,' Cork says, 'without getting any writer's-block equivalent.'

He'd draft up enemy movement patterns and formations on a 13x13 square paper grid, then type the cell numbers into a homemade map editor to lay out the levels.

But even with the engine already built, development had its share of challenges. 'Because of the colour and machine limitations in those days, I couldn't assume all [256] colours were available.' VGA graphics set at 256 colours was the emerging standard of the time, but 16-colour EGA was more common, and many people were still running PCs with an old CGA card or a Hercules graphics adapter. To reach the widest possible audience, Cork needed a way to make the game run on PCs that were limited to just four-colour or monochrome displays. For this Cork turned to a friend called Chris Wood, who showed him how to write colour remap tables that would automatically adapt to different colour depth settings.

Another friend and former colleague called Martin Holland then agreed to draw the graphics. But around two-thirds of the way through development, Holland grew tired of working after-hours, and Cork grew tired of driving Holland back and forth between their respective homes in Wigan and Preston (both in northwest England). As a compromise, Cork took Holland's existing graphics for the game and changed the colour palettes to make them look new, then he put them into the remaining levels as best he could.

Cork thought it'd be difficult to work with an American publisher, so he made a deal with a British company called Precision Software Publishing (PSP) – which also served as the UK distributor for Epic MegaGames. 'Unbeknownst to me at the time though, Epic were already getting pissed off with PSP,' recalls Cork, 'apparently over unpaid royalties or something.'

Cork encountered his first warning that something wasn't right when he returned home after a visit to PSP's office and got an angry phone call from the company owner. Cork recalls he had been given a boxed author's copy during his visit, but PSP's owner accused him of stealing.

'So I then got a lawyer and he voided the contract with them,' says Cork, 'though with their requested proviso that they could sell the physical stocks they'd made – which, like Epic, I never saw any money from that I remember.'

Cork later heard from a PSP staff member that Epic had pulled out of their arrangement with PSP, and soon after that Epic boss Tim Sweeney called with an offer to sell *Overkill* directly. He jumped at the chance.

Sweeney's newly hired right-hand man Mark Rein, id Software president turned Epic MegaGames vice-president of marketing, flew over to the UK for a week, underdressed for the cold English weather after a misunderstanding between Rein and Cork: 'Before flying out to the UK, Mark had asked me what temperature it was where I was sitting,' explains Cork, 'and I thought he meant in my home office, so I said 80 Fahrenheit. Apparently he thought I meant the temperature in general, so when I turned up at Preston train station to collect him he was outside dressed only in a thin Hawaiian shirt, no coat, while everyone else was bundled up against a typical cold and wet British day.'

Rein was there to get *Overkill* ready for its second release, which required little changing other than a new title screen, updated version number and ordering information, and some added advertising screens for Epic's recently released *Jill of the Jungle* game.

Jill of the Jungle, meanwhile, was Epic's effort to outshine Apogee's spate of hit shareware platformers. Tim Sweeney did the programming and design work on it himself, his focus squarely on how to beat *Commander Keen*.

'*Commander Keen* was an EGA game with PC speaker sound effects and AdLib music,' he later told *Gamasutra*. 'So we went one step further and had digitised sound effects and VGA graphics.' And to break with the monotony of games starring men, he made his hero a woman too.

Sweeney had started working on the game several months after he released the first version of *ZZT*, beginning, as before, with an editing tool. This time he'd started with a specific genre in mind, however, and so he'd coded not just a tile-based environment but also basic world physics – gravity and normal forces, so that if a player walked or jumped off a platform, they'd fall, but also so that if they landed on a solid surface they would stick to it and not just fall forever.

He finished *Jill* in June 1992 and immediately saw Epic's fortunes improve. *Jill* was getting 20 to 30 orders every day – 10 times more than *ZZT* – and drawing attention to Epic's other new games, the most intriguing of which was called *Castle of the Winds* (also released in June 1992).

Castle had come from Microsoft engineer Rick Saada, who began working on the game in the late 1980s to help him get more familiar with the Windows API (application programming interface) – as he saw that's where the company's future lay. He was a big fan of roguelikes – especially *Hack*, *Larn*, and *Omega* – so he fiddled around with a Norse-inspired graphical dungeon crawler (with a heavy dose of *Dungeons & Dragons* mixed into the combat system).

This was a spare-time, learning-focused endeavour, so progress moved along in fits and starts as Saada slowly wrote and rewrote different chunks of the game to fit whatever ideas seemed cool to him at the time. But he sought feedback from his Microsoft colleagues and by the time Windows 3.0 came out, in mid-1990, he knew he had the makings of something good. Development got more serious then. He added in palette animation and 256-colour support and he watched in curiosity as the shareware games market exploded in popularity.

Come May 1992 he was finished, and he had Tim Sweeney convincing him that he should let Epic handle the distribution for him. They'd put part one of the game, *A Question of Vengeance*, out as shareware and give anyone who registered (for $25) a copy of part two: *Lifthransir's Bane*.

'It turned out to be a great decision for me,' Saada later told the *Vacant Ritual Assembly* zine, 'because while I only got a piece of the pie, instead of all of it, it was a much larger pie.' Indeed, with help from Epic's global distribution reach and name recognition, *Castle of the Winds* brought in a strong 12,000–14,000 registrations – far more than Saada would have been likely to get on his own.

Jill of the Jungle and *Castle of the Winds* together were transformative for Epic's business. Where sales revenue for the whole of 1991 had been a respectable $25,000, by September 1992 they'd reached that much *per month* (and *Jill* would hit fifth on the Shareware Top Ten charts the following month, wedged between seven Apogee games, a shoot-'em-up called *Galactix*, and Nels Anderson's *Mah Jongg*). This bolstered revenue afforded Sweeney the budget to expand his operations – both to bring in more external developers and other collaborators, and to hire internally – hence the arrival of Mark Rein shortly before they picked up *Overkill* distribution.

With id still on their side, however, Apogee retained the edge in the shareware games business. And now that *Wolfenstein 3D*'s success had dwarfed everything else ever done in shareware games, id were obviously going to keep focusing on fast-action 3D. But Miller worried how much longer the partnership would last.

'I knew that id wasn't going to be our partner forever,' he says. 'They were getting so big that I knew at some point they would realise they didn't really need us anymore.'

Apogee needed to invest internal resources into 3D games, both as a move into the future and as a kind of insurance policy. That way they'd be prepared to handle the rapid shifts that id had set in motion in the games industry, and to cushion the blow when id moved on.

John Romero had suggested they sign a deal for a *Wolfenstein 3D*-based shooter from former Softdisk employees Mike Maynard and Jim Row, and that seemed like a good idea, but it wasn't a long-term solution. The only way to safeguard their future was to build an in-house development team that could rival id. So they set plans in motion to get their own technology, not built by id, and for that they turned to teenage programmer Ken Silverman – whose 1993 shareware oddity *Ken's Labyrinth* sported graphics and underlying technology similar to *Wolfenstein 3D* but a design that was out of this world.

Ken's game

Silverman had been tinkering with computers and programming since he was eight years old. He'd started on a TI-99/4A, designing levels with his older brother for a *Pac-Man* game, then soon surpassed his sibling as he delved deeply into making simple games using TI BASIC. Sometimes his dad would bring home other computers from work, and Silverman tinkered with games programming on them too. In 1988 he got his first PC and promptly installed QuickBASIC for further adventures in game-making, then in 1990 he finally gave in to his parents' efforts to push him into C. His games got more advanced – no more board games or card games or two-dimensional chase-the-dot games, but rather things like a competitive *Tetris* game he called *Kentris* and a Mario-wearing-rocket-boots-style platformer called *Super Silverbrothers* (both from 1991).

Ken's Labryinth

Programmed by Ken Silverman
Art by Andrew Cotter and Ken Silverman

Original music by Ken Silverman
Boards by Andrew Cotter and Ken Silverman

SCORE: 0 LIFE: WEAPON:
TIME: 100%   3   1 1 0 0
BOARD: 7 Tim   0 0 0 \

Ken's Labyrinth was a step up again for the coding whiz-kid, who began work on the game on 16 June 1992, one week after he saw *Wolfenstein 3D* for the first time – ostensibly because his brother played id's Nazi-killing hit constantly, but also out of fascination with the raycasting technology. He hoped to draw his sibling's attention to a game made somewhat closer to home.

Like id's engine architect John Carmack, Silverman worked primarily from instinct – solving problems and studying new programming techniques as and when he needed them. The teenager found he had a knack for the complex mathematics involved in fast 3D rendering of bitmapped graphics and lines projected out into the distance, and in just a few months he had a working prototype of a game with technical underpinnings that rivalled *Wolfenstein 3D*. He called it Walken – a portmanteau of 'walk' and 'Ken' – and tapped his friend Andy Cotter to help him fill it with placeholder content that would test out his engine.

Walls were stitched together from a mismatch of seemingly random textures – cross-stitch wallpaper, four different kinds of bricks, an overlapping colour wheel, hastily drawn images, and so on – each room different to the last. Where *Wolfenstein 3D* hid secret rooms behind walk-through wall sections that looked indistinguishable from the regular variety, Walken labelled them plainly with an instruction blithely painted on: 'walk through this wall'. Everything was improvised and created on a whim because it sounded like fun.

> We had no plan for the game. I would visit him each weekend with my box of floppies. For the first hour, we would take turns showing off our latest features. Perhaps I fixed some bugs and got the slot machine working better. Andy would show off his latest map with placeholder art. Sometimes he would come up with something really clever, like a wall texture that just happened to exactly match my ceiling and

floor colours – a sky. I would then make that work better for the next week… We drew whatever we could. If it looked good, we kept it, [but] neither of us were great artists.

Their drawing tool for creating the graphics was a tedious-to-use, homemade QuickBASIC editor with limited features – little more than just placing individual pixels, changing all pixels of a certain colour, floodfilling an area, and what Silverman describes as 'a few other weird effects'.

Enemies, bullets, and obstacles were no less unpolished. Sound effects were recorded by Silverman himself, sampled from his own voice (for instance, a giant 8-ball rolling into a room and falling down a hole would exclaim 'aaahhhh!'). It had an unusual charm, this odd, technically brilliant game with a fever-dream design. Walken was completely without pretence, and the perfect proof of concept for what it would later become.

Silverman's father recognised that Ken had made something with commercial potential, so he encouraged the teenager to contact software companies about it. Thus in October Ken sent a demo build off to 15 publishers. One publisher, Apogee, showed interest. But to publish with Apogee, Scott Miller told the teenager, he'd need to make large-scale changes to the code and design. Walken wouldn't just need polishing or extending; it'd need to be rebuilt – almost from scratch.

His parents didn't like that at all. He needed to focus on school. He was in his final year of high school, and they didn't want to see the project drag into college. After consulting with them, he turned down Apogee's offer and decided to finish the game alone. With Andy Cotter's continued assistance on art and design, Walken became *Ken's Labyrinth* and evolved into a full-featured, fever-dream, minimal-violence alternative to *Wolfenstein 3D*.

The pair improved or redid much of the placeholder art, extended the game to 27 levels, and devised a silly story about alien scientists using the labyrinth to test the worthiness of humans to avoid being 'blown into a million pieces, each the size of a pea'. Silverman also added more features to his engine – such as warp zones, a strafe key (for moving side to side), doors that opened and closed, AdLib music (which he composed himself), shootable walls, 3D shading, death and level-completion animations, and new technical features such as Sound Blaster support, better data compression, and extended memory support.

Ken's Labyrinth was then self-published as shareware on 1 January 1993, with a promise that players could buy two additional level packs (ten levels a piece) for $15 each or $25 as a set. For a further $10, he'd also throw in the complete set of musical compositions and – once it was finished – a developers' toolkit with which players could make their own levels or modify the game.

Silverman had no idea how well it would do. He knew his friends and relatives seemed to like the game, and that had been enough to get his dad's approval to release it, but beyond that? *Who knows*, he thought.

He recalls that the next few months were 'pretty crazy'. Fans wrote in with praise for the game, some also sending in the registration fee, while companies called to offer him a job. But he ignored most of it. He had to finish high school.

Epic MegaGames made an offer he and his father liked, however. They wanted to republish the game, with minimal changes, and were willing to offer a 40 per cent royalty (slightly higher than Apogee's earlier offer of 35 per cent) as part of the deal. This time Silverman said yes, and to ensure he could stay focused on school his father got a stipulation put into the contract that it had to be released no later than March 1993.

And so it was that just two months after Epic signed on as publisher, they released *Ken's Labyrinth* version 2.0. It offered further-improved graphics, around half of which were redrawn or added by artist Mikko Iho from the Future Crew demoscene group. And it had an improved design and engine technology, courtesy of advice from Tim Sweeney and game designer Cliff Bleszinski.

The story was revamped and expanded, too. The goal now was to rescue the player character's dog, Sparky, added by Mark Rein after he saw a wooden dog at Silverman's house, and find him a safe place to hide before the player turned to the challenge of defeating alien leader Ken. Epic also switched the game to their standard shareware pricing model ($30 to get the second and third episodes plus a 'free' bonus disk containing other Epic-published games).

Ken's Labyrinth was only a modest success by the standards set by Epic and Apogee's bigger titles, with Silverman's cut of earnings across the two releases up around the $25,000 mark. But it was well received and opened new doors for Silverman, who turned his attention next to another test game. He called it Build, and he approached it in much the same way as he had *Ken's Labyrinth* – as a digital whiteboard for testing out his ideas and new 3D programming tricks. Impressed by the technology, Mark Rein tried to get him interested in coding the engine for a baseball game. Silverman declined. 'I didn't care for sports games, and it seemed like a waste of my talents,' he recalls.

Besides, he didn't even know what a game 'engine' was. At least, not yet – and indeed, with Apogee poised to snap him up, he was about to find out.

CHAPTER 10

Maelstrom

Andrew Welch was a college student on summer break in 1992 when he came upon a Usenet post that made his blood boil. Its author insisted with the utmost certainty that the low-end Macintosh IIsi was too slow to do decent animation on. Welch disagreed.

He'd only made one game up to that point – a simple black-and-white *Wheel of Fortune* game called *Wacky Wheel* that he'd released as shareware in 1990, as he'd been doing for years with his homemade fonts. But he'd also taught himself Assembly language for the Macs of the era, and he was sure he could do exactly what this Usenet poster thought impossible.

'So I set out to prove this guy wrong,' Welch told me in an interview for *The Secret History of Mac Gaming*, 'because it's always fun to try to prove to someone on the Internet that they're wrong.'

Welch soon had an animation engine written that proved his point, but he didn't stop there. He had spent much of his youth hanging out at the local arcade, playing games like *Asteroids* and *Centipede* for hours every day after school, so he decided to turn it into an *Asteroids*-style game. He handled all the code (in Assembly language), design, and audio (with help from his college buddies), while two Internet pals of his contributed title artwork and 3D asteroid renderings that would lend the game an extra layer of polish.

The final game, *Maelstrom*, had the air of a rap album from the era. It freely sampled from pop culture, with movie and TV audio snippets, popular music riffs, and random things from life around him at the Rochester Institute of Technology in upstate New York: fart noises, *Star Trek* and *Ren & Stimpy* recordings, and a Marine Corps yelp (because he had friends in the Marines), to name just a few. It was edgy and cool and a breath of fresh air, and in November 1992 he self-published it as shareware, for any Mac with a 256-colour display, under the company name Ambrosia Software.

A message in the bottom-right corner of the main menu screen stated 'This game is not free; please pay if you play!' while a shareware notice in the game's 'About *Maelstrom*' screens asked that people send Welch $15 to register the game and encourage him and his friends 'to create more high-quality games' (and, implicitly, to release bugfix and feature-addition updates to the game).

This was a tough time in the Mac gaming scene. The Mac's personal computer market share was nearing its lifetime peak of 12 per cent, and Apple had great momentum driving them forward, but the Motorola 68k processor family that powered Macs at the time could not reliably keep up with the Intel CPUs of the day. And few commercial publishers were willing to invest in Mac versions of their games, which required specialised programmers who knew the system inside-out.

Maelstrom was a rare beacon of brilliance on a platform that had seen little original game development since the 1980s, and rarer still it was a brilliant *action* game – not a puzzler or a point-and-click adventure or a flight simulation, the genres that were well-catered for by those few other high-quality Mac-original games, but rather a game of fast-action reflexes.

Mac gamers took to it instantly. Within weeks, Welch found his mailbox stuffed full of letters and cheques from all over the world. (He and his friends liked to look each place up online.) And every day more registrations would come in.

Eventually *Maelstrom* would receive a Shareware Industry Award and numerous other plaudits, but its main legacy was in creating a new shareware powerhouse. After its surprise success, Welch found himself at a crossroads. He had been studying photojournalism, intent on a career in that industry, but this shareware thing seemed like it was really taking off for him. At the pressing of one of his customers, the renowned *National Geographic* photographer Rick Smolan, he considered his future.

Smolan advised him to focus his energies on his shareware business. The photojournalism business was changing fast, and he had low odds of success in the field. Welch gave it some thought, then agreed. He officially incorporated Ambrosia Software in August 1993. He even managed to convince his bank to give him a merchant account so that he could accept credit card payments – at a time when selling things online was considered high-risk.

And so, with his roommate's help, Ambrosia Software became the Macintosh world's equivalent to Apogee Software and Epic MegaGames – a shareware-focused, online-based games publisher that divided its resources between in-house and externally developed titles, and that traded on the strength of its reputation.

Ambrosia published shareware utilities too – lots of them – but *Maelstrom* was the real money-spinner. By the end of 1993, *Maelstrom* had been registered around 6,000 times (equating to some $90,000 or so in turnover). Over its lifetime it would receive significantly more than that.

More games emerged soon after. Welch's next title was a chemistry-inspired puzzler called *Chiral* – adapted and rewritten from a game he'd acquired the rights and code to (for $1,500) from an Australian high-school student. The goal was to create inert molecules on a grid by bonding new atoms from a fast-filling vial with other atoms within existing molecules, taking care to use up all the required bonds for each atom. It was easy to learn the basics, but extremely hard to master, and it earned a loyal following. But its high-minded concept failed to capture the popular imagination like *Maelstrom* had, and thus *Chiral* only garnered modest sales. Not so for Ambrosia's next two games, however – the internally developed *Apeiron*, which gave the same remix treatment to *Centipede* that *Maelstrom* had done for *Asteroids*, and the externally created *Swoop*.

Just as Scott Miller and Tim Sweeney had turned to online message boards and the demoscene to find potential developers to work with, Welch scoured America Online and Usenet for talented programmers and artists. One day he spotted a programmer on the Usenet group comp.sys.mac.programmer.games who was working on a game and seemed to know what he was talking about. That game turned out to be a twist on the hit arcade shoot-'em-up *Galaxian*, which was perfect for Ambrosia, so Welch pitched this programmer, David Wareing, on publishing with him.

Ambrosia could offer brand recognition, customer payment and support infrastructure, software testing, and technical support through the various software libraries that Welch and his tech support guru 'Cajun' David Richard had created. Wareing jumped at the opportunity. 'Game development was hard enough without having to worry about that stuff,' Wareing told me in an interview for *The Secret History of Mac Gaming*.

Over the next few years, Ambrosia would publish several more games through the same arrangement, including Wareing's own *Mars Rising* vertically scrolling shoot-'em-up; Wareing and Alex Metcalf's joint effort on the *Pengo*-inspired *Bubble Trouble*; Juri Munkki's abstract-looking multiplayer first-person shooter *Avara*; and Matt Burch's *Escape Velocity*.

Each game earned a passionate following within the Mac community, but it was *Escape Velocity* that would finally eclipse *Maelstrom*'s success.

Creator Matt Burch had first devised the game as a straightforward *Asteroids*-style shooter, not unlike *Maelstrom*, shortly after he started college. But he was a year or two ahead of his peers – having completed most of the credits he needed for an electrical engineering degree before he left high school – and rather than attend classes he'd already completed he opted to instead fiddle with computers.

Most of his time hence went into expanding his space game. He drew inspiration from Edward Elmer 'Doc' Smith's mid-twentieth-century science fiction novels, which presented readers with fantastical stories of adventure throughout the universe – each filled with incredible technologies and weapons and vast alien civilisations. And he looked to the rocket ship model-building catalogues he'd loved growing up, along with the grandeur and technologies of *Star Wars* and *Star Trek*, and most of all to his imaginings of the influential 1984 space game *Elite* – which had wowed players with its enormous procedurally generated universe, wireframe-3D graphics, trading, piracy, combat, and unprecedented scale and freedom of exploration.

Burch had not been one of those players. Despite *Elite*'s obvious and significant influence on his own space game, he had never played it. He had *owned* it when he was ten years old, but he had lost the included Lenslok copy protection device – a prism that unscrambled an on-screen code – on the way home. The store wouldn't let him return or exchange his copy, so he was stuck with his dud. Instead of playing *Elite*, he read the manual over and over, enraptured by the short story included in its pages and by the detail in the game's design – imagining what a great video game it must be.

And so, *Escape Velocity* was a two-dimensional interpretation of his childhood dreams of *Elite* combined with his contemporary conjurings of the experience of playing early video game *Spacewar!* as described in the book *Hackers*. By the time he completed development in May 1996, *Escape Velocity* had grown to include several dozen planets and moons spread across a miniature universe, many inhabited by twenty-third-century citizens of one faction or the other in an intergalactic war to which players could enlist or ignore entirely – perhaps focusing instead on merchant service or piracy or mercenary protection.

It was, like *Elite*, an epic game of extraordinary freedom, and Ambrosia fans adored it. They shared stories, traded discoveries, and embarked on their own adventures in game design by modifying or adding to the game, which had – similar to *ZZT*, *DOOM* (see next chapter), and Ambrosia's own *Maelstrom* – been built with a plug-in architecture that allowed easy modification.

Between the epic space adventure and a thriving modding community, *Escape Velocity* drew a huge audience. It paid Burch's way through college and reportedly netted him a cool $80,000 in royalties in the game's first year on the market, according to an October 1997 article about Ambrosia published in the Rochester *Democrat and Chronicle* newspaper.

The company itself had expanded to a staff of six employees (and a small army of external developers) by this point, with sales revenue across its full catalogue of shareware games and utilities pushing towards the million-dollar mark – up from around $300,000 two years earlier. And it would grow bigger still in the years to come, but it wasn't the only success story in the Mac shareware games scene.

Others thriving on a smaller scale included solo developer Stuart Cheshire, whose networked-multiplayer game *Bolo* seemed to be played by nearly every online-connected Mac user in the world – such was the magnitude of its popularity. Every month

Kathoon

Escape
Velocity

New
Pilot

Open
Pilot

Quit
EV

Enter
Ship

Set
Prefs

About
EV...

hidia

lagon

What? How dare you! Prepare to die!

Greetings

Beg for Mercy

End Communication

Pirate Clipper
Status: Hostile

Antare

Shield
Fuel

Stellar Navigation
New Ireland

No secondary Weapon

Clipper

Shield 100% Pirate

Time: 25
Speed:
Multiple

Credits:
83,240

us   Si

yvin

Soc

Quake is a world continually shaken by seismic
tremors. Anyone who lands here immediately blasts
off again and heads for Opal, Quake's sister world and
a far more calming place. Of course, anyone with any
sense at all wouldn't come to Quake in the first place.

Leave

III, Sirg

Fuel: 0
Cargo:
Equip
Credits:
106,644

Day: 35

from its release in 1992 to its abandonment in the late 90s, tens of thousands of people would congregate in small groups for matches over a LAN or online, all hurriedly scooting around in their little tanks – each hoping to snag control of a supply depot before anyone else could kit it out with fortifications.

People traded custom maps of all shapes and sizes, fit for all kinds of different play styles, while others built (shareware) map-making utilities to facilitate their creation. Some made computer-controlled opponents called 'brains' to allow for practice matches or to bolster the numbers when player counts were low. They had player registries for finding opponents who lived in the same state or country. And they even recorded matches and shared the replays online, in the process turning some moments between a few friends into the stuff of myth and legend.

Cheshire had originally designed the top-down-perspective tank warfare game in 1987 for BBC Micro computers. He first tested that original version with 50 feet of networking cable strung between his room and his friend's, then expanded and improved the game for a while until he realised it needed to be on a modern platform like the Mac or PC if it were to ever reach a wide audience. (He chose the Mac because it had built-in networking capabilities, a standardised graphical user interface, and just one screen mode to worry about.)

He was a graduate student at Stanford University in April 1992, still readying the game for release, when it leaked out to Mac FTP sites and Usenet. But this didn't concern him – the game was made to be shared. He told people it was unstable beta software and let them have their fun. *Bolo* would be shareware, but he'd only ask for payment after he'd made it stable. (And even then he chose the pure 'pay if you like it' shareware model, at a requested price of $25/£15.)

By the time that happened around a year later, *Bolo* was already getting 20,000 matches played on public networks each month – with many more known to be happening on private office and college networks as well as within Apple's own internal network. Numbers would continue to grow from there, only declining after the march of technology left the game trailing behind more modern network games that supported higher resolutions (the game still ran in a 512 by 342-pixel window), easier netplay set-up, and newer versions of Mac OS.

(Cheshire had planned – and begun working on – a big update that would have fixed these issues and added a rudimentary 3D mode, but then he got a job at Apple in 1998 and had to stop development in accordance with company rules about independent software projects.)

Old-school role-playing game *Realmz* would meet a similar fate – fading away in the early 2000s not through lack of customer interest but rather fading revenues and a lack of developer support. It had been first released in 1994 by Tim Phillips, a civil engineer and army reservist who'd spent a tour of duty in Iraq and Saudi Arabia during Operation Desert Storm in 1991. Working as a supply sergeant, he'd whiled away the hours reading the same copy of *Macworld* magazine over and over – gazing longingly at the Mac IIsi computer on its cover.

When he got back to the States, Phillips dropped $1,500 he'd saved up to buy a Mac IIsi of his own. At first it was just a hobby for tinkering with, but it soon transformed into a game project. With his wife 320 miles away finishing her master's degree and a serious knee injury keeping him largely immobile while he waited for surgery, he started learning how to program in C. And to make that more enjoyable, he focused his learning experience into creating a game.

After three years of development, in April 1994, *Realmz* was done. It was an *Ultima*-style fantasy RPG – not for any particular reason except that it seemed like a fun thing to do – that hearkened back to an earlier time in the genre's history, with a design and an interface that felt closer to games from the late 1980s than to contemporary commercial titles like *Jagged Alliance*.

Phillips published the game for the RPG-poor Mac as shareware. To his delight, it was a resounding success. Mac gamers and critics rallied behind it, praising its polished, non-linear scenario design and writing – with a story following a group of heroes from an 'honest city' called Bywater that's ruled by 'a kind king' but is now under threat from a cult of spider worshippers. *Inside Mac Games* said it was 'easily in the same class as commercial games'. *MacUser* called it the best shareware Mac game of the year. And in 1997 *MacFormat* declared it the second-best shareware game they'd featured up to that point (after the Mac port of *DOOM*).

Sales were strong enough that Phillips was able to quit his job to focus on *Realmz* full-time, whereupon he and his friends built more scenarios (each sold separately) and put together a scenario editor companion app so that fans could create their own games in the *Realmz* engine. Before long there were hundreds of fan-made scenarios, the best of which Phillips helped publish as official shareware add-ons to the game.

Phillips harboured bigger ambitions than just one ever-evolving, community-driven fantasy RPG, though. He wanted to do a sci-fi RPG, too, and he thought he could use his company's growing recognition to publish other people's games on his highly trafficked website and take a cut of their profits.

Over the next several years he'd do this with several games across a range of genres – including platform game *Monkey Shines* and its sequel, puzzle games *Squish* and *King of Parking*, and fantasy RPG *Exile*.

Jeff Vogel's *Exile* (1995) was by far the most popular of these. Unlike Phillips, Vogel made his old-school, *Ultima*-inspired RPG specifically to fill a perceived gap in the market. He'd bought his first Mac at the beginning of 1994, finding to his disappointment that there weren't any games like the ones he'd loved on his Apple II in the 1980s. To relieve the stress and misery he was feeling in his graduate studies in mathematics, he decided he'd make one himself.

Its title and theme would fit the mood of its development: *Exile: Escape from the Pit* – an enormous quest to break out from the underworld in a fantasy land where the scum of society are literally thrown into a giant, inescapable pit, but also, for Vogel, a desperate attempt to escape the torment of his own making that was graduate school. (Or as he told me in an interview for *The Secret History of Mac Gaming*, 'to maintain my sanity'.)

Despite the game's enormous size and scope – with a campaign that lasted upwards of sixty or seventy hours of playtime – it took Vogel just seven months to create. He finished at the beginning of January 1995, whereupon he thought on a lark that maybe some people might like to pay money for it. After a chance encounter with Tim Phillips on Usenet, he made a deal to publish through Fantasoft.

Phillips did a brief test release in an AOL group first, where it met with such a strong initial reception that news of its impending release was excitedly discussed in the Usenet group comp.sys.mac.games. By the end of the month they were ready to go public, and, before they'd even finished pushing it out to all the usual shareware channels, the Mac gaming community was already buzzing with excitement. *Exile* looked like an early *Ultima* game (by then a decade-plus old, depending on the version), but it also *played* like an early *Ultima* game. Its engine was rough and unpolished, and its graphics stank, but the core game was brilliant.

Sales were slow at first, though, perhaps because so much of the game – some 20–30 hours of content – was available to unregistered players. But things picked up rapidly once *Exile* got included in the July 1995 subscriber CD for *Macworld* magazine, which expanded his reach from Internet-connected *Realmz* fans to the entire Mac community. More reviews and magazine coverdisc placements soon followed, along with a Windows port and a sequel, and the steady flow of living-wage money coming in gave Vogel the confidence to drop out of grad school and go full-time with games.

Monkey business

Meanwhile, as Ambrosia captivated Mac gaming audiences with its arcade remixes, and community-centric efforts like *Bolo* and *Realmz* established themselves as Macintosh shareware mainstays, another Mac-focused shareware company called Freeverse Software was making a name for itself with quirky, humorous renditions of popular card games. Freeverse had similar roots to Ambrosia. Founder Ian Lynch Smith had graduated college in 1992 with a degree in cognitive science and specialisation in artificial intelligence (AI). Then while pondering what to do next with his life he'd moved into a sharehouse with several aspiring screenwriters and taken a job as a computer expert for a temp agency.

In his spare time, he learned how to code Mac software on his PowerBook 160c graduation present – skills that he put to use the best way he knew how.

His first program was a jazzed-up version of the popular four-player card game Hearts. He put in silly sound effects, colourful hand-drawn graphics, and a multitude of customisation options, and he made the most of his AI thesis to code up some capable computer-controlled opponents. *Hearts Deluxe* was published in 1993 as shareware, with a requested donation of $15. It quickly took off, tapping into a passionate Hearts community that Lynch

Smith didn't realise existed, and subsequently won a *MacUser* Shareware Award.

The following year he moved back to his family home in New York, whereupon he set up shop in his old bedroom. His brother Colin suggested he call the company 'World Wide Ian'. But he thought the name Freeverse would work better.

He spent his days adding new features and more opponents to *Hearts Deluxe*, as well as porting it to Windows, writing a second game (a puzzle game called *Enigma*), sourcing packaging for floppy disk mail-outs, building a website for taking credit card orders (which was only possible thanks to his telling the credit card company that he ran a bodega), and procrastinating with game-playing and cartoon-watching. 'The early days were fun, but fairly unfocused,' he told me when I was researching *The Secret History of Mac Gaming*.

Colin coming on as a partner in 1995 helped give the business a smattering more focus, but it wasn't until the pair decided to use their skills and business infrastructure to produce and publish other people's games that Freeverse began to thrive.

Their modus operandi was a little more specific than Apogee, Epic, and Ambrosia. They recognised that they each had strong artistic and design sensibilities (and pretty soon would also hire a brilliant in-house artist), and they'd seen how their first two games appealed to a broad audience, so they searched for passionate hobbyist coders with family-friendly ideas who struggled with art or user-experience design. Their approach was then to offer a partnership deal, rather than just a publishing or distribution arrangement. They'd do all the art, sound, menus, etc. in-house while the external coder handled all the game logic.

They published games across all genres, but Freeverse's biggest successes were all card games. *Hearts Deluxe* and its sequel *3D Hearts Deluxe* – plus spin-offs like *Classic Cribbage* and

Spades Deluxe – were beloved not just for their raft of options and excellent AI but also for their quirky humour. And this humour would be put front and centre in *Burning Monkey Solitaire* (1999) – a collection of solitaire card games wherein an audience of primates watches and mocks the player in speech-bubble dialogue, delivered in a similar tone to the heckling *Muppets* characters Statler and Waldorf.

As beloved and successful as they were in the Mac shareware scene, however, neither Freeverse nor Ambrosia (nor Fantasoft, for that matter) ever registered more than a blip in the larger PC shareware scene. Only Jeff Vogel, breaking out on his own post-*Exile II* under the label Spiderweb Software, would ever pull off the transition to cross-platform Mac/PC shareware games publishing.

But in spite of the two platforms' obvious isolation from each other, the rise of shareware on the Mac – attributable as it was to the absence of commercial games in popular genres like RPGs and classic arcade games – had no doubt been helped by the shareware concept's rapidly growing public mindshare. The positive feedback loops spurred on by the early successes of the Mac zealots at Freeverse and Ambrosia were a key factor too, for sure, but everyone in shareware really owed their upwards trajectory to one game released back around the time that Freeverse and Ambrosia were just getting started. One game that changed everything.

PROVIDED BY id FREE OF CHARGE • SUGGESTED RETAIL PRICE $9.00 • id SOFTWARE, ©1993

CHAPTER 11

DOOM

It seemed there was no stopping id Software. *Commander Keen* had given them their freedom, and *Wolfenstein 3D*'s mega-success had earned them the financial cushion to do anything. But all they wanted was to beat the last game – to outdo both themselves and everyone else. And at the centre of that drive was a push for ever-better technology. By the time *Wolfenstein 3D*'s commercial prequel *Spear of Destiny* hit retail shelves, Carmack had already built a new engine.

This one had texture-mapped floors and ceilings – not just walls. It supported diminished lighting, which meant things far away could recede into the shadows, disappearing into the distance. And it had variable-height rooms, allowing for elevated platforms where projectile-throwing enemies could hang out, and most exciting of all it allowed for non-orthogonal walls – which meant that rooms could be odd-shaped, with walls jutting out at any arbitrary angle from each other, rather than the traditional rectangular, boxed design that had defined first-person-perspective games up until then.

It ran at half the speed of *Wolfenstein 3D*'s engine, but they were thinking about doing a 3D *Keen* game next – so that wouldn't matter. At least not until they saw it in action. Everyone but Tom Hall suddenly got excited about doing another shooter, which meant Carmack would have to optimise the hell out of his engine to restore that sense of speed. Briefly they considered a proposal from 20th Century Fox to do a licensed *Aliens* shooter, but they didn't like the idea of giving up their creative independence, so they considered how they could follow up *Wolfenstein 3D* with something new. Fighting aliens in space was old hat. This time it could be about fighting *demons* in space. This time it could be called *DOOM*.

First they had demons to exorcise internally. They'd done great out of their relationship with Apogee, but some members of the team wanted id to pull away from the shareware giant and go solo. Word from Shawn Green at Apogee was that too many staff there were slacking off and playing games when they should be taking orders, and some people were having trouble getting through to buy the game over the phone. Plus Apogee's ordering system was a disorganised mess, with orders written on scraps of paper rather than typed directly into a computer system.

Scott Miller and George Broussard were their friends, but they realised that Apogee was starting to hold them back. Instead of sharing profits 50–50, they could handle everything themselves and keep 100 per cent. So just as Miller had predicted months before, id Software would forge ahead alone.

The tension within the team didn't end there. Tom Hall wanted *DOOM* to have a story – an actual narrative pervading through the design, with an emotional pay-off much deeper than the impulsiveness of *Wolfenstein 3D*. John Carmack disagreed; story didn't matter, and it should get out of the way as quickly as possible. After months of disagreement, Carmack got his way, backed up by the rest of the team (who recognised the strength of his engine once again lay in speed). Hall was then asked to leave before development finished, his levels reworked by his replacement Sandy Petersen and his name pulled (*not* unanimously, it's worth noting) from the credits.

John Romero recalls that level design on *DOOM* was one of the hardest things on the game because they had to break

out of their old way of thinking. 'Before *DOOM*,' he explains, 'everything was 90 degrees.' Fixed-height ceilings, uniform lighting, right-angled walls – that's all that 3D game engines could do. *DOOM* changed all that, but the team struggled for months to get out of the mindset they'd built up over the previous decade – both from playing maze games and working on id's early stuff.

Romero says he eventually had to come up with a rule: 'If you make an area in your level that I could have made in *Wolfenstein*, you failed.'

First-of-its-kind level design and a cutting-edge engine weren't the full extent of *DOOM*'s innovations or appeal. Also critical were the punchy, brash sound effects, the wild, new weapons (including a chainsaw and the BFG, or 'Big Fucking Gun'), its ratcheted-up levels of gore, its support for networked multiplayer, and its all-in-one WAD file format – which contained all the data needed to run a level (its layout/geometry, character sprites, textures, and everything else).

Fans had started modifying *Wolfenstein 3D* to make their own levels and art almost as soon as it came out, but id had never intended for that to happen and so *Wolfenstein 3D* modding had involved a convoluted process of data extraction and editing.

With *DOOM*, id came prepared. 'We immediately put the data format of the maps up so people could write their own editors,' Romero says. *DOOM* thus spawned a thriving cottage industry not only of mapmakers and modders but also of modding toolmakers – many of whom sold their tools as shareware.

DOOM itself was sold as shareware, too – id may have walked away from Apogee, but they weren't about to abandon the business model that had made them rich.

They were in fact going to improve it.

Their business guy Jay Wilbur hadn't had any luck calling around the big newspapers and magazines. *DOOM* had lots of buzz, but it was almost all underground – online mostly, spread within the shareware scene and branching out into the more plugged-in PC gaming magazines. To make *DOOM* sell as the game-changer that it was, he needed to innovate its marketing.

He knew that *DOOM* would sell itself, if people just had a chance to play it, so he devised a plan to get the game into the hands of as many people as possible by subverting the retail distribution model. As John Romero recalls:

> We basically went and bought up all these different shareware games that had different publishers on them. And we contacted them and we told them we're going to come

out with this game *DOOM* and it's going to be shareware, and what we want is for you to take the shareware version – the first episode – to download. You take it, put it on a disk, don't charge more than nine bucks, and you get to keep all the profit you get. We want none of it. And so they're like, oh my God, yes.

It was a win-win arrangement. Retail distributors were incentivised to help promote *DOOM* by selling its shareware episode, then when people inevitably fell in love with the game they'd pay id for the other episodes. 'And so when you went to the store,' Romero recalls, 'there were like 10 different boxes of *DOOM* from 10 different companies. They all had the same shareware in it. It's like whatever box looked best is the one that won all the sales.'

PC gamers had *DOOM* frenzy. British games magazine *PC Zone* narrated the final minutes of anticipation on CompuServe as a preamble to their review. 'I was almost sick of this program before it appeared,' wrote resident shareware expert Mark Burgess, in disbelief at the panic and hype he'd seen for the game. *DOOM* was due for release on 10 December, so one fan dutifully posted at 5:23 a.m. Eastern Time (id was in Texas, which is an hour earlier than that) to ask why the game was not yet available.

'What's going on here anyway!!!!' they wrote. 'I demand *DOOM* be released immediately!!!!'

Two hours later, Burgess noted, 'all hell broke loose' as hundreds of gamers poured online to demand its immediate release – which ironically was delayed because they'd clogged up the disk's storage space to such an extent that id couldn't finish uploading the game. (Jay Wilbur had similar issues the night before with uploading to the University of Wisconsin's FTP server, which had so many users logging in hoping to download the game that he was initially locked out.)

Meanwhile BBSs and FTP servers around America crashed under the immense load of hundreds of thousands of people clamouring to download the game on day one. Worse for universities around the country, people were jumping straight into the multiplayer once they had the game – and they kept crashing the university networks.

DOOM had been hyped for months by fans wowed at the early teasers of id's next-generation technology, yet now that it was out they were stunned. *PC Zone*'s Burgess summed up the sentiment in the conclusion to his review: 'id has exceeded all expectations with *DOOM*; it won't be equalled, let alone surpassed, for a long time.'

DOOM blew everything else out of the water. *Byte* called it 'heroinware'. *Computer Gaming World* said it set 'a new benchmark' in games technology. *Compute!* referred to a new dawn in PC gaming. Only *Edge* broke ranks among the games and technology press, complaining in an infamous and widely mocked review about the game's simplicity before concluding: 'If only you could talk to these creatures, then perhaps you could try and make friends with them, form alliances... Now, that would be interesting.'

Newspapers praised it, too, though many, including the *Orlando Sentinel*, pointed also to its addictive qualities and the positive and negative toll it could have on people's lives. 'If you play it for hours it can make you paranoid,' one computer science student was quoted as saying. 'People were hugging the walls instead of walking down the middle of the halls.' Another source, an unnamed pharmacist, told the paper that he used the game to let off steam by imagining the demons were difficult patients.

Most recognised that it was a landmark achieved, regardless. The *Houston Chronicle* cited fun, realistic movement, an 'enthralling' sense of detail, and its four-player 'deathmatches' among the reasons for its success, adding that it was not just a great game but also 'the coming of age of shareware'.

They turned a profit on day one and quickly climbed to $100,000 in orders every day. It would take longer to conquer the mainstream, but *DOOM* had already transformed the industry. Now anything that wasn't a 3D shooter seemed old hat. Everyone was either talking about it or playing it (or likely both), from the low-level workers at games publishers and big software companies to the elite developers working on the next big commercial games, all the way up to the top executives at the biggest games and technology companies – many of whom spent the next Computer Game Developers Conference discussing how they should respond to *DOOM*'s success with their own marketing and product development strategies.

For Apogee it was a long-expected reality check. They may not have seen *this* coming, but they'd been anticipating a paradigm shift since *Wolfenstein 3D*. Still, it was unfortunate timing for two of their most promising new games.

One, *Blake Stone: Aliens of Gold*, had been developed by id's successors at *Gamer's Edge*, Jim Row and Mike Maynard – who themselves left Softdisk to work on the game. They'd cooked up an excellent sci-fi shooter with a few neat enhancements on the *Wolfenstein 3D* engine – including switches that could unlock doors on a different level (reachable via an elevator), one-way doors, automapping, and bio-technician 'informants' that would help the player rather than try to kill them. The game reviewed well, but it released just one week before *DOOM* and was thoroughly buried and forgotten beneath the avalanche of *DOOM* hype.

Side-scrolling shoot-'em-up *Halloween Harry* fared much better. It was a remake of a game of the same name made in 1985 for Australian home computer the Microbee by John Passfield when he was in high school. He'd seen *Ghostbusters* a short time before and so wanted to do a haunted house platform game. Six weeks later he'd submitted it to a local publisher and they'd put it out commercially (earning him pocket money rather than riches).

Several years later a friend of his had found out about the game and suggested they start a company together with a *Harry* remake as their first game. An initial prototype on the Amiga in AMOS – which was not at all well-suited to a fast-action platformer – eventually gave way to a DOS version when they met a couple of programmers (Rob Crane and Tony Ball) who were into PCs. 'They started doing really cool things that were way better than what I was doing on the AMOS version,' Passfield recalls. 'They had things like parallax scrolling and all this really cool stuff in it. So we started working with them.'

After a while they showed the game to a local distributor called Manaccom, which made a deal to publish the game in Australia and connected them to Apogee for international sales. (Though their naivety meant that Manaccom would take a large cut out of their royalties from Apogee.)

Harry had shifted dramatically from its roots by this point. Rather than a ghost hunter searching a haunted house for a malevolent witch, it would star a marine wiping out aliens in a mission to save the human race. And that of course meant a trusty arsenal of big, bad weapons, the most popular of which would prove to be a flamethrower. Ammunition for these weapons came from vending machines scattered throughout the game, paid for with coins picked up from defeated monsters.

The game's design was cheap and nasty in all the ways that games often were in those days – regularly breaking cardinal rules of good design with tricks like slime monsters hidden out of sight, biting at your ankles, and zombies that charged out of nowhere. But it looked so good and sounded so great – and flying around levels with the jetpack was so much fun – that Apogee fans adored it. The company's primarily US-based audience found its title confusing, however. It wasn't a Halloween-themed game, so why did it say Halloween in the title?

Scott Miller would eventually convince the team to change the name to *Alien Carnage* for its version 2.0 update and retail release, giving it another big influx of sales, though *DOOM* frenzy limited its impact.

Passfield remembers well his first sighting of *DOOM*, shortly before they finished *Halloween Harry* version 1.0:

> We were so happy with ourselves and how good our game looked. Then we were at Manaccom and they said, 'Check out this new game.' And it turned out it was *DOOM*. It was like looking 10 years in the future and going, 'That's now?!' And it was coming out just shortly after we were launching. We thought we had a cutting-edge game with this parallax scrolling and everything. And suddenly seeing *DOOM* – oh my God, these guys are just so far ahead of where we are (laughs). And I think luckily – I'm pretty sure we were the top of the shareware charts for like a month or so before *DOOM* hit. But that was the writing on the wall.

The 2D action-platformer was as good as dead, and everyone knew it – especially Apogee, which had already begun racing to catch up. They had one internal project in the works: a *Wolfenstein 3D* spin-off called *Rise of the Triad*, with id co-founder Tom Hall as lead designer, and would soon also start up development on a 3D *Duke Nukem* game using *Ken's Labyrinth* creator Ken Silverman's next-generation technology – the Build Engine. But it would be a while before either of those were ready, so in the meantime they kept pushing out platformers and shoot-'em-ups, waiting for their moment to strike.

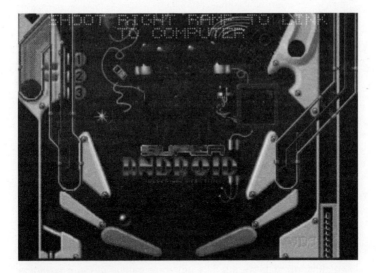

Pinball jazz

While id forged ahead with the burgeoning new first-person shooter genre and Apogee raced to play catch-up, Epic hesitated. Tim Sweeney didn't think he had the programming skill to make a comparable 3D engine. He'd been shocked by *Wolfenstein 3D*'s technology, and now *DOOM* had leaped even further ahead. He couldn't imagine how he'd ever catch up.

Epic wasn't exactly hurting from the absence of a *DOOM* killer in their catalogue, though. They'd had a huge hit that same year (1993) with James Schmalz's *Epic Pinball* – an Assembly-coded, vertically scrolling pinball game with realistic physics.

The idea had come from Finnish demoscene group Future Crew, whom Sweeney had been trying to recruit since the early days of Epic. They'd built a brilliant pinball demo that Epic couldn't convince them to turn into a full shareware release, so Sweeney asked Schmalz to look at it.

Schmalz had worked with Epic for a while by that point. He was at university when he'd made a game for them called

Solar Winds, an RPG and multidirectional shooter about bounty hunter Jake Stone's adventures through space.

Schmalz later recalled in an interview with the *Noclip* YouTube series that he was earning about $1,200 a month from *Solar Winds* royalties, and when he'd started building *Epic Pinball* he thought he'd double or triple it. 'My first cheque was like $50,000,' he said. In the first year after the game came out, he made around $1 million. *Epic Pinball*, which *PC Zone* declared 'easily as good' as any commercial pinball package (and better than most), would go toe-to-toe with the best shareware had to offer, ultimately finishing third, by Epic's reckoning, in the list of bestselling shareware games ever.

Its sequel, *Extreme Pinball*, and commercial spin-off *Silverball*, both developed by Schmalz's new company, Digital Extremes, would earn Epic millions more.

And that wasn't their only new hit, either. In a flurry of other new games released in 1993 and '94, two others had an outsized influence: August 1994 platformer *Jazz Jackrabbit* and October 1994 fighting game *One Must Fall 2097*.

Jazz Jackrabbit had come from the dream-team pairing of demoscene programmer Arjan Brussee (from acclaimed Ultra Force group) with hotshot teenage designer Cliff Bleszinski, who had started teaching himself to make PC games just three years earlier, aged 15.

He'd made rapid progress. His first game was a text adventure made in Visual Basic called *The Palace of Deceit*, self-published for DOS just months after he got his first computer. Then the following year he made an improved version for Windows 3.1, with hand-drawn Windows Paint graphics and an interface inspired by ICOM Simulations' *MacVenture* series of point-and-click adventure games.

He distributed the game on CompuServe, with an order form that included the question 'How old will the person be who

will play this game?' Bleszinski also left a note at the end of the game's documentation imploring people to register to support his passion and help pay for his impending college tuition, adding that 'not only will you get a great product and a company who stands behind it, you will help me to join a company like Sierra or Lucasfilm to make the greatest games ever someday.'

He went one step closer to his dream with his next game, a graphic adventure called *Dare to Dream*, which followed a troubled ten-year-old boy as he solved problems in his subconscious (and which channelled Bleszinski's real-life grief from his father's sudden passing in 1990). Rather than distribute this one on his own, he submitted the game to Epic – which had been actively soliciting proposals from emerging game developers through periodic talent calls across multiple online platforms. Sweeney said yes, and they published the game in 1993. Bleszinski was 17 when it came out.

He later admitted in a Reddit AMA ('Ask Me Anything') that it had actually been outsold by *The Palace of Deceit* 'by a factor of four to one'. But that didn't matter, because now the teenager was in on the ground floor at one of the fastest-growing games companies in the world. Sweeney liked to send him work-in-progress builds of upcoming games for testing and feedback. 'He'd write off his big list of what's good about this game and what needs to be fixed,' Sweeney later told writer Tom Bissell for a *New Yorker* profile of Bleszinski. 'Cliff's lists kept growing bigger and bigger.'

One day Sweeney sent him a prototype for a run-and-gun side-scrolling platformer with a silky-smooth frame rate and a suite of editing tools that were simple enough for a non-programmer like Bleszinski to understand. 'I immediately took to the tools like a fish to water and began crafting what I originally called Rambo Rabbit,' Bleszinski wrote in a blog post years later, 'because nothing seemed cooler than a rabbit with a gun.'

Gradually this character morphed from purple to green and its name changed to Jazz Jackrabbit. For several months they worked remotely – Bleszinski in California, Brussee in the Netherlands, communicating with each other over the phone as Brussee expanded and improved the engine while Bleszinski designed the levels (and *Epic Pinball* composer Robert Allen stepped in to do the music). Towards the end of development they also brought on animator Nick Stadler, who tried to lend the main character more of a classic Warner Bros animation vibe.

A summer of crunch then followed as Bleszinski and Brussee crammed into a temporary sharehouse with Sweeney, Schmalz, and *One Must Fall* creator Rob Elam, polishing levels and crushing bugs to get it ready for release.

Jazz Jackrabbit emerged from its development bunker on 30 July 1994, with six episodes in total (the first of which, containing eleven levels, was released as shareware). Epic pitched it as the PC's answer to *Sonic the Hedgehog*, and they weren't far off. *Jazz* was fast, funky, and cool, with a lot more precision-platforming than *Sonic* but a vibe that otherwise matched Sega's popular mascot game. And its stellar technical achievements – 60 frames per second 256-colour graphics, 8-channel digital music, demoscene-inspired plasma and particle effects – both impressed DOS gamers of the day and gave them a chance for a cheap (and controversial) dig at Apogee. An 'APOGEE' cheat code included in the game's CD version, released a few months later with three additional episodes, would put the game into a slowed-down 16-colour 'Apology Mode' – a move that amused many fans but caused such a backlash online (and from Apogee) that they removed it from later updates.

Meanwhile Epic's next-most-popular game of the time, *One Must Fall: 2097*, a rare console-style fighting game designed specifically for PC, had been picked up for publishing soon after brothers Rob and Ryan Elam released a tech demo called *One Must Fall* in May 1993, following months of public development on FidoNet.

Their idea had been to make the PC's answer to popular two-player arcade fighting game *Street Fighter II*, which featured a variety of martial arts experts engaging in a series of best-of-three, one-on-one close-quarters fights. But their vision quickly morphed into something more futuristic when they realised they could make it about giant robots instead of humans.

Not only would that be cooler, they thought, but also it would help Rob to finish the art, which he'd been making in Deluxe Paint from video capture frames of himself doing the different fighting moves. By switching to robots he could save production time, because then he wouldn't have to hand-draw everything – and instead could use 3D modelling software to create the fighters.

To accommodate the new theme, they changed the title to WAR Machines and contacted Tim Sweeney at Epic, who made a deal to publish it later that year.

The game was then delayed repeatedly as the Elam brothers struggled to achieve their vision. Come March 1994, they settled on a final name – *One Must Fall: 2097* – and promised two separate releases. The first would feature 'a normal, fight-till-you-win tournament', Ryan Elam wrote in a public update, with three out of the full ten giant mechs and four pilots (the characters that control the mechs) playable. There'd be nine fights to win, then 'a nice, wonderful beg screen' (literally a screen asking that people send in money for the product). The second release, due at the same time, would be an add-on tournament mode in which players could create their own pilot and build their own mech.

But plans changed, and the game did too. A month later Ryan Elam revealed there'd be a single game with a story mode about 'your struggle to win what is probably the best job in the galaxy', a tournament mode 'where you begin with a Jaguar robot and build the most powerful fighter you can', and notable features including stereo sound ('even on the Sound Blaster') and at least three unique special moves per character.

The game would be out 15 June, he added. For real this time.

On 10 October 1994, Epic finally released *One Must Fall: 2097*. They'd promised it would be worth the wait, and fans and critics agreed: *One Must Fall: 2097* was by far and away the best fighting game on PC – 'bar none', emphasised *Computer Game Review*. Its graphics and audio fight commentary weren't much to get excited about, they agreed, but the tournament mode (which included provisions for robot repairs and both robot and pilot upgrades between fights) and the fighting itself were both deemed masterful. *PC Format* even rated it the second-best arcade game of the year – ahead of the PC version of *Mortal Kombat* and behind its Epic stablemate *Jazz Jackrabbit*.

Sales were strong, too, and they got a modest boost from the arrival of online multiplayer in a July 1995 update, but *One Must Fall* could never compete with its better-funded competition – which quickly forged ahead – and it struggled to keep pace with the runaway success of *Jazz Jackrabbit*.

All the same, Epic and the Elam brothers forged plans for a sequel – but that would eventually be scrapped through concerns that the genre had shifted to 3D. (Rob Elam would eventually make that 3D sequel, titled *One Must Fall: Battlegrounds*, without Epic's help. He published it commercially in 2003.)

Epic weren't resting there. They put out a holiday level set for *Jazz Jackrabbit*, along with the critically acclaimed vertical-scrolling shoot-'em-up *Tyrian*, plus baseball management sim *Epic Baseball*, platformer *Xargon* (from Allen Pilgrim), and first-person space combat shooter *Radix: Beyond the Void* – which was a blend of *DOOM* and Interplay's hit six-degrees-of-freedom shooter *Descent*. And they made a distribution deal with a small, new shareware publisher called Safari Software.

But their sights were set on a different challenge – a new realm to conquer. And their days in shareware were numbered.

Shareware Version 1.0

This game requires 17.3 megs of free hard drive space to install.

C:\DUKE3D_

To install this program, we will need to know what directory on
your hard drive that we can copy the game files into.

You may either select one of your own or you may accept the default setting
listed above. If you choose to accept this setting, just press [ENTER],
otherwise enter your own directory. After you have typed in a directory name,
press [ENTER] to continue with the installation process.

CHAPTER 12

Shareware Edition

Come 1995, the shareware games scene was in major upheaval. *DOOM*'s success had triggered a wave of new entrants to the scene, most trying to copy its apparent path to riches – which was perceived simplistically (but not incorrectly) as a multi-level 'shareware edition' demo, with included ordering instructions, to whet the appetites of gamers everywhere, then a full-version retail release.

The three big players in shareware had all dabbled in retail partnerships for years by this point. There were dozens of 'rackware' retail shareware distributors who'd put unregistered versions of games – either individually or in collections – in convenience stores and big-box retailers, in some instances sharing a small cut of the profits with the authors. Apogee and id had also done deals with FormGen for retail episodes of *Commander Keen*, *Blake Stone*, and *Wolfenstein 3D*. And Epic had had a boxed version of *Castle of the Winds* sold in Wal-Mart stores.

But this was different. Retail was no longer a side channel where they could pick up a bit of extra revenue – it was fast becoming a primary channel.

This kind of transition was not unprecedented. In the 1980s several shareware companies focused on utilities and productivity tools had transitioned to retail distribution and sales

221

channels. Even Jim Knopf, one of the pioneers of shareware, had guided his company Buttonware completely out of the shareware business.

It was also not unexpected – at least in retrospect. Both Apogee and id had been founded in part out of a failure to garner interest through conventional commercial channels for what were actually bankable, marketable ideas. And Tim Sweeney had always harboured ambitions for Epic that stretched beyond the shareware realm. In his first company newsletter, published in September 1992, he'd celebrated their successes in becoming the world's second-largest publisher of shareware entertainment while in the same breath turning his sights on a bigger target: 'We are in the big leagues now,' he wrote. 'Our team's competitors are the big guys: Sierra. Origin. Brøderbund. MicroProse. Their products are the standards by which we will be judged.'

They weren't just going to compete with deeper-pocketed commercial publishers, Sweeney promised; they would beat them. And beat them on their own terms. They would *blow them away* with unparalleled advances in graphics, storylines, animation, and music 'that's ages ahead of the rest of the computer world'.

For a while, shareware could do that. Shareware could support the creation of advanced, breakthrough games like *Epic Pinball* and *Jazz Jackrabbit*, and *Wolfenstein 3D*, *DOOM*, and *Duke Nukem*. Not anymore.

Now they needed bigger teams and bigger budgets. Now they really were competing with the giants of commercial games publishing – because now everyone was doing shareware (or pretending to).

When *Commander Keen* came out, John Romero remembers, 'Within the shareware market it was like a meltdown. It was huge. [But] outside of it, shareware was a joke. Commercial publishers were not paying attention at all.' And so it was barely noticed. Then *Wolfenstein 3D* started to change that. It was being played in the offices of technology giants like Microsoft and several leading game publishers, including Lucasfilm Games and Origin. But none of them could fully get their heads around it. *This is free? How can this be free?*

Then just as they were coming to terms with *Wolfenstein 3D*'s success, *DOOM* came along and blew up bigger than any game before it – commercial or shareware. This time the games industry saw it happen in real time. They'd spent the previous year thinking about shareware and its intrinsic connection to the growing success of id Software, Apogee, and Epic. Now they saw its power, and they concluded that it was the chance to try before you buy that made the difference.

A partial game, released and distributed freely, as a taster – a demonstration – of the full experience: that was what they needed to copy. And so began the precipitous rise of the game demo, long regarded mainly as a tool for showing work-in-progress builds to industry peers but now recognised as a marketing technique unto itself.

First off the ranks were games that had roots in shareware, such as *Descent*, a six-degrees-of-freedom hybrid of first-person shooters and space-flight sims. It featured nausea-inducing banking and rolling seen through the cockpit of a compact spacecraft that players piloted through claustrophobic tunnels and wide-open chambers in a mining facility on the Moon (and then onto other locations), blasting virus-infected robots and rescuing trapped miners along the way (while flipping upside down so many times that it became impossible to tell which way was up).

Descent had briefly been on the books at Apogee, after its creators pitched Scott Miller on the game and he funded its early development. But he'd cast them adrift when he didn't see it coming together as he'd envisioned, and in a mad rush to pitch other publishers before money ran out they'd landed a deal with Interplay – one of the largest PC game publishers in the world at the time.

Interplay founder and CEO Brian Fargo decided to retain plans to release *Descent* as shareware, in addition to the retail version. 'I've always loved doing creative marketing ideas,' he explains, 'and I thought the product could use the extra boost of visibility.' *Descent* was a great game, but it had not been greatly anticipated, so he thought a shareware release might generate some extra buzz – which it absolutely did, dominating online discussions for weeks afterwards.

In this case, *Descent*'s shareware edition contained seven out of the full thirty levels – a large chunk of the full game, in keeping with the shareware model used by Apogee, id, and Epic. But more often shareware editions of commercial games were much smaller. Publishers hated the idea of giving part of their game away freely, and they felt like the Apogee model of publishing a quarter or a third of the full game as shareware was far too generous. One or two levels should be enough, they thought – all people really need is a little taste.

But still, even a *taste* of the actual game was a step up from the old days. Shareware – and *DOOM* in particular – had forced deep-pocketed commercial publishers to start showing their games. If they didn't, they were viewed with suspicion – like they must have something to hide. 'We were forcing everybody to start showing their gameplay,' Romero says, 'and put it out there so people have a more informed choice when they make a decision to play a game, so that they're not going to get ripped off.

'For the commercial producers,' he adds, 'they're like, "Wow, we can't screw around anymore. We can't actually sell empty promises."'

Their window of opportunity to capitalise on *DOOM* fervour with knock-off versions of their own would close fast, too, because shareware's best and brightest were making their play for the retail world not only through commercially published standalone episodes of their shareware games but also with full retail releases of their new 3D games.

In 1995, id published a commercial version of *DOOM* called *Ultimate DOOM* – with all three original episodes plus a fourth new one to give buyers more value for their money. That same year, with help from GT Interactive, they published *Hexen: Beyond Heretic*, a retail-only sequel to shareware first-person shooter *Heretic* (both developed by Raven Software).

Realms beyond

Meanwhile Apogee had been making moves into retail as well. They'd tested the waters with commercial spin-offs of *Blake Stone* and their new game *Rise of the Triad* – which had begun its three-year development as a *Wolfenstein 3D* sequel. When those went well, they'd also made deals with FormGen and GT Interactive to publish retail versions of most of their games.

On one occasion they'd gone the other way, too, with a shareware sequel to Australian animator Lindsay Whipp's *Baron Baldric* – an Amiga and PC side-scrolling platformer published in Australia only by Electronic Arts in 1992 (on the proviso that he design and supply his own packaging for the game, which he says left him with 'small' earnings once this material cost was deducted from his income from the deal). Local shareware publisher Manaccom then re-released the game as shareware, with one extra level added to entice buyers, before referring him to Apogee to allow the sequel, *Mystic Towers*, to have wider distribution.

But between their retail spin-offs and republishing experiments and id's massive success with 3D, it was clear to

Apogee heads Scott Miller and George Broussard that 3D was the future – for the industry, and for Apogee. 'We realised we couldn't really be sidetracked and distracted by these non-3D games anymore,' Miller says. 'So we really kind of phased things out.'

To aid in the transition, they started a new publishing label in July 1994: 3D Realms. The Apogee name would continue as their company name and their brand for 2D games, while 3D Realms would serve as their trading name on all 3D titles – starting with Terminal Reality's combat flight sim *Terminal Velocity* (1995), which had its retail version published just weeks after the shareware episode went online.

This 3D Realms label would morph into the company's public identity in 1996. 'We decided to put all our bets going forward on 3D Realms – only games that were more high-end, 3D, fully immersive experiences,' remembers Miller. 'And so we basically got out of the 2D market.'

Their final Apogee release would be *Stargunner* in November 1996, but their last notable 2D releases both came two years earlier, in 1994, at the beginning of their 3D transition. The first of the pair, *Raptor: Call of the Shadows* (released 1 April), was a critically acclaimed, fan-favourite, vertical-scrolling shoot-'em-up that proved 2D could still swing big numbers for the company – with an estimated 80,000-plus sales, which put it first or second on Apogee's bestselling 2D games (alongside *Duke Nukem*).

The other notable 2D Apogee release of 1994 was much more offbeat – and mired in controversy.

The story starts in 1992, when programmer Andy Edwardson and artist Shaun Gadalla collaborated on a side-scrolling shareware shooter called *Phylox*, which was published through a few different small-time shareware distributors around the world. That work helped them get a contract with a Belgian company called Copysoft.

Copysoft had briefly concerned itself with the Amiga before shifting over to PC shareware and inventing a squirrel character called Skunny that goes on adventures through knock-off versions of popular games. (There would be six in total across 1993–4, plus a low-budget commercial 'Special Edition' release in 1995.)

Copysoft founder Philippe Mercier's business strategy was to recruit promising young programmers and artists on CompuServe and hire them to make these games, uncredited, and release them as shareware (under the Apogee model). He started with *Skunny: Back to the Forest* – pitched as a *Sonic*-killer with 256-colour 'hand-painted' graphics, parallax scrolling, gamepad support, 'Fast! Fast! Scrolling', two playable characters (Skunny and Rosie, distinguished from each other by their clothing), and automatic 'smart' saving of player progress.

The goal in this first game was to traipse through the forest fighting off crazed insects and battling an evil mastermind called King Toad in order to rescue Skunny's friends. It wasn't especially original, but it made a strong enough (positive) impression that it was widely shared and distributed.

Three more games followed almost immediately after, each echoing the first game's light-yet-generic tone and repeating the message that Skunny was a children-, animal-, and sticky-nut-pudding-loving squirrel. There was a second platformer called *Save Our Pizzas*, wherein Skunny travels back in time to retrieve 'the recipe of the Pizza'; a poorly regarded *Moon Patrol* clone called *Lost in Space*, which involved retrieving 'all our TV satellite dishes' from the Moon and rescuing captive astronauts from large-nosed green aliens; and *Desert Raid*, a game so underdone and basic that *PC Games* magazine scored it 9 out of 100 in their review.

Gadalla and Edwardson had meanwhile been tooling around with a demo for an animal-filled racing game based on Nintendo's popular *Mario* spin-off *Super Mario Kart*. Through trial and error and painstakingly analysing *Mario Kart*, Edwardson built a pseudo-3D engine that mimicked the Super Nintendo's Mode 7 technology – which combined scaling and rotation to make flat background images look like 3D landscapes sprawling out towards the horizon, thereby enabling *Mario Kart* to adopt a behind-the-racer perspective.

Once they had a working prototype (around December 1993, with the working title Wacky Kart), the pair sent it to Copysoft. 'They were quite excited and put a few screenshots of it on CompuServe,' Edwardson later wrote. But he and Gadalla weren't happy with Copysoft, which refused to pay them royalties. When Scott Miller started negotiations to publish the game through Apogee, they delivered an ultimatum to Copysoft: pay us royalties or we won't continue development. Copysoft declined, so they decided to jump ship.

They made a deal to publish directly with Apogee and sent Copysoft a cheque to buy their way out of their contract – paying back the £25,000 they'd been paid. And that was that... or so they thought.

While Gadalla and Edwardson laboured away on their game, now retitled *Wacky Wheels*, polishing the graphics and engine, fine-tuning the design, and sneaking in a cameo appearance from the Dopefish character from *Commander Keen*, Copysoft was secretly making their own game based on the original prototype – a feat made easier by the fact that Edwardson had accidentally included the source code when he sent it to them.

So when Edwardson was busy adding modem play to the game, along with various other features that Apogee's testing team (and Joe Siegler in particular) had pressed for, Copysoft took their opportunity to go to market first and release *Skunny Kart*.

The pair were heartbroken, and furious. 'There was no way Copysoft had the ability to write an engine like that from scratch,' Edwardson reflected in the Apogee FAQ. They cried foul and threatened legal action. Copysoft countered that the original prototype code was their intellectual property, as it had been created on equipment they'd given Gadalla and Edwardson under contract, and therefore *Wacky Wheels* – as a derivative of that prototype – was also theirs. To avoid years of legal wrangling, Copysoft's US representative told *PC Gamer*, they offered Apogee a non-exclusive licence to market *Wacky Wheels* for a pre-determined percentage of the sales generated. Apogee didn't like that and counter-offered 10 per cent of gross sales if *Skunny Kart* was pulled from the market, which Copysoft declined.

At an impasse, and seemingly poised to head to court, the two companies then decided to each let the other be. Their games weren't *exactly* alike, despite the shared point of origin – *Wacky Wheels* had racers starting side by side in a row, whereas *Skunny Kart* had them lined up *Mario Kart*-style, plus the courses and racers were all different, and *Wacky Wheels* had more game modes and more refined graphics. And litigation is expensive, anyway, so they could just let the market figure it out.

Skunny Kart remained available, rated by magazines and fans alike as the best Skunny game by far, while *Wacky Wheels* came out to mostly positive reception a short time later – deemed just slightly better in a close race by German magazine *Aktueller Software Markt* and given the seal of approval by *PC Gamer*, which noted that 'manoeuvring a shark around a racetrack firing hedgehogs at a pelican is actually a hell of a lot of fun.'

Both Apogee and the PC games market were trending down a different path, however. Gritty 3D realism – delivered in gory, violent packages – was in vogue, not playful cartoony tomfoolery.

By this point Apogee's new 3D Realms division was already deep in the trenches working on their Build Engine *DOOM* killer *Duke Nukem 3D* (shortened to *Duke 3D* in casual or

character-limited usage): a game that would be to *Duke Nukem* what *Wolfenstein 3D* had been to *Castle Wolfenstein*.

With *Duke 3D*, the 3D Realms team wanted to chart a different course for the burgeoning first-person-shooter genre. Where id Software emphasised the purity of action, reaction, and speed – just guns, blood, and level design, perfected, presented, and delicately balanced like the best roller coaster you could ever be on – 3D Realms was about character and wit.

'id [Software] had a philosophy of just *to-the-bone* gameplay,' says Miller. Faceless, fearless characters (*DOOM*'s protagonist was even called 'Doomguy') beating back hordes of generic, though frightening, brilliantly rendered monsters. 'We added a lot of meat to that bone.' They did this in the form of jokes, wise-cracks, mutant pig cops, and interaction with objects in the environment – like vending machines that dispensed drinks, pinball machines players could enjoy in-game, toilets that flushed, a cinema with a loaded projector, and much more. They even had pole dancers who could be tipped a few bucks to flash their pixellated breasts.

The press went wild for it. *PC PowerPlay* wrote that it 'injected new life into the genre' just when it was becoming passé. *Computer Player* said it 'supersedes *DOOM* in almost every respect'. *Next Generation* noted that it 'has everything *DOOM* doesn't, but it also doesn't leave anything out that made *DOOM* a classic' and it was 'by far the best of the new-wave shooters'. A year later *Computer Gaming World* would rate it the 37th best game of all time.

But its January 1996 shareware release was talked about as though it were a preview release – a demo – rather than the first episode of a three-episode game, and as such most reviews didn't come until after the retail version hit stores in May – a month after episodes two and three became available via shareware registration.

As with *DOOM*, the fact that it was shareware had proved critical to its 3.5-million-copies-sold success, with players raving online about how cool its first level was and how awesome its interactive elements were. But with retail and shareware releases side by side, shareware had become synonymous with demo.

Being shareware had complicated repercussions for id's next big game, *Quake*, thanks to a bungled experiment whereby the shareware edition was sold at retail with the paid episodes already on the CD – unlockable via a code received upon ordering from id over the phone. It was intended as a way to cut out the middleman and streamline the shareware ordering process, as id recognised that the lion's share of sales would come at retail, but it proved disastrous when a group of hackers figured out how to bypass the copy protection – and hence cut id out of the deal too.

All the same, though, the *Quake* shareware box was reportedly the sixth bestselling computer game in the US that year, with the full retail *Quake* box in a distant 20th place (at around 250,000 copies shipped nationwide, on the way to a 373,000 retail sales tally in its first 12 months).

Valuable software

It wasn't only Apogee, Epic, and id Software making big gains and profitable shareware-to-retail partnerships in the mid-1990s. Propelled by the combination of increasing market size, ever-improving shareware distribution and consumer awareness, and the halo-effect cast by *DOOM* over the entire shareware games business, numerous other companies and individual authors were making a play for the big time.

One of the more successful efforts came from MVP Software, a small shareware publisher in Grand Rapids,

Michigan, that was founded in 1985 as a hobby venture by philosophy professor Dave Snyder. In the early years Snyder sold software via mail order for the Sanyo 550 series of computers, marketing direct to end-users in magazine ads, then when his university job evaporated he started to search for new ways to earn a living. He tried selling other people's software through his hobby business, ran a newsletter called Christian Educational Computing, and worked a series of odd jobs. 'He sold insurance, he sold encyclopaedias, he sold siding,' his son Chris recalls. But through it all he continued trying to develop MVP into a viable business.

'He spent a lot of time online, especially CompuServe. A lot of BBSs as well.' Chris doesn't know how it happened, but his dad eventually settled on running a shareware PC games publishing business. 'And he would be doing the promotion, he would do the sales, he'd do the tech support,' Chris adds. 'He was a one-man shop for that. If a customer had a question, he would be answering the phone.'

MVP's first DOS game was a simple top-down maze-action game called *RoboMaze*, developed by programmer Keith Laverty in 1989. A pair of sequels followed in 1991, each nothing alike. *RoboMaze II* was a multi-screen (no scrolling) action-platformer where players scurry, jump, and shoot their way through a tower to win freedom from a repressive dictator. *RoboMaze III*, meanwhile, was more in line with the sprawling fantasy of *The Legend of Zelda* – right down to an old man in a cave giving the hero a sword to 'slay the evil ones'. Rather than a side-view platformer, it was a slanted-perspective top-down adventure through caves, forests, cities, and secret dungeons.

Despite the large discrepancy in gameplay and theme, all three games shared the same overarching storyline and all had sparse graphics – with colourful and detailed sprites drawn onto a stark black background.

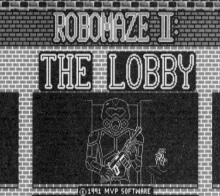

ROBOMAZE II:
THE LOBBY

© 1991 MVP SOFTWARE

WRITTEN BY KEITH LAVERTY
WITH: JASON PELLERIN, DANIEL NUTTALL, MELODY SMITH

MONEY   0

MONEY   210   19

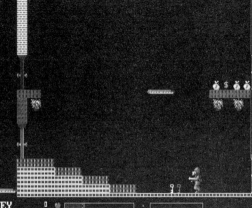

MONEY   0

Snyder published them under an Apogee-style episodic model. The first volume of each game was free (and in a press release for *RoboMaze III* he emphasised that it was not a demo but rather 'a complete game in its own right, with its own storyline and graphics') while the others could be ordered either direct from MVP or via one of its retail distributors. *RoboMaze III* buyers would also receive a multicolour game map and a 15-page printed manual, with its shareware episode pitched to retail customers as 'a free bonus game'.

The *RoboMaze* games were a resounding success for MVP. An impressive 40,000 retail sales in four months for *RoboMaze II* added to tens of thousands of shareware registrations across the two games to give Snyder the push he needed to turn MVP into his full-time job.

After the initial *RoboMaze* successes in 1991, however, MVP Software struggled to generate enough revenue to support Dave Snyder and his family. To supplement his income, Snyder took on a part-time sales job towards the end of 1993. But that didn't last long. In a family Christmas letter in 1994, his wife wrote that in February 'several things began to fall into place' for the business. They had several new products out, most sold both directly to end-users via shareware and in boxes distributed through several nationwide retail chains. And that year they'd found particular success through a retail version of the game *Sand Storm*, which was the bestselling game in Kmart for four months.

In a letter to MVP's international shareware distributors the previous year, Snyder also noted that *Sand Storm* had been named Top Pick and Top Download by AOL, though their bestseller at that point (by a slim margin) was alternative-history World War II flight simulator *Corncob 3D* – an editor's choice pick from *Shareware Magazine* and a nominee for two Shareware Industry Awards.

Corncob had been released independently by Kevin Stokes in 1991 with an engine written entirely in Intel 8086 Assembly language, its 3D physics models worked out by hand by Stokes – at the time a physics graduate student at Duke University – and his friend George. Stokes had uploaded the game to every BBS he could find, calling long distance all around the US, but one day in 1992 he'd received a call from Dave Snyder – who pitched him on working together.

Snyder and Stokes made a deal to republish *Corncob* through MVP, with a mission-builder program and a 130-mission expansion called *The Other Worlds Campaign* available to people who paid the $20 registration fee. The full *Deluxe* version ended up being sold at Kmart (alongside *Sand Storm*) for $5.95, of which Stokes later wrote he received around 30 cents. (Kmart took around half, then the retail distributor took most of what remained before MVP took its little slice – smaller than Stokes' – and Stokes got what was left at the end.)

Multiple income streams were not just a happy accident for MVP; they were critical elements of Snyder's business strategy. In a January 1994 insider newsletter, Snyder wrote that it was no longer possible to succeed without products that were competitive in both retail and shareware markets. Going forward, he added, 'We'll continue to pursue a marketing strategy based on a diversity of channels.' They were reaching deeper into pay-per-download services, shareware, direct mail, hardware bundling, and low- and medium-cost retail as well as more speciality retail.

This new strategy had the knock-on effect of increasing tension between MVP and shareware distributors. Snyder had been frustrated by less-scrupulous vendors for years, but now he had products in direct competition with them. Catalogue, computer-club, and other non-retail vendors were still permitted to sell MVP's shareware games, as long as they were clear that these were unregistered versions, but 'rackware' vendors that targeted retail channels needed written permission from Snyder.

Many ignored the missive. Likely they never even bothered to read it. So Dave Snyder went on the assault.

If a distributor put an MVP Software product on their CD without his permission, he'd sue them. His son Chris remembers 'one particularly egregious case' involving a company that called itself MVP Publishing, but most were just doing quick-buck slapped-together CD compilations with no thought to the contents.

> And usually these companies would either get shut down or they would settle and we'd end up with a bunch of these CDs as part of the settlement terms. I mean, these companies never really had much money, I don't think. And the main goal was to get it off the shelves.
>
> So we would sometimes be including them for free with our [registered games] – you know, sending them out. Because at that point, as long as we weren't selling them, there wasn't an issue. People wouldn't have that complaint. But I remember we had boxes and boxes of these compilations that we'd gotten that way.

When he wasn't fighting against unauthorised distribution of his products, Snyder was invariably hustling for more business. He was constantly on the phone or sending emails to drum up new licensing and distribution deals or to oversee work on MVP's upcoming games.

At that point in time (1994), their big upcoming games were *Pickle Wars*, a non-violent platformer about repelling an invasion of pickle-shaped aliens by former Apogee developer Karen Crowther, bridge (the card game) simulation *MVP Bridge*, and digital board game *Rings of the Magi* by David Bollinger.

The second of these, *MVP Bridge*, would define the later direction of the company, but it was the third, *Rings of the Magi*, that raised the company's profile.

Rings of the Magi had begun as an untitled, experimental toy project of developer David Bollinger's over a decade earlier. 'There wasn't the glut of match-three games that exist today,' recalls Bollinger, 'but one of the mechanics that interested me was grid-based "physics", where moving one cell caused others to move, or fall/collapse, or connect/combine, or interact in some other way.'

In one experiment, he made it such that the circles on a grid could only be manipulated indirectly via arrow buttons that exerted force in a particular direction (one button might make all rings that are parallel to it slide to the right, for instance). It was a cool little mechanic, but Bollinger had no plans to do anything with it. He was a tinkerer, making free graphics and physics demos for the game development community and prototypes for his own amusement.

But then in the early 1990s, while doing beta testing on the MVP-published game *Cargo Bay*, he struck up a friendship with developer Steve Blackwood. 'One thing led to another,' Bollinger recalls, 'and eventually Steve suggested that we team up, with him serving as producer, in order to bring one of my ideas to MVP Software for possible publishing.' They went with his circle-pushing prototype.

Bollinger at first struggled to find a suitable conceptual hook to wrap around his old prototype, but one day 'while staring at the outlines' of its circles, he suddenly saw them as rings. A wealth of Tolkien-esque ideas bombarded his mind, giving him his *Rings of the Magi* name and a suitable mystical story conceit.

Bollinger's hacked-together programmer art went through multiple iterations to get it to a pitch-worthy state, then he and Blackwood took it to Dave Snyder, who promptly arranged for a professional artist and musician to help turn it into a polished product.

MVP published the game for DOS in 1994 and then Windows in 1995, earning Best Puzzle & Logic Game recognition in the

1996 Ziff Davis Shareware Awards, along with five-star reviews from several shareware critics. But its success and acclaim had little impact on MVP's business strategy, which doubled down on the fast-emerging casual games market on Windows.

That move would pay off handsomely for a few years, as the company did some of its best-ever business, but their high-royalties/low-commission sales model and a few bad choices in an ever-changing market squandered much of MVP's financial windfall. In particular, a deal with Microsoft to make games for the ill-fated Windows ME at the close of the decade seemed like a huge boon but ultimately proved more distraction than profit for Snyder. Meanwhile, an online gaming service called Classic Entertainment Online cost more money and took longer to develop than expected and a few game projects hit delays of their own.

These blunders took their toll. Eventually MVP ran out of money, and in the early 2000s Snyder was forced to change occupation to selling insurance and financial planning. He continued to run MVP as a shareware-focused side business until his sudden death in a car accident in 2007.

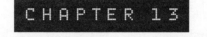

CHAPTER 13

Pretty Good Shareware

The shareware scene in the early 90s had been defined by the rise of the shareware titans, but as their focus began to split and shift away so too did the overarching character of the shareware scene. The post-*DOOM*, post-*Duke 3D*, increasingly overexposed and oversaturated shareware world, by contrast, would be marked by the rise of the shareware specialists. This would be the era of the boutique one- or two-person studios that earned their money and (modest) fame within the confines of a niche.

As always in the shareware scene, some studios would last longer than others. Many struck fire once, then struggled a few times to recapture it before fizzling out of the business – as was the case with Bob Mancarella, who had such a hit with his Mac and Windows 95 shareware mini-golf game *Gopher Golf* (1994–6) that the Mac version got picked up for a commercial release by MacSoft.

Mancarella received around 20,000 registrations for the game (around 16,000 on Mac and the rest on Windows, at $15 a pop), which he'd distributed in a demo-ware format – limited to three holes per included course, plus no saving or loading of player-made courses, until a valid registration code was entered.

But his initial follow-up effort – the first-person-perspective action-light exploration and puzzle-focused Mac game *Giza*

(1996) – fared poorly, as did a 'quick toy' he made called *SpiralGraphics*. And then a return to mini-golf with *Goofy Golf Deluxe* (1999) – which swapped cartoony gophers for claymation graphics – did little to reverse his fortunes. 'I had hoped it would come off as more of a professional effort,' he recalls. But income from the game fell short of his expectations – 'probably to do with the fact I tried to double the price and switch to CD-only distribution [of the registered version],' he suggests. After around four years in shareware, with four titles to his name, Mancarella felt he had no choice but 'to go and get a real job'.

Others, like *Capture the Flag* author Richard Carr, shared a similar fate. Carr had made three further shareware games after his 1992 non-violent strategy hit – DOS educational game *Mix and Match*, real-time and turn-based strategy hybrid *Treasure Island*, and a turn-based twist on *Treasure Island* called *Pirate Battles*. But even with the industry goodwill and press connections Carr had made through *Capture the Flag*, he struggled to earn any noteworthy sums from these later games and decided not to test his wife's patience any longer – so he gave up on games and got a software industry job as a programmer.

Mike 'Zugg' Potter's zMUD serves as a fine counterpoint for the viability of a shareware games business in the late 90s – provided it targeted a narrow niche. zMUD was a client program for connecting to MUDs (multi-user dungeons), a kind of text-based online multiplayer role-playing game invented in the late 1970s, with its notable features including a graphical user interface (rather than pure text), various advanced tools for veteran MUD players, and a first-of-its-kind auto-generated graphical map of a MUD's environment.

Potter initially published the program as a free hobby project in August 1995, then around a year later decided to switch to a shareware model with his version 4.1 update – which introduced a 30-day (later changed to a 30-execution) limit for unregistered users.

To facilitate payment of the $20 registration fee (which included free updates to subsequent versions of the program), Potter turned to a new online payments processing service called Kagi – which was arguably the first e-commerce service of the new Internet age to be purpose-built for selling software. (Another, Digital River, may have been founded slightly before Kagi but didn't sign up its first software developer until August 1996, while others such as Register Now!, ShareIt!, and RegSoft emerged soon after.)

Kagi had launched in September 1994 with five shareware utility programs, including popular Mac FTP client Anarchie, then steadily expanded as word spread among the Mac and Apple Newton faithful – and later, from May 1995 onwards, among Windows programmers too.

It had begun shortly before that as a hobby project for Berkeley-based programmer Kee Nethery, who noticed that people would sometimes post on software mailing lists to ask for help registering a shareware program. Their cheque had been returned, the letter unopened, and their email to the author bounced – did anyone know how to pay for the software? Nethery thought he could solve the problem. He had a permanent mailing address, a domain name, and a credit card merchant account, so once he had his first shareware author on board (Anarchie developer Peter Lewis) he decided to build Kagi and see if it caught on.

He initially ran the website and payment processing systems off two old Macintosh computers (a Mac IIci and Mac Classic) in his bedroom, squeezed onto a small desk next to the bed. Space was so cramped in the early days that he had to roll his chair out of the way to let his wife pass when she wanted to go to bed. But by the time Potter found the platform, Kagi was a thriving full-time enterprise for Nethery – who employed his wife and friends to help run the business.

By the end of 1996, there were over 1,000 products selling through Kagi – most of them shareware Mac and Windows programs (a small proportion of which were games or games-related utilities). And zMUD was among the bestsellers, ranked 11th on both sales quantity and gross income for the final three months of the year. It would remain comfortably in the top twenty on both quantity and income rankings for the next three years, peaking at number two on the rolling three-month and twelve-month charts in late 1998.

Those sales weren't trivial in number, either. By February 1997, zMUD had a thousand registered users. By September Potter was earning enough money to quit his day job and work on zMUD full time. In August 1999, spurred on by a positive CNET review and an editor's choice award from ZDNet, he surpassed 20,000 paid customers – with no signs that things were slowing down (and indeed they wouldn't for another few years, though Potter remained dedicated to zMUD and its eventual CMUD successor for a further decade after that).

Going solo

This sort of low-key, steady success was common among professional shareware authors, many of whom lived for years off service to a narrow niche. Usually that meant maintaining just one or two specific applications that were regularly updated and rewritten with better features and support for the latest system updates. But in one case the niche was instead a steady flow of new games within a few related genres.

Such was the modus operandi of dancer-turned-game-developer William Soleau, publishing under the name Soleau Software through the entirety of the 1990s.

Soleau had found his way to game development slowly. He'd made physical games with cardboard and cards as a kid, but the idea of creating a computer game was entirely new to him when he bought his first computer, a Commodore 64, in 1983. 'I had to load the operating system with a tape cartridge,' he recalls. 'And I was fascinated just by the medium.'

He'd been around computers before. In college he'd learned the basics of punch-card programming for mainframe and mini-computers. But here was a little machine he could call his own, and it came with a book about programming in BASIC.

Quickly he caught the programming bug. 'My first program I think was called File-O,' he says. It was like a modern-day notes app – useful for saving and searching through random thoughts, shopping lists, to-do lists, and so on. He wrote it to help manage his appointments and schedules when he was travelling around on tour as a ballet dancer. Then he wrote more programs, each meant to solve a particular problem (one was for monitoring expenses, for instance).

In 1984 he began to transition from dancer to choreographer – from performing to programming the flow and movements and staging of a ballet – and around a year later he decided to try making a game. It was a simple ASCII graphics game he called *Car Race*. 'You take this car through this course and you can't crash into oil slicks and stuff like that,' he recalls. Soleau enjoyed the process of creating it so much that he made another game, and then another and another. He'd take the computer with him on tour, as his ballet company travelled all around the world, and put his downtime into learning more programming.

At some point he started uploading his games to CompuServe for other people to enjoy, and then a little while later he started to ask for donations from anyone who enjoyed them. He'd code in a count variable that tracked how many times someone hit the button to play again (rather than exiting). If they played two or more rounds in one session then they'd see a message soliciting feedback via CompuServe or a letter and asking for a $5 or $10 donation 'if you found this game worthwhile'.

Around the same time, in 1988, Soleau switched to a PC and released another ASCII racing game, *Race Car*, followed in March 1989 by a new game he called *Seeker of Wisdom*. Then he made a set of text-mode maze games: *RatMaze, MadMaze, BumpMaze,* and *BlindMaze.* Each was a variant on the same core idea: move through a maze and try to complete a given objective within some other specific constraint. *MadMaze* and *BlindMaze,* for instance, both involved searching for an artefact by blowing holes in walls and exploring a maze, of which the player could only see a small portion at a time, while managing their character's oxygen levels. *RatMaze,* by contrast, was more of a straightforward cat-and-mouse game where the goal was to grab the stars scattered through the maze before one of the pursuing X characters could catch you.

At one point – he doesn't recall when exactly – Soleau returned from a month-long tour overseas and went to the post office to collect his mail. To his surprise, they had a whole bag full of letters for him. 'And there was $10 in each one of those letters,' he recalls. 'I probably made more money in that one event than I did dancing – because we weren't getting paid that much money. And I started thinking to myself, *Wow,* that *many people found this interesting.*'

On hearing the news, his friend and fellow dancer Kevin Santee suggested that maybe he should start a games company. He didn't act on it right away – he kept publishing shareware games under his own name for another year or so, but this planted the seed for what would in 1991 become Soleau Software.

As his shareware earnings increased so too did his free time – he reduced his workload as a choreographer and stopped dancing in companies. And his games made a corresponding step up in graphical fidelity. Soleau's 13 games released in 1990 all offered CGA colour graphics, eschewing his previous reliance on text-mode visuals. (Which brought him in line with the graphical standards of a few years' prior, as even in the shareware world the PC games industry had largely moved up to the successor of CGA: EGA graphics.)

Of those thirteen, one asked players to collect gold and push boxes around to trap enemies, another was a *Risk*-style digital board game, and four were different kinds of number puzzles: a falling-block colour-matching game called *Cuber*, a column-colouring game called *Plotz*, and two Othello/Reversi variants called *Iago* and *Doubolo*. Four others were variants of popular commercial game *Pipe Mania* (also known as *Pipe Dream*) – which involved connecting pipes on a grid to construct a path for onrushing sewer slime to drain through. Two of these, *Up the Wall* and *Main Break*, were simple keyboard-controlled clones of the core pipe-laying gameplay loop, while the other two, *Jungle Jack* and *Runoff*, tried to re-theme the game (as canal-digging in an uncharted jungle and path-laying for a woodland marathon, respectively).

Every year Soleau added multiple new games to his catalogue, most of them similarly grouped into just a handful of core ideas – and all strictly non-violent. He liked to create puzzle and strategy games that were heavy on logic, even if they were presented as traditional platformers – as in the case of *Ladder Man* (1992), which had players use a portable ladder rather than a jump ability to traverse environments. Pressing the spacebar would activate the ladder, which extended two tiles above the character's head, but if the player stepped off the ladder (or any object) onto empty space, they'd fall to the next solid tile.

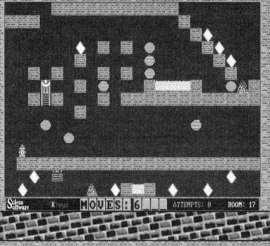

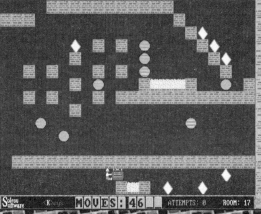

Navigation thus became a test of wits rather than of dexterity – because for Soleau that was the joy of both playing and designing games: puzzling out the logic of it.

His go-to genres were strategic maze games, block-pushing/ carrying puzzle games styled after *Sokoban*, move-your-men-to-the-other-side-before-your-opponent games (usually involving some sort of logic puzzle whereby the men automatically move forward whenever a path is cleared for them), *Risk*-style strategic conquest wargames, and *Pipe Mania* variants.

'I would write a game and then the next game I wrote might be an adaption of the same game, with different graphics,' Soleau explains. 'But I'd have one or two elements that were different, because that's the only way it would be interesting for me.' Along the way he'd make notes about which games were selling well and which were selling poorly, then he'd try to hold onto elements from the popular games for future efforts.

He soon brought on his friend Kevin Santee as business partner, to help him grow and manage the business. Soleau would make the games while Santee took care of company financials and order fulfilment.

Soleau had no interest in adopting the Apogee model whole hog, but he – like many other shareware authors – took the essence of the idea: to offer more content to anyone who pays. He devised a system whereby a single unlock code would open up the full experience and shut off the shareware nag screens or start delays, and rather than invest in a complicated licence generation and validation process he baked that one code into the game. 'It didn't matter whether you were John Boesky or Bill Soleau,' he explains. 'It's the same code.'

This, he figured, would be enough to pull in the honest people, and the rest were never going to pay anyway – so what difference did it make if they could just look up the code on the Internet?

It worked well enough, at least, to keep him and Kevin Santee focused on the company full-time – or close to it – through most of the 1990s. Most years they'd earn around $40,000 apiece, after business expenses, although in one particularly strong year they doubled that, thanks in large part to a load of extra income through royalties from games licensed for CD-ROM shareware collections sold in big US retailers like Wal-Mart.

The biggest money-makers were DOS games *Oilcap* (1996; lay pipes for oil to go through, as in *Pipe Mania*), *Ant Run* (1996; same idea except with ants and the pipes are fixed pieces that need to be rotated as the ant runs through), and *Isle Wars* (1994; a computerised take on the *Risk* board game, with added natural disasters and rebellions), along with Windows game *Score a Million* (2000; general knowledge trivia where players must complete a bingo-style line of correct answers on the board in order to win).

Over the course of the decade, Soleau published more than 60 shareware DOS games plus roughly that number again across Windows, Mac, and Web titles – some of which were sold not as shareware but as licensed commercial titles (they did a *Saturday Night Live* CD-ROM, for instance). This output of over 100 games in a decade was second only to Tommy's Toys (see Chapter 3) in sheer volume, and incredibly they were nearly all made by William Soleau himself – the only exceptions being a small series of games by brothers Doug and Larry Murk, who initially contacted Soleau in 1993 with a request to publish their puzzle-platformer *Block-Man*.

'At the time I was thinking, oh, maybe Soleau Software will be a conglomeration of logic programmers,' Soleau recalls, 'and we'll bundle under Soleau Software, but I'll have many programmers. I won't have to write all the games myself.' But it soon petered out and Soleau Software continued to be a one-man development house (with Kevin Santee and Santee's wife, former dancer Katie Langan, still helping on the business and marketing side).

Soleau found the same joy in game development as in choreography. They were one and the same to him – just problems to be solved, concepts to be explored, challenges to overcome.

> I churned out game after game after game. And for me as a choreographer, honestly, I have 100 ballets in companies around the world, and I'm not interested once the ballet is finished. It's over. I want to get a new set of paints and paint on a new canvas and start something new. And that's sort of the way I was with game programming. I mean, once I did *Isle Wars*, for example, which is like *Risk*, but added different, other elements, I was like, 'OK, it's over. Let's do another' – just something else that challenges me, programming wise and intellectually, that would be a fun game to interact with.

He knew that he'd have better results if he cleaned up and polished his games, with professional art and sound, but he just couldn't do it. He was unceasingly driven to move on to the next project. The next coding problem to solve. The next thing to create.

But as the 90s faded, after a decade of running the company together, Soleau and Santee found themselves getting restless. They'd just won an Association of Shareware Professionals award for best non-violent game, and business was still strong, but they could see the business changing. 'We weren't writing the type of games that were starting to come out [on top] at the turn of the century,' Soleau says. 'And these big games – you know, we couldn't compete there.'

In any case, Soleau felt an itch to get back into choreography and Santee needed to increase his income to support a growing family – so he wanted to go back to school to get a CPA (an accounting qualification). They decided to start winding things down, and then in 2003 Soleau Software went onto life support. (Then in November 2020, tired of running tech support on these games he'd made decades ago for long-obsolete hardware and operating systems, Soleau shut the company down entirely.)

Good solitaire

Several niche-focused developers had in the meantime built on the successes of Soleau, Carr, MVP Software, Everett Kaser Software, Nels Anderson, and others in establishing a market for casual-oriented shareware games. New names emerged like LavaMind, Cyna Games, Goodsol, SolSuite, Synthetic Reality, SoftSpot Software, and Silver Creek Entertainment, all renowned for their thoughtful puzzle games and/or card games. And with them came hit new shareware games, bringing in hundreds of thousands of downloads and tens of thousands of dollars (or more) in registrations – games like *Hardwood Solitaire, Pretty Good Solitaire, Kyodai Mahjongg,* and *Gazillionaire,* a kind of intergalactic twist on *Monopoly* that went from shareware in 1994 to commercial in 1996 and back to shareware again after a 1997 *Deluxe* update.

Likely the most successful of this new breed of casual-market shareware games companies was Tom Warfield's Goodsol.

Warfield had known about shareware since the model first emerged in the early 1980s, back when he was in college. He'd watched it grow with interest, but it wasn't until 1994 that he decided to try making a shareware program himself.

He was teaching mathematics at a community college at the time and had just started learning Microsoft Visual Basic. He'd already played around with it a bit but needed more experience

SHAREWARE HEROES

to become confident with the language, so he decided to make a
Windows 3.1 solitaire game and release it as shareware.

He wasn't sure if there'd be any money in doing it, but he
uploaded his game to CompuServe and AOL and asked people
to pay $5 if they liked it. 'A month later I got a cheque for $5,' he
recalls. Then two more cheques came in. This was good, but he
thought maybe he could do better – so he started again, this time
with a set of four solitaire games: *Baker's Dozen, Golf, Fourteen Out*,
and *Yukon*, each with unlimited undos and redos – because he'd
been annoyed at the lack of an undo option in other solitaire
programs he'd tried.

'I put it out to a few friends,' Warfield says. One of them
worked at Microsoft. 'He said, "Well, you know, this is pretty
good." And that became the name.' *Tom's Pretty Good Solitaire.* But
before he published it online, his friend suggested he should
add a game called FreeCell – because they were about to release
Windows 95 with a version of that built in.

With the fifth game added in, Warfield published *Tom's Pretty
Good Solitaire* on 19 July 1995. Almost immediately the cheques
came trickling in from CompuServe and AOL forum-goers, and
soon from BBS users too – thanks to a $50 service called Author
Direct that he paid to upload his game to all the major BBSs.

The money wasn't much at first, but each time he released a
new update – adding new features and more kinds of solitaire –
it seemed to grow his audience, so he made a habit of regularly
improving his game. 'I basically spent the summer of '95 just
writing solitaire games,' he recalls. 'And by the end of the summer
I had like 30 [included in the program].' By contrast, most people
making shareware solitaire games had just one – a Klondike game
or a FreeCell game or some other popular game on its own. Even
commercial solitaire packages rarely had more than a few.

The sheer volume of options made Warfield's shareware
solitaire package stand out from the considerable pack of

competitors. And his timing was perfect. Windows 3.1 and Windows 95 were inspiring millions of people to buy their first personal computer and at the same time the Internet had just entered a period of explosive growth – reaching an estimated 16 million global users in December 1995 before leaping to 36 million by December 1996. And when they went online looking for a fun, familiar-looking game to play, they invariably saw *Tom's Pretty Good Solitaire* and decided to give it a whirl.

With his 30-game version 2.0 release, Warfield dropped his name from the title – now simply *Pretty Good Solitaire* – and upped the price to $12. Then version 2.1, released seven months later (in June 1996), doubled the solitaire-game tally again, and version 2.2 from February 1997 rounded it up to an even hundred. And he didn't stop there.

By mid-1998, he'd hit 200, then 300 less than a year later, and on and on, new solitaire games and game variants plucked from books of solitaire as well as fan suggestions and requests – and even the occasional original addition, designed by Warfield himself in response to fan feedback about this or that form of solitaire being either too easy or too hard.

Along the way he inadvertently found himself at the head of a shareware solitaire empire. In 1996 he expanded his games catalogue with 11 variants of Forty Thieves that he packaged into a program called *Napoleon Solitaire*, which came also with a 'Game Wizard' that let players create their own variants. Then that same year he noticed a lot of people were asking him for a standalone Windows 3.1 FreeCell game so that they could enjoy it in the same way as their Windows 95 counterparts could with *Microsoft FreeCell*.

They could buy *Pretty Good Solitaire*, sure, but that would get them a whole lot of solitaire games they didn't care about. Similarly, the *Microsoft Windows Entertainment Pack* retail product included a Windows 3.1 version of FreeCell, but it was hard to find and had other games they didn't want. Warfield realised he had an opportunity to corner the market for such a game, and it'd only take him a day to rip it out of *Pretty Good Solitaire* and craft a new interface.

Thus emerged *FreeCell Plus*, released on 25 January 1996, with a requested $10 registration ($2 cheaper than *Pretty Good Solitaire*, which soon got a price hike to $19) from anyone who used it beyond the 30-day evaluation period. 'It wasn't a huge seller by any means,' Warfield recalls, 'but it did a little bit and it just kept selling and selling. Even past 2000.'

It had taken him a day to build and cost $50 to market (via Author Direct), but over the following nine years – during which time he only made minor updates and additions to the game – it would receive thousands of registrations.

Meanwhile, Warfield finally made a Windows 95 version of *Pretty Good Solitaire* in 1997, kicking it off in July with 160 different kinds of solitaire and a new shareware nag screen that changed over time. During the first 30 days it'd show variants of the usual 'this is an unregistered shareware version for evaluation purposes only' and 'if you enjoy this game please register via [any of the listed sales channels]' that had by the mid-90s become a standard across much of the shareware industry.

'Then I think it was like day 34 or 37,' Warfield says, 'I decided to put in a nag about "Please feed my cats."' It'd show a picture of one of his two cats, Lady Jane, whom he and his wife had adopted in 1996, and a note that buying the game would get them more of the tuna treats they loved.

> I mean, it was crazy how much that worked – because you would get comments. Even on the mail orders you would see it on the comment line on the mail-order forms, and in the emails you would get it. It was an amazingly effective way to get people who I guess were on the fence. Because they'd already been using it for over 30 days. They were past their

30-day free trial period – because I let it go beyond that back then. And they would order because of seeing the little cat. (laughs)

So I don't know how much money that picture of the cat made me, but it's a lot. I mean it really helped a lot. It probably made hundreds of thousands [of dollars]. It's just crazy.

The nature of the business had changed considerably by this point. In the early years, people learned about shareware primarily through word of mouth – from friends, family, colleagues, and magazine and newspaper articles. But the rise of the World Wide Web brought with it a shift to online shareware repositories and reviews sites.

Two cows

People would now find shareware by looking for it – rarely for that specific program, but rather for something in a given category. Like a puzzle game or action game or card game. They'd go to web portals and search engines like Yahoo (which initially was just a big hierarchical directory linking to a variety of web pages about different things), Lycos, Excite, AltaVista, or GoTo.com (which allowed webmasters to pay as little as one cent per click for a top search result, thereby generating huge traffic to a website at low cost). If someone was steeped in gaming culture, they'd load up a specialist games site like Happy Puppy or Games Domain to read reviews and check the charts before they grabbed the latest wares.

Or they'd go to a general software repository and look at what was trending. Notable examples included Jumbo, SoftSeek, Shareware.com, Shareware Junkies, TUCOWS, CNET's Download.

com (which had been created in consultation with shareware expert Michael 'Dr File Finder' Callahan), and ZDNet's Software Library (also known as HotFiles.com and based on Public Brand Software's catalogue), but there were many others.

The most visible ones were CNET's and ZDNet's repositories, as both had tech-focused media empires driving traffic their way. Download.com generally had the better traffic numbers of the two, but for Tom Warfield it was very much the other way around, with his biggest download numbers coming via ZDNet. (At least until CNET bought them out and redirected their site to Download.com.)

Another of Warfield's favourites was called WinSite, which he describes as more of an FTP download site than a website. 'It was really nice to upload your file there and point to there to download,' he says. 'Because you could have your file there and not have bandwidth charges.' This was not so much a cost issue for him as a logistical one, as most web hosts divided their servers into multiple virtual servers that had fixed bandwidth allowances to keep the pricing fair. Warfield remembers that he was kicked off a paid web hosting service for using too much bandwidth – when he was happy to pay more – and had to then spread his small, roughly 1MB, game download across as many web hosts as possible. (In 2001 he'd give in and set up his own server to host his website and game downloads.)

There were so many of these shareware websites – hundreds in all at their late-90s/early-2000s peak – that a cottage industry emerged where shareware authors could pay small businesses to submit the latest versions of their software. Warfield remembers that he hired a woman in Virginia to do this for him: 'She charged me a certain amount per program per month, and she'd go and she'd just submit those things to all those different sites.'

Arguably the biggest and most influential of them all was TUCOWS – though its origins were much humbler in intent than the other big download sites. Its earliest incarnation began in 1991 when founder Scott Swedorski, then a recent college graduate, took a job at a library consortium as a system administrator for an initiative called FALCON (Flint Area Library Cooperative Online Network). 'At the time people started hearing more and more about getting online,' he recalls, 'but there was no simple way to do it unless you wanted to use something like AOL or Prodigy.'

Swedorski wanted to help library patrons navigate what the online world had to offer, and so he came up with a simple one-page document. 'It highlighted some applications with instructions on how to install and use them,' he says.

But quickly the document expanded to two pages, then three, then four, and so on, and in his spare time Swedorski decided to teach himself HTML and turn it into a website. He called it The Ultimate Collection of Winsock Software – referencing its focus on Windows networking software. Fans called it UCOWS or TUCOWS for short (in September 1995 it would officially become TUCOWS after the purchase of a tucows.com domain name).

'In the beginning, it was sparse,' recalls Swedorski. 'The Web now has no end to the content, but back then you could visit all the websites out there in a few hours. But one by one, day by day, more apps became available.' And if it was at least a half-decent freeware or shareware program, TUCOWS would have it listed and rated, ready for any of its thousands (later millions) of visitors to download.

By 1994, when TUCOWS first went live on the World Wide Web, the collection had grown to over 500 applications listed, now spread across all categories of software. Swedorski personally tested each one and gave it a rating out of five, and he wouldn't list anything he'd rated at less than three. This was crucial for helping visitors make sense of the litany of choices available, but it upset more than a few developers who were furious at a lower-than-expected rating or a refusal to list their program. Swedorski was adamant, however, that there be human-curated quality control, and he often saw developers reap the rewards (with boosted downloads and, where applicable, shareware registrations) when they took his feedback on board and submitted improved versions of their work.

The site quickly grew to the point where Swedorski needed to mirror its contents on multiple servers – scattered around the globe – to balance server load, to maximise download speeds, and to help ISPs (Internet Service Providers) reduce their operational costs by shifting content onto local servers. 'There was no automation,' Swedorski notes, 'so each time I made a change, I kept a log on a sheet of paper, and when I was all done updating the primary site, I had to FTP all those files to each mirror site.'

In 1996 TUCOWS was acquired by one of its first mirror sites, the Toronto-based Internet Direct, and they gave Swedorski an operating budget with which he could hire a small staff to help with software ratings and site administration. Just in time, it seems, because TUCOWS had exploded in popularity amidst ongoing word-of-mouth and search-engine discovery as well as a rapidly growing shareware community and frequent mentions in newspaper and magazine articles about the burgeoning online space.

Within a year of its acquisition, TUCOWS had added sections for Mac and OS/2 software, expanded to over 180 mirror sites (or affiliates, as they were also called) scattered across six continents, received around fifty awards (including a place in *PC Magazine*'s Web 100 over three consecutive years), become a top-50 site on the Internet (in terms of traffic volume), and grown to over 300 million pageviews a month across all the mirror sites.

In 1997 the site also began to monetise, after years of being an entirely free, hobby-driven service. Advertisers had discovered the Internet, and they were willing to pay top dollar for the privilege to place banners that would be seen by the site's millions of daily visitors. And while Swedorski disliked ad revenue, he saw the need for it to pay their running costs, so he allowed one ad – and later two – per page.

It did nothing to harm TUCOWS' growth. By 1998, it was rated 16th most popular site on the Internet and had an average of 1.4 million hits a day. There were now nearly 600 mirror sites and 27 full-time employees, and people could buy either a 'Best of TUCOWS' CD-ROM that had over 350 applications – all rated four cows or better by a TUCOWS reviewer – or an 'every few months' Best of TUCOWS Subscription Plan with semi-regular CD-ROM collections of highly rated new and updated software.

But even with these curation efforts, and other efforts such as the TUCOWS Pick of the Week – plus similar initiatives at competitors like Download.com and ZDNet – the shareware scene was getting mighty crowded. Shareware could still be profitable, but – somewhat ironically, given the ease of mass distribution and online payment collection – turning a profit was getting trickier. Worse, shareware's reputation was once again getting shaky, as too many programs labelled shareware were turning out to be time-limited or functionally restricted demos (often derisively called 'crippleware').

But as segments of the shareware scene embraced unscrupulous, unethical business strategies in pursuit of a quick buck, others still clung to the principles of old. And some of them even thrived.

Audio is using WaveOut

V 1.3

Seumas McNally's

By **LONGBOW DIGITAL ARTS**

F1: Backgrounds (Textured Half-Bright Black)
F3: Players (1)
F4: Difficulty (Normal)
F5: In-Game Music (Disabled)
F6: Swap Audio (Normal)
F7: Display (Full Screen)
F9: Go to DX-Ball 2 Web Page

	Thru Brick		Extra Life		Kill Paddle		Expand Paddle
	Set-Off Exploding		Level Warp		Shrink Ball		Shrink Paddle
	FireBall		Zap Bricks		Fast Ball		Split Ball
	Shooting Paddle		Slow Ball		Super Shrink		Mega Ball
	Grab Paddle		Expand Exploding		Falling Bricks		Eight Ball

DX-Ball 2 Copyright 1998-1999 by Longbow Digital Arts.
Music Copyright 1998-1999 by Eric Gieseke (SideWind@txdirect.net)

CHAPTER 14

Fade Out

By the time the dust had settled on *Quake* and *Duke Nukem 3D*, the professional shareware games market was past its zenith. Little remained at the top end of the scene besides the two holdouts (Ambrosia and Freeverse) on the Mac side. But shareware at the level of the individual developer still very much had some life left in it. And before it faded from public view, shareware would find one last spate of success – a few final hits to see it off into its twilight years.

Perhaps the biggest hit of them all – and one of the most surprising success stories ever to come out of the shareware scene – was a simple little puzzle game called *Snood*.

Its creator Dave Dobson had followed shareware since he started college in 1987 and played a shareware DOS version of the famous 1960s PDP-1 mini-computer game *Spacewar* (one of the earliest computer games ever created). 'I really liked the [shareware] concept and the community,' Dobson says, 'especially when I shifted over to using a lot more Macs in grad school [1991–7], because it was becoming harder then to buy Mac software in stores.'

At first he'd get shareware from BBSs, then from early Mac-focused FTP sites, and from 1994 onwards – when the general availability of the World Wide Web made online publishing easier – he'd make his own shareware games too. He had a PC at home at the time, so his first title was a *Minesweeper* clone called *Bombs*

Away! – which he published (to scant sales) directly from his new homepage. Then the following year he and his wife bought a Mac and he began learning how to use shareware game-creation tool Sprite Animation Toolkit, which powered dozens of 90s Mac shareware games.

Come 1996, Dobson had it figured out well enough to publish something new. He released *Centaurian*, a multi-directional shooter inspired by 1981 Midway arcade release *Bosconian*, 1995 Mac shareware game *Glypha III*, and elements of several other space-themed computer and arcade games. It involved piloting a single spacecraft tasked with wiping out starbases, located sector by sector using a mini-map in the corner of the screen, while simultaneously dodging mines, destroying rival ships, and earning credits to outfit the craft with better weapons.

Players of the unregistered version got access to just eight of the game's sixty zones, and registration ($18) also granted the ability to save and load games and edit levels.

Mac game review sites loved it – 9.5 out of 10 from *Mac Gamer's Ledge*, four stars from *Mac Game Gate*, 4.5 stars from *The Mac Games Headquarters* – and Dobson thought he had a great success on his hands when he earned over a thousand dollars from sales in its first year (and around triple that amount overall).

But his next game would make it look like an abject failure in comparison. He wanted to make a game for his wife, who disliked the frenetic, fast-action games that he favoured. She enjoyed puzzle games like *Tetris*, and other games that relied more on thinking and strategy than quick reflexes. Dobson thought a homegrown version of *Puzzle Bobble* – released Stateside as *Bust-a-Move* – would do the trick. It was an arcade game from two years earlier that had been rapidly working its way – either officially or unofficially (or both) – onto everything and anything that could run it.

The player controlled a 'pointer' that shot coloured bubbles up the screen, the goal being to aim these shots such that bubbles of the same colour were touching. Once three or more bubbles of the same colour formed a chain, they'd pop, and any bubbles hanging off them would fall off the screen. Every so often a new row of bubbles would appear at the top of the screen, pushing everything down, and the player would lose if the lowest line of bubbles crossed a line near the bottom of the screen. And because it was an arcade game, the designers had made sure that most players would struggle to last more than a few minutes by adding an extra element of restrictiveness – a time limit on every shot, before the pointer fired automatically, to force snap decisions that would inevitably lead to the player either putting more money into the machine or leaving so that somebody else could play (and pay).

Rather than bubbles, Dobson's version, *Snood*, would feature a variety of smiley- and not-so-smiley-faced creatures that he called Snoods – differentiated not only by colour but also by shape and facial expression to maximise accessibility for people with vision impairments. And to make the game more fun for his wife, he cut the timer out of the game. *Snood* would let players take as long as they liked on *every* shot – calmly picking their spot or stepping away to think over a strategy while doing other things. (There was still a pervading sense of danger, though, courtesy of a 'Danger Meter' that dropped a new line of Snoods onto the top of the screen after a certain number of moves.)

This simple change would prove critical to the game's ultimate success. Reviewers – nearly all of whom gave high ratings – uniformly praised the accessibility of the game. Competitive-minded types could relish the online scoreboards, tournaments (for registered players only), and higher difficulty levels, while everyone else could hop in and out of the game as the mood took them (or as their daily lives allowed) – vibing with it as their go-to Zen game.

The initial Mac release on 17 June 1996 steadily gathered momentum as word passed around about this oddly illustrated, brilliantly designed *Puzzle Bobble* variant. By February 1997, when version 2.0 came out, *Snood* had over 900 registered users and – by Dobson's estimate – thousands of unregistered players worldwide.

Registration, done mostly via snail mail, cost $10 and allowed for custom difficulty settings, custom level sets, and tournaments for up to six players. It also removed the game's shareware nag messages – a recording of Dobson saying '*Please!*' at start-up, plus various silly poems that came up every so often after 100 unregistered games. In a curious, unintentional parallel to Tom Warfield's 'Please feed my cats' message on *Pretty Good Solitaire*, one poem read: 'Dave's kids need clothes, Dave's kids need food, Dave's kids need haircuts – Please register Snood!' Another went: 'The poems are bad, They keep getting worse, Register now, To stop all the verse.'

Around the same time, Dobson finished his Ph.D. and took a job as an assistant professor of geology at Guilford College in North Carolina. Then he bought a new PC and started creating DOS and Windows versions of the game – a slow process, as first he had to learn the basics of Microsoft's graphics and audio library DirectX, then convert all his graphics and sounds to a PC format, learn how to handle mouse and keyboard input in Windows, port over his main game code, get it working, add menus, and then finally go through the many cycles of testing and bug-fixing that every software release requires.

He finally got it stable enough to release officially in February 1999, whereupon *Snood* began its transformation from minor shareware success to viral Internet sensation. The signs were there early when newspaper columnists started to casually slip mention of the game into their articles. Australian humourist Danny Katz joked in the opening paragraphs of a November

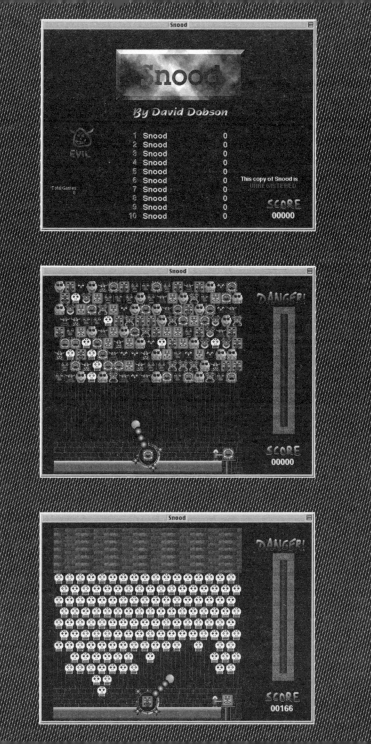

article that it was 'what I do for most of my day as a professional newspaper columnist', for instance, while in Pennsylvania, *Sentinel* columnist Kurt Wanfried playfully called himself a *Snood* addict and noted that his non-gamer wife and boss played the game too. Then word started to spread about famous people like *Jurassic Park* author Michael Crichton playing the game. (Crichton wrote in a letter accompanying his registration payment that playing *Snood* had delayed his next book.)

Every week *Snood* fervour grew stronger as it swept through colleges and workplaces around America and drew fans in from around the world. In late 1999 Dobson brought on a business partner, intellectual-property lawyer Jeff Grogin, who began to offer licensing and merchandising opportunities, and then in 2001 *Snood* suddenly exploded in popularity.

The trigger was a widely syndicated *Philadelphia Inquirer* feature in which one college student was quoted as saying, 'You can pretty much go into any dorm and people have it on their laptop.' The article referenced student newspapers that celebrated people reaching their thousandth or ten-thousandth game of *Snood*, and it noted the growing cultural reach of the game – which was already making its way into TV shows and commercials and getting referenced in parody songs.

By this point *Snood* had racked up 30,000 registrations (now priced at $14.95), with more than a million downloads from its official website alone. Its daily download tally outstripped what even the most popular game listed on CNET's Download.com would receive in a week. But it was about to get a whole lot bigger.

By the time another widely syndicated news article calling *Snood* 'a fad sweeping the country' emerged a year later, *Snood* downloads had surpassed 5 million and a market-research firm had estimated it was the ninth most-played game in America. *Snood* was helping people grieve for lost loved ones, process cancer diagnoses, slack off from work or study, learn to use a mouse, stick to a new diet, and keep their mind active post-retirement. It had become one of the defining games of its generation.

And things still hadn't slowed down much come 2004, by which point Dobson estimated there were 10–15 million copies 'floating around' alongside a commercial *Game Boy Advance* port and a variety of official merchandise products.

Growing pains

The Mac's leading shareware publishers had meanwhile been forced to diversify their businesses to retain their market standing. The end of the 1990s was a tough time in Mac software. The future looked bright for Apple, which had bought NeXT and in so doing welcomed back co-founder Steve Jobs after a decade out in the cold, and which had introduced innovative, popular new computers like the iMac and iBook. But their market share was at an all-time low, and their most loyal devotees were caught in the middle of a difficult transition to a completely new operating system – from the 'Classic Mac' era that ended with holdover update Mac OS 9 in 1999 to the new Mac OS X that entered public beta a year later.

Many of the smaller commercial and shareware publishers went out of business in the transition, but Ambrosia and Freeverse were big enough to ride it out and nimble enough to adapt. For Freeverse, the trick was introducing an online subscription service that let people play many of their games – such as *Classic Cribbage*, *Spades Deluxe*, and *Burning Monkey Puzzle Lab* – over the Internet, while also forging commercial partnerships. These deals would never earn them much money (to their chagrin), but they greatly aided their standing with Apple and the press.

'It was one of our pet peeves that no one took shareware seriously,' co-founder Colin Lynch Smith told me during a

Secret History of Mac Gaming interview, 'even though it was just a distribution method and didn't indicate anything about the nature of the game.'

But once they had boxes on the shelf, suddenly magazines were willing to cover their output and Apple Developer Relations were happy to take their calls – which meant more partnerships, more eyeballs on their games catalogue, and more games downloaded and bought from their website. And it helped, too, that they were able to publish quality games outside of their usual wheelhouse, like online RPG *Arcane Arena* and *Wingnuts: Temporal Navigator,* a silly shoot-'em-up where players fight a time-travelling pilot ace who enjoys tacos and soap operas.

Ambrosia Software was likewise delving into new genres, with fantasy RPGs *Cythera* and *Pillars of Garendall* and side-scrolling platformer *Ferazel's Wand* – a homage to the best of 16-bit console platformers by the creator of their surprise hit *Harry the Handsome Executive,* a comedy-laden action-adventure about a middle manager at 'ScumCo' fighting off poltergeists and sentient office equipment while scooting around on a swivel chair.

But they found consistent success with shareware games increasingly elusive after the turn of the century. An *Escape Velocity* sequel called *EV Nova* (built by a team of modders) met some acclaim and boasted a thriving fan community, but original games *Sketchfighter 4000 Alpha* (a hand-drawn shoot-'em-up), *Redline* (a racing game), *The Adventures of El Ballo* (a quirky platformer), and *GooBall* (an arcade-style puzzler) – among others – struggled to move the market, despite good-to-great reviews. And Mac ports of PC indie hits like *Darwinia* and *Aquaria* fared only a little better.

Ambrosia owner Andrew Welch was as staunchly committed to shareware as ever, but he gradually concluded that it wasn't worth staying in games. They'd always distinguished themselves by offering commercial-calibre games at shareware prices, but the development costs needed to remain competitive had become too high for him to stomach, so he changed Ambrosia's focus to utilities – which had always been a strong background source of revenue for the company – and small productivity apps. After a while they just stopped making games entirely.

They weren't the only ones feeling like the shareware games dream was slipping away.

Shareware had been keeping the Atari ST and Amiga gaming scenes alive for years at this point, with the odd commercial-calibre masterpiece like *Starball* (a 1994 Atari ST pinball game) making a big splash in a small puddle, plus programmers like Dave Munsie (creator of excellent arcade clones *Asteroidia* and *Frantick*) coding away at new titles out of joy more so than a desire to earn money. (Indeed, Munsie later told the Atari Legend website that he could count the number of shareware registrations he received 'on two hands and two feet'.)

But now those releases were becoming further and further apart as people increasingly fled the long-since-discontinued ST and Amiga systems for other computer platforms. There would later be a small-scale resurgence on both the ST and Amiga, as small groups of hobbyists returned to the system they loved to make and play games for fun, but shareware (and licenceware) was as good as over.

Going for broke

The PC had the opposite problem, albeit leading to much the same results. The audience was huge, but so was the volume of shareware content. Finding a way through the noise had become harder than ever before, even with high-end graphics – as Paul Lauzon painfully learned firsthand.

He'd quit a job writing software and debugging custom hardware for the aviation industry, eager to pursue new challenges and make his dream computer game. He envisioned something like the *Star Wars X-Wing* and *TIE Fighter* games (1993 and '94, respectively), but with full control over the spaceship's movement so he could actually enjoy the detail in the graphics.

'I also wanted to go very fast toward planets and moons and be able to fly on their surface,' he adds. And he was determined that his game, *Star Quest 1 in the 27th century*, would pull it off.

'At first I was working alone,' he recalls. He shopped for books related to every aspect of game development and planned as much of the game as he could. But soon he realised he lacked the talent needed to do the graphics and audio, so he posted job ads to recruit help.

He hired mostly students (they were cheap) and converted his basement into a development studio, with tables, chairs, PCs, and a local network. At its peak, his team swelled to thirteen people, though most worked from home as he couldn't afford to buy more than four computers.

Lauzon made most of the key development decisions, though each team member was empowered to create their own mission scenarios, and all together they'd try things out and give feedback. They went hard on presentation, throwing in advanced real-time lighting and shading techniques plus planetary atmospheres, animated texture-mapping, and layered pseudo-3D sound. Yet despite their extensive ambitions, Lauzon's limited self-funded budget meant he had to do the bulk of the programming work himself – the core game logic, graphics engine, interfaces, much of the toolchain used to make the game's content, and even large chunks of the mission logic, all while managing the team and doing the non-development work.

Even with him taking on so much of the workload himself, somewhere along the way Lauzon ran out of money. Rather than lay off all his staff and give up, he offered them royalties based on profit – plus interest on unpaid wages – if they stayed on. But those royalties would never come. *Star Quest 1* never turned a profit.

After turning down offers from larger commercial publishers that offered just 10 per cent in royalties, Lauzon made licensing deals with a few small non-exclusive publishers. None of these delivered any of the contracted money other than an initial payment. He self-published a shareware version in late 1995.

Doing his best to market the game himself, Lauzon took out a small ad in the back pages of *PC Gamer* and contacted every games magazine he could find. UK-based *PC Answers* reviewed it soon after, rating it 79 out of 100 but bemoaning its lack of innovation. German magazine *PC Games* put the game on its coverdisc. Another German magazine, *PC Joker*, eventually ran a brief review in 1997 – rating it just 39 out of 100 – complaining of an uneven design and what by then were outdated graphics (such was the rapid rate of 3D graphics evolution in the late 90s).

Its turbulent development had taken a toll on the final game, with a solid first impression on players quickly giving way to an understanding that it was compromised in both vision and presentation. Worse, the fact that it was shareware exposed these weaknesses to players taking advantage of the try-before-you-buy system, even as the model allowed it to spread with a near-zero marketing budget. Lauzon had dreamed too large – pushed too far, too soon. And it almost ruined him.

The game's shareware sales numbered just 'a few thousand', while a planned sequel failed to get funding and a spin-off multiplayer game they made for commercial publisher Infogrames fell victim to bad luck – the Oceanline online gaming network it had been built for was shut down just after they'd finished development, forcing the publisher to release a stripped-down single-player-only version.

By the end things had gotten so bad that the bank threatened to sell Lauzon's house. He had no choice but to shut down the studio, his dream in tatters and his mental health at breaking point. 'It took me about 10 years to recuperate and pay back the bank and employees everything I owed them,' he recalls, 'plus some small interest I had promised.'

An epic leap

While Paul Lauzon overreached and overextended himself, and failed, Epic were thriving from Tim Sweeney and Mark Rein's more measured, incremental approach to meeting their ambitions. And by the mid-90s they were ready for another major advancement.

Back in 1994, fresh from his smash hit *Epic Pinball*, James Schmalz had started looking into 3D programming and built a texture-mapped demo that caught Tim Sweeney's eye. Sweeney had previously been reluctant to join Apogee in the race to outdo id Software, as it seemed too much of a stretch for his programming talents, but this demo changed his mind. Maybe he could do 3D after all. Schmalz and Sweeney then began pushing to create a game (*Unreal*) and an engine comparable to id's latest tech but with design tools that were easier to use.

To meet their vision, like Apogee before them, they had no choice but to pool their best talent and hire more full-time staff. Where before Epic's games had been created by small teams consisting of no more than a few core people and one or two others, now they had a growing team of twenty-plus people on one new title. The finances no longer made sense for shareware.

In April 1996 the *Washington Post* reported that Epic's revenues were split 70–30 between direct sales (i.e. shareware) and retail partnerships, but that was all about to change. Between the shift to

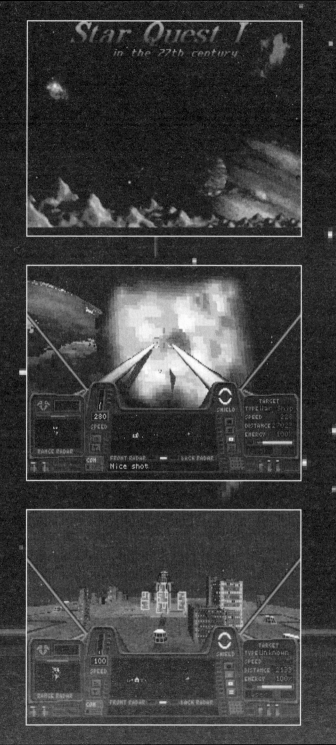

3D and the adoption of shareware by major publishers, Epic had to turn to outside funding sources and big-bet retail distribution deals to remain competitive. That year they made their debut at the leading industry trade show Electronic Entertainment Expo (E3) – five years after publishing their first game.

They kept releasing shareware builds of most of their games for another few years (some, such as sci-fi real-time-strategy title *7th Legion*, released as shareware *after* they were available at retail), but the company that once called itself Epic *Mega*Games (now just Epic Games) to conceal its amateur roots was finally going to take its leap into the big time. And they'd never look back.

Adapting to the web

With Apogee making near-identical moves out of shareware post-*Duke 3D*, id Software gone from the scene post-*Quake*, and long-time shareware publishers MVP and Soleau winding down their operations (because of declining revenues and an itch to return to ballet choreography, respectively), PC games shareware suddenly looked very different. The highly polished commercial-calibre fare was all but gone, and shareware seemed to once again be the realm of the amateurs and hobbyists.

But there were still plenty of good games coming through, and there were still a few game developers who could earn a living making shareware.

The most successful may well have been *Pretty Good Solitaire* author Tom Warfield, who had built tremendous momentum off the back of his unexpected successes in the mid-90s. But rather than diversifying or making lots of new games that were like his old games, like others who had found themselves with a strong audience in shareware, he'd decided to treat his hit game as *the* product.

In much the same way that Microsoft would regularly update Windows and Word and its other core apps, charging money every time there was a major upgrade, *Pretty Good Solitaire* would regularly add new features and solitaire games and other improvements. In that way, *Pretty Good Solitaire* begat *Pretty Good Solitaire 97* and *Win 3.1*, then *Pretty Good Solitaire 98*, then *99*, then *2k*, then *Quest Edition*, then *500* (to celebrate reaching 500 built-in games), and so on – with most major version upgrades given a unique name to make them easier to distinguish as improved versions.

Warfield's attitude was that 'the first version is just the first version'. And so he rarely bothered releasing new products. 'Because it's hard enough to get a success,' he explains, 'so to try and come up with another success and another success over and over again – it seems like a lot of work. Whereas if you've got one success, you can work on it and try to make it better and make it a bigger success.'

Even his rare releases of things that weren't *Pretty Good Solitaire* updates fed into this narrowly focused effort to keep one core product fresh. In 1998 he was contacted by another developer, Michael McCulloch, who'd created a game called *Free Solitaire*. It was a 'completely free' collection of ten popular solitaire games with built-in advertisements, and McCulloch was hoping that Warfield – the king of Windows solitaire games – could help him get more exposure for it.

Warfield agreed to list *Free Solitaire* on his website (which brought huge traffic in from websites dedicated to telling people about great free software), and to split the proceeds from that and a paid upgrade called *Solitaire Plus* with McCulloch. And he positioned them as essentially being lower-tier versions of his core product – lite (*Free Solitaire*), standard (*Solitaire Plus*), and pro (*Pretty Good Solitaire*), to use the terminology of today.

This late-90s/early-2000s era was the most successful in Goodsol's history. Warfield had strong momentum from *Pretty*

Good Solitaire, which was winning awards and topping shareware charts, plus big web traffic from *Free Solitaire*, which was driving sales of his premium products, and he was getting retail sales through a deal with eGames to publish reskinned commercial versions in big-box retailers under the *Solitaire Master* moniker.

And on top of all of that, this was also the peak era for shareware distribution and reviews sites – which were just then beginning a phase of mass consolidation and closures (driven mainly by ZDNet and CNET buying out most of their competition in 1999 and 2000, before CNET acquired ZDNet in late 2000).

Warfield was one of a few professional shareware game authors who peaked around this time. Another of the big success stories was with Steve Pavlina's Dexterity Software.

Pavlina had started Dexterity Software in 1994 and published a few games under the label, including a collection of 'coffee-break games' designed by his partner of the time, Erin, but he'd not found much success. Then one day in 1999 he decided he'd been playing it too safe, so he studied the market and looked for areas where he could stand out. Most shareware games were clones of older games, he realised, or they were violent action games. To stand out, he needed to be original, non-violent, and creative.

He spent the next four months writing and rewriting a five-page design document for a logic-puzzle game called *Dweep*, iterating until he felt he had it right. It would be about a little purple furry creature that needs to rescue its children and manoeuvre its way out of a variety of scary, dangerous situations – dodging deadly obstacles like laser beams and bombs not with quick reflexes but rather through clever strategy and creative problem solving.

After he finished his design document, it took Pavlina just two months to build the game. He released it on 1 June 1999 to critical acclaim. TUCOWS, ZDNet, and Shareware Junkies all gave it five stars, while Download.com marked the game as an Editors' Pick. As his audience grew, he began receiving requests for more content and complaints that the creature Dweep moved too slowly – so he added speed control and released a paid expansion pack, then another expansion pack soon after.

As more feedback came in, he kept refining and updating the game. But he also relentlessly tweaked his business. He tried marketing cross-promotions with other games, ran ads, redesigned and rearranged his website, overhauled his ordering process, changed the price, changed the content included in the free version, and set up an official forum for players to discuss the game and post custom levels.

The initial release had been popular, and it was good enough to win a Shareware Industry Award, but it was this constant refinement that made Pavlina's business a successful one.

Before *Dweep*, he'd been earning about $300 a month combined from all of Dexterity's prior shareware titles. 'Six months after its release,' he wrote in a gamedev.net forum post, '[*Dweep*] was making about $3000 per month, which is what I needed to cover all my living expenses and business expenses.' With a price rise from $9.95 to $24.95 for a *Dweep Gold* release, plus three more awards, he added, 'Sales kept going up from there.'

Unlike Warfield, however, Pavlina wouldn't stick around long term. In 2001 he branched out to publishing other people's games as well as his own, and began to build a strong brand in the games industry with his game-development business advice articles, but then in 2004 he had a change of heart and retired from the business to pursue motivational speaking and personal development blogging instead.

In the meantime there were plenty of others trying to capitalise on the growing ubiquity of the Internet and

Internet-based commerce through shareware. The late 1990s and early 2000s were a veritable cornucopia of independent creators trying their luck with web-based distribution.

As with the early 90s shareware boom, most failed completely – releasing just one or two titles that took on none of the wisdom that people like Steve Pavlina tried to impart to the industry. But some made a small splash, like graphical roguelike *UnReal World* – which had been slowly building an audience since 1992 but made big strides forward in the late 90s when it pivoted from a traditional dungeon-focused, fantasy-themed roguelike design to incorporate wilderness survival elements (including crafting and climate modelling) and real Iron Age Nordic history.

Likewise, Dutch one-man studio Wiering Software hit its peak at this time after years of quiet preparation. Creator Mike Wiering had entered the scene accidentally in 1994 with a four-level *Mario* clone he made to practise VGA programming and test his in-development engine. He'd not intended to distribute the game, but it nevertheless wound up in public – hacked and redistributed by another programmer as $15 shareware under the title *Mario!!!*, then shared all over the world. (Golfer Tiger Woods was even recorded playing the game during a TV interview.) When Wiering found out, years later in 2001, he released his original version as a free download with source code.

In the meantime, he created an original *Mario*-like platformer called *Charlie the Duck* (*Charlie de Eend* in his native Netherlands) and a free *Mario Kart*-style racing game called *Super Worms.* Then in 1997 he released the more obviously *Mario*-derived *Super Angelo,* complete with a moustachioed main character, followed by another platformer called *Sint Nicolaas* in 1998. This latter game drew inspiration from the local traditions that had morphed into the American vision of Santa Claus, with players running and leaping across rooftops to collect and

SINT NICOLAAS

STORY

Sint Nicolaas has been robbed! The thieves
have taken his big sack full of presents and
gingerbread cookies. In their run however,
they weren't careful and presents started
dropping out of the sack. Now Sint only has
to collect the fallen cookies and presents
and bring them to the right chimneys.

Ok

SINT × 2   TIME: 2:11   ● × 6   SCORE: 000002200

SINT × 0   TIME: 2:38   ● × 4   SCORE: 000007050

deliver all the presents and gingerbread cookies that had been dropped after thieves tried to abscond with Sint Nicolaas's sack.

In 2001 Wiering got serious. He started publishing under the name Wiering Software and released a sequel to his most popular game, *Charlie the Duck*, with hopes of earning enough from registrations that he could go full-time on developing his next game. This sequel, *Charlie II*, was a more polished game than its predecessor, and it earned plaudits to match – 8 out of 10 and a 'one of the best executed games of this type' comment from *GameTunnel*; four cows and a 'popular' designation from TUCOWS; and four stars from DOSGames.com, along with the winning trophy in the Best Action/Arcade Game category of the Shareware Industry Awards (where it beat Retro64's *Warheads SE* and id Software's *Quake III: Arena* demo version).

But while it sold reasonably well, it never blew up big, and – aside from a single *Charlie II Expansion Pack* in 2006 – Wiering Software spent the next several years simply re-releasing and updating all their existing games, instead of making another new game.

Wiering also published a free TileStudio development tool to help other authors make games more easily, but it too failed to catch on widely – only resulting in around a dozen published games (and no doubt many more prototypes and student games).

Making a mark

By contrast, part-time shareware author Balázs Rózsa had a much bigger impact.

Rózsa had been inspired to make a game of his own after he played *DOOM*. At first he didn't know what to make, but then one day in 1995 he suddenly had the idea to do a physics-based motorbike simulation. It wouldn't be a traditional racing game, however. Each course would instead be a puzzle to solve. Players would have to collect the tokens strewn about a level as quickly as possible before heading to the exit. To represent these graphically, he put in the first things that came to his mind – apples and flowers – thinking he'd change them to something else later (he never did).

Players used the cursor keys to carefully balance acceleration, braking, and shifting the rider's weight, navigating complex, jagged 2D environments in fits and starts so as not to send their rider toppling forwards or backwards to the ground. A tap of the spacebar would flip the bike in the opposite direction (so the powered rear wheel became the unpowered front wheel, and vice versa) to allow for more supernatural feats and a variety of physics exploits. But if the rider touched a 'killer object' or hit their head on any part of the environment, they'd die and the level would begin anew.

Rózsa and his brother built 24 levels for the game, each expanding on the skills and techniques required to complete the previous stages – such as pixel-perfect flips through the air or tipping the bike so that one wheel rolls over a ledge and the rider hangs upside down, suspended off one wheel, to grab a hard-to-reach apple or navigate a tight space. Rózsa called it *Action SuperCross*, and on 11 February 1997 he put the game out into the world – the first eight levels available free and the other sixteen requiring a $30 registration.

Immediately the game started to build an audience, thanks in large part to a Game of the Month feature in Finnish magazine *MikroBitti*, but it wouldn't take off until a year later when version 1.2 introduced a level editor and expanded the internal level count to 16 in the shareware edition and 42 overall.

Rózsa wasn't getting rich from it by any means, and he remained gainfully employed as a programmer outside of the games industry throughout this time, but his little game spread like wildfire across the nascent World Wide Web. Fans traded tips, tricks, and levels, and ranked their high scores by country. They arranged time trial tournaments, too, including a pair of *Action SuperCross* World Cups – where the best players in the world grouped into teams that competed for the fastest times on new, previously unseen levels. It even got to the desk of Rockstar Games boss Sam Houser, who remarked to *PC Gamer UK* that 'the feel of the bike is un-f***ing-believable.' Houser commissioned a Game Boy port, adapted to the licence for famous American motorcycle stunt performer Evel Knievel, that struggled to recapture the original's thrilling physics-based bike handling.

A Windows *Action SuperCross* sequel called *Elasto Mania* – or *Elma* for short – followed on 2 February 2000, with tweaked physics, improved graphics, split-screen local multiplayer, new levels, a price drop to \$9.95, and various other changes.

Again the game found a particularly strong audience in Finland, which was also the heartland of immensely popular real-time *Worms* variants *MoleZ* (originally released under a traditional donation-based shareware model in 1997, but made freeware in 1999 after the developer lost its source code) and *Liero* (a freeware clone of *MoleZ*).

But this time the game was more than merely popular. It was everywhere. Just as *Scorched Earth* had conquered high school and university computer labs around the world in the 1990s, *Elasto Mania* did the same in the 2000s. It even got a brief, upbeat mention in *Computer Gaming World* (which had continued to ignore shareware, but for the rare article or sidebar).

Fan tournaments continued unabated, as the best players raced to not only set new world records but also to invent new tricks and play styles in what quickly became northern Europe's favourite e-sport. But eventually the lack of updates from Rózsa – now working a more demanding day job – took their

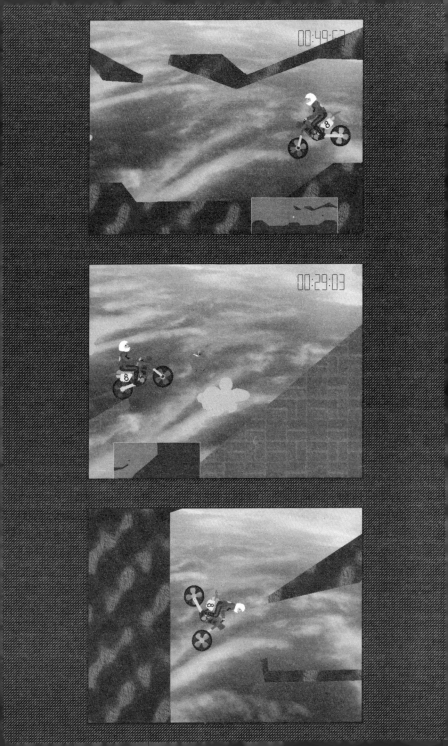

toll and the community contracted. (Though it never died out completely, and today is in the midst of a resurgence after Rózsa sold the rights to a group of fans that are moving forward with a remastered edition.)

Similarly popular – though not as long lasting – was Beermat Software's 1998 Windows remake of 1980s DOS game *Dope Wars*, which in turn had been one of many imitations of John E. Dell's 1984 business simulation *Drug Wars*. The game involved buying and selling different kinds of drugs while trying to stay alive and out of prison. There were no fancy graphics and no characters to manipulate – just a range of menus, buttons, and text displays. But millions of people rallied around the game, all drawn to the unusual premise and then hooked on the challenge of managing price fluctuations and police interference – plus the economics of trenchcoat storage space, random muggings, paying off debt, and buying guns for protection.

As *Dope Wars* for Windows took CNET's Download.com by storm, rushing to the top of the charts and to its first million downloads in less than a year, Beermat expanded the game with global leaderboards, loan sharks, more travel options, and hospital visits (later expanded to allow for the possibility of a 'nasty doctor' that steals stuff). By 2005 the game had more than 6.5 million downloads from Download.com alone – having been near the top of the most-popular charts for almost its entire life.

DX-Ball 2 (1998) by Longbow Digital Arts managed similar numbers over the same period, except its downloads mostly came directly from its own website. It sprang from the mind of teenager and Longbow founder Seumas McNally, who had helped out with the 3D graphics and level design of Michael P. Welch's original *DX-Ball* in 1996. Welch in turn was the creator of *Scorched Tanks*, an Amiga version of perennial DOS favourite *Scorched Earth*, and he had created *DX-Ball* in response to his wife's preference for shareware Amiga *Breakout* variant *MegaBall*

(1990–5) over *Scorched Tanks*. (And to complete the chain of influence, *MegaBall* was created by brothers Al and Ed Mackey because they weren't happy with any of the *Breakout*-style games they'd seen on the Amiga.)

The convoluted backstory to its creation belied the elegance of its design. *DX-Ball 2*, like its predecessors, took *Breakout* and edged it nearer to perfection. It had smooth and responsive controls with varied level designs that never let the game turn stale – exploding bricks, fireballs, invisible bricks, invincible bricks, 'throughballs' that would pass through bricks, ray-traced balls, textured bricks, plasma effects, lasers, and even a level editor for creating or installing custom levels (complete with alternative graphics).

It was all beautifully tuned to balance difficulty against accessibility, with the ball slowly accelerating over time to constantly turn the heat up on players. And those struggling with the requisite dexterity to handle fast and precise mouse movements could turn to the built-in 'kid mode' for a dialled-back experience that enlarged the ball and paddle, slowed the ball speed, and excluded a few of the nastier power-ups (like the ones that made the ball tiny). There was also hotseat multiplayer, where up to four players could compete for the highest score, plus leaderboards and cheat codes for the hardcore players to dig into.

ZDNet called it 'the quintessential Windows *Breakout* game', while Games Domain reviewer James Kay praised its propensity to make players lose track of time – noting that expectations of 'a quick five-minute game' could easily give way to an hour-long sojourn through twenty-five boards.

McNally opted for one of the most tried-and-true shareware models: a fully functioning free game consisting of twenty-four boards, divided into six sets of four (in three different graphical styles), with a *DX-Ball 2* Board Pack (which expanded the game to 150 boards, or six sets of twenty-five) available for $15 from BuyDirect.com or via mail order.

Sales were strong (McNally wrote in July 1999 that it had sold 'thousands') though not extraordinary, but the shareware version was widely acclaimed and a consistent audience favourite. Over the next several years *DX-Ball 2* would receive an estimated 5 million downloads, and its reputation as one of the best shareware games of its time earned McNally a place in the book *Game Design: Secrets of the Sages* – where he was blunt about the power of the Internet as a distribution vehicle for games: 'What it boils down to,' he told book author Marc Saltzman, 'is having a kickass product,' before noting that he'd seen many shareware games that should never have been released at all (even as freeware).

McNally had good reason to be forthright. He'd defied the fate set before him to make *DX-Ball 2* such a stellar *Breakout* variant. He was diagnosed with Hodgkin lymphoma in 1997, aged 18, with a bad prognosis. Starlight Foundation Canada had subsequently sponsored a trip to Texas to spend an afternoon and evening with his hero, master programmer and id Software co-founder John Carmack, in June 1998. Then, filled with inspiration and a sense of tenacity, desperate not to let his declining health deny him his dreams, he'd marched on with his new game projects.

DX-Ball 2 was one of these, developed with assistance from his immediate family – mum, Wendy, on the board designs, father, Jim, on audio, and brother Philippe on additional graphics. The other, bigger project was called *Tread Marks*. Here, again, the plan was to make the game with his family as his development team and publish as shareware, but this time McNally had a more ambitious vision.

Inspired by John Carmack's innovative 3D engine technology at id Software, he pushed to not only make a kickass off-road combat racing game but also to break new ground in game programming. In *Tread Marks*, tanks (initially gun-toting dune buggies, but tanks 'seemed a lot cooler') would leave permanent tread marks in the soil and their weapons would disfigure the terrain around them. Some weapons would blow holes and craters in the landscape, others would deposit mounds of dirt to create hills where none were before. Players could craft rivers and trenches, invent shortcuts, give their rivals new obstacles to avoid, and listen to the destruction and racing around them in 3D positional audio.

And in keeping with the trends of the day, there'd also be a fast-paced multiplayer deathmatch mode plus full, easy customisability and modding.

Deep into development, McNally entered the game in the second Independent Games Festival awards. The judges shortlisted it for multiple award categories (including the grand prize). But McNally focused not on the immense achievement, or its dizzying promise of likely future success, but on the reality of his situation. John Carmack later wrote that McNally had admitted in an email soon after that he hoped he could 'make it' to completion.

'Not "be a huge success" or "beat the competition",' Carmack remembered. 'Just "make it".'

Make it he did. Just. The *Tread Marks* shareware version launched on 3 January 2000, with three maps, three tanks, all the weapons, and all the single-player modes (but limited multiplayer). The full version followed 11 days later, deemed so big it needed to be shipped on a CD via Digital River.

In March McNally travelled to California with his family to attend the Game Developers Conference, of which the Independent Games Festival is one part. At the IGF awards ceremony on 10 March, confined to a wheelchair and assisted by an oxygen tank, he accepted three awards for *Tread Marks*: technical excellence, game design, and the grand prize.

MPH

CONCUSSION

100

0

RELOADING

RELOADING

Now playing music file "sound/music/camptown.mp3"

His health visibly declining, McNally remained hopeful and defiant. 'Sometimes it gets in the way a bit; sometimes it sort of helps spur me on,' he told CBC Radio in an interview shortly after receiving the award.

He died on 21 March. A month later, the Independent Games Festival renamed its grand prize in his honour ('The Seumas McNally Grand Prize'), while his family vowed to carry his legacy on and continue operating his company Longbow Digital Arts – though they would soon shift away from shareware to pure online retail.

Tread Marks also marked something of a last hurrah for high-achieving shareware games. It was the first and last winner of the main IGF prize to self-identify as shareware, and the last shareware game to be widely covered in the games media.

This wasn't because shareware was dead – quite the opposite. Shareware never died. Rather it faded out of collective consciousness. It went out of vogue. It became irrelevant, and as such its flawed use as shorthand for independent software would soon give way to the more descriptive term 'indie'. Shareware had defined itself as being a point of difference – a radical new way to sell software without the costly chains of boxed retail distribution; a faster, more direct, and more honest way to reach a customer. But now the term was no longer needed because shareware – in its various guises – had become normalised.

Now everyone had demos, and demos served the same purpose as shareware – to allow people to make an informed choice about what they bought, separating hype from reality. The only difference was they gave away less of the product for free.

For years, shareware's biggest proponents had been mocked for their unflinching mantra that 'one day all software will be sold this way'. But even they could never have imagined just how right they were.

[CTRL]+
[ALT]+
[HOME]

Coda – Free to Play

It was always the essence of shareware – free to try, free to share, free to enjoy, but not *truly* free. Shareware was free as in freedom, a democratised model of software distribution wherein there was an expectation that some of the time, from some of the users/players, money would change hands. You could pay for something more – such as customer support, additional features, free updates, more levels and episodes, a map editor, a printed manual, and so on. Or you could settle for what you had and just enjoy *that* as best you could.

At the height of the mobile gaming gold rush, critics coined a new term for it: freemium, an oxymoronic portmanteau of free and premium.

This is the way of the world now. And really it's just a new form of shareware.

There are, in a sense, four ages of shareware. They overlap each other, but are still more or less distinct. The first age was those early years of 'user-supported software', where you had a lightly incentivised mass patronage system that in retrospect was a forerunner to present-day platforms like Patreon. The second age saw the rise of the Apogee model, where the bulk of the story in this book resides. The third was the age of the demo, a bastardisation of the Apogee model driven partly by the greed of commercial publishers – who muscled their way in on an independent software scene – and partly by the difficulty of applying the Apogee model across all software forms.

This third age accepted that some games (and most non-game software) just didn't lend themselves well to an episodic model. They needed a different incentive, and past experience had shown it needed to be aggressively applied in order to have a decent installs-to-payments ratio. Hence the rise of the strictly enforced 30-day free trial and the 'crippleware' (or one-level) demo in the late 1990s – both concepts that had been around much earlier but which now became normalised industry practice with the advent of instant digital order fulfilment and easy to implement but hard to work around trial-period enforcement.

We're now in the fourth age of shareware. The age of free with an asterisk. Free except you have the option of purchasing paid unlocks for extra levels or characters or hats, or of upgrading to a 'pro' version. Free with premium downloadable content that you buy separately and install via your game console's storefront or a launcher program like Steam. Free with built-in advertising, where your time and attention is monetised to show annoying ads for things you probably don't care about (but which you may now be incentivised to watch because they grant you more free in-game stuff). Free with microtransactions, a nifty way to shake more money out of people by charging real money for cosmetic customisations, finite virtual goods, or pseudo-random 'loot'.

And in the most cynical form, free to play, pay to win – where the microtransactions are not just for cosmetic items or extra content but rather for more 'energy' or time tokens with which to engage in more in-game activities or, in a multiplayer game, some form of unfair advantage. It might be a special 'premium' form of ammunition that does extra damage, or it could be a perk that lets you run faster or jump farther or soak up more damage than a player that hasn't spent that money – anything that makes non-paying customers second-class citizens of the game's world.

Taken across all its forms, free to play – and this new model *freemium* – is the norm now. The traditional pay-upfront models are the exception rather than the rule. Games that cost money are 'premium products', where before they were simply products.

The biggest games in the world are nearly all free-to-play with microtransactions – *Fortnite* (Epic's latest hit), *Genshin Impact*, *ROBLOX*, *FIFA Ultimate Team*, *Grand Theft Auto V*, *Free Fire*, *Honor of Kings*, *League of Legends*, *PUBG Mobile*, *Call of Duty Mobile*, *Candy Crush Saga*, and so on. Premium games haven't gone anywhere, but in both money and popularity they're second best.

In 2020, only two non-free games – *Animal Crossing: New Horizons* and *Call of Duty: Modern Warfare*, a premium game with added microtransactions – were ranked in SuperData Research's yearly top ten highest-grossing games list. If trends continue, at some point in the next few years free games will hold every spot on the list.

And the numbers involved here are astronomically big. Some two dozen free-to-play mobile games released in the past decade have generated over a billion dollars in lifetime revenue. Multiple free-to-play PC and console games have achieved the same feat.

Shareware's founding fathers had made clear that they saw the model as an experiment in economics – to see if giving software away and merely *asking* for payment could be a profitable enterprise. Forty years later, there's no doubt whatsoever: 'free' can be very profitable indeed.

Developer Spotlights

Ambrosia Software

TAGLINE: None
FOUNDED: 1993
YEARS ACTIVE IN SHAREWARE: 1992–2018
KEY PEOPLE: Andrew Welch (founder), David 'Cajun' Richard (technical service manager), Matt Burch (game developer), Ben Spees (game developer)
KEY GAMES: *Maelstrom* (1992), *Escape Velocity* (1996)

Ambrosia was to the Mac shareware scene what Apogee was to the PC: the cutting-edge publisher of cool games that made professional shareware development seem attainable. Their *Maelstrom* and *Escape Velocity* games in particular stood out among the best shareware on any platform.

FUN FACT: For almost the entire company's life, they shared an office with a smack-talking parrot called Hector (who doubled as enforcer of the 30-day trial limits).

Apogee Software

TAGLINES: 'The Height of Gaming Excitement' / 'Apogee Means Action!'
FOUNDED: 1987
YEARS ACTIVE IN SHAREWARE: 1987–96 (also sold shareware as 3D Realms, 1995–7)
KEY PEOPLE: Scott Miller (founder), George Broussard (co-owner)
KEY GAMES: *Kingdom of Kroz* (1987), *Commander Keen* (1990), *Duke Nukem* (1991), *Wolfenstein 3D* (1992), *Duke Nukem 3D* (1996)

The first major shareware games company, and one of the world's earliest indie game publishers. Apogee invented the episodic shareware model that transformed the games industry, created multiple major game franchises, helped id Software get started and published several of the highest-grossing shareware games.

FUN FACT: Apogee had planned to offer free games for the lifetime of the company to the first person to find a hidden message 'Call Apogee and say "Aardwolf"' in *Wolfenstein 3D*, but cancelled the promotion when fans created game editing tools.

Epic MegaGames

TAGLINE: 'The New Name in Computer Entertainment'
FOUNDED: 1991
YEARS ACTIVE IN SHAREWARE: 1991–7
KEY PEOPLE: Tim Sweeney (founder), Mark Rein (business VP), Cliff Bleszinski (game designer), Jamie Schmalz (game developer)

KEY GAMES: *ZZT* (1991), *Epic Pinball* (1993), *Jazz Jackrabbit* (1994), *Unreal* (1998)

They've long since ditched the 'Mega' from the name and become a true giant of the industry with their *Fortnite* game and Unreal Engine technology, but Epic was always shifting the conversation right from the start – ever innovating and pushing to build upon the examples set by trailblazers like Apogee.

FUN FACT: Epic's original name was Potomac Computer Systems, after a computer consultancy that never got off the ground, but Tim Sweeney wanted his then-tiny operation to sound more like an important games publisher.

Freeverse

TAGLINE: None
FOUNDED: 1994
YEARS ACTIVE IN SHAREWARE: 1994–2013
KEY PEOPLE: Ian and Colin Lynch Smith (co-founders), Steve Tze (art director)
KEY GAMES: *Hearts Deluxe* (1993), *Burning Monkey Solitaire* (1999)

The Mac shareware world's all-star jokesters, beloved for their silly software toys, witty press releases, stylish graphics, and family-friendly game design with loads of monkey humour.

FUN FACT: Their most famous work, the singing smiley face *Jared: The Butcher of Song*, was based on an actual recording of Ian and Colin's other brother Jared showing off a new song he'd learned while overseas.

Goodsol Development

TAGLINES: 'The world's most popular shareware solitaire games' / 'Solitaire the way it was meant to be.'
FOUNDED: 1994
YEARS ACTIVE IN SHAREWARE: 1994 to present
KEY PEOPLE: Tom Warfield (founder)
KEY GAMES: *Pretty Good Solitaire* (1995)

Goodsol weren't the first company to embrace the concept of games as a service, but they were one of the first to get rich from it. Their model was brilliant in its simplicity: regular paid and unpaid updates to a small and focused catalogue of solitaire games – still going strong more than 25 years later.

FUN FACT: Goodsol's most successful marketing technique turned out to be including a picture of one of Warfield's cats in one of the dozens of *Pretty Good Solitaire*'s registration nag messages.

Gray Design Associates

TAGLINE: 'Entertainment & Educational programs for your PC!'
FOUNDED: 1990
YEARS ACTIVE IN SHAREWARE: 1990 to present
KEY PEOPLE: David P. Gray (founder)
KEY GAMES: *Hugo's House of Horrors* (1990)

David Gray was the man who proved that adventure games could work (financially speaking) as shareware. His bestselling *Hugo* trilogy stood out from the pack of also-ran platformers before he tinkered with the emerging first-person shooter genre with *Nitemare-3D* and ultimately settled in for the long-lived casual title *Jigsaws Galore*.

FUN FACT: While the *Hugo* games are often compared to the LucasArts SCUMM adventures, Gray had not played them beforehand. His chief gaming influences were *Leisure Suit Larry*, *Captain Comic*, and *Colossal Cave Adventure*.

id Software

TAGLINE: 'We're In Demand!' (only used in *Keen 1*)
FOUNDED: 1990
YEARS ACTIVE IN SHAREWARE: 1990–6
KEY PEOPLE: John Romero, John Carmack, Tom Hall, Adrian Carmack (co-founders)
KEY GAMES: *Commander Keen* (1990), *Wolfenstein 3D* (1992), *DOOM* (1993), *Quake* (1996)

Founded by a breakaway group of Softdisk employees after an offer from Apogee to publish a *Super Mario*-style game as shareware, id quickly came into their own. *Wolfenstein 3D* proved shareware's strength, then *DOOM* made them superstars.

FUN FACT: Their first-person-perspective 3D games transformed the industry, but id only adopted this viewpoint because drawing a person on the screen for a traditional third-person perspective would have wasted critical CPU cycles needed to make the games run fast.

MoraffWare

TAGLINE: None
FOUNDED: 1988
YEARS ACTIVE IN SHAREWARE: 1988–2018
KEY PEOPLE: Steve Moraff (founder)
KEY GAMES: *Moraff's Revenge* (1988)

No shareware developer's output was more instantly recognisable than MoraffWare, a mostly one-man operation renowned for its quirky style. Today's indie auteurs have much to thank the likes of Steve Moraff for, for carving out a niche in which weird games could thrive.

FUN FACT: When his shareware business slowed down after around 20 years in operation, Steve Moraff made software to help people learn Chinese.

MVP Software

TAGLINE: 'The Winner's Choice'
FOUNDED: 1985
YEARS ACTIVE IN SHAREWARE: 1989–2013
KEY PEOPLE: Dave Snyder (founder)
KEY GAMES: *RoboMaze II* and *III* (1991), *Corncob 3D* (1992), *MVP Bridge* (1994), *Rings of the Magi* (1994)

MVP were effectively the Apogee of the casual games space, a shareware publisher that worked with external developers on high-quality fare for non-enthusiast gamers. And they made a decent business out of it for most of the 1990s shareware heyday.

FUN FACT: Founder Dave Snyder, a former philosophy professor, tried several new professions before he landed on shareware publishing – including encyclopaedia salesman and running a newsletter called Christian Educational Computing.

Soleau Software

TAGLINE: 'Non-Violent Strategy Logic Games For The Entire Family'
FOUNDED: 1991, following five years of hobby development
YEARS ACTIVE IN SHAREWARE: 1991–2020
KEY PEOPLE: William Soleau (founder), Kevin Santee (general manager)
KEY GAMES: *Isle Wars* (1994), *Oilcap* (1996)

A decade-long game publishing odyssey from ballet dancer and choreographer William Soleau, who designed his games around the same feeling he loved about both programming and choreography: as a problem-solving challenge, subtly varied, where no two products are exactly alike.

FUN FACT: Soleau choreographed his first ballet, a pas de deux, in 1984, just one year before he made his first game.

Glossary

APOGEE MODEL – A popular and successful model of shareware game distribution in which the first episode/volume/level set is free and the rest are available via direct order.

ASSOCIATION OF SHAREWARE PROFESSIONALS (ASP) – A trade organisation that represented the interests both of shareware authors and customers, acting simultaneously as industry advocate, watchdog, and gatekeeper.

BULLETIN BOARD SYSTEM (BBS) – An online text-based service, typically run out of a person's home, that can be accessed directly via dial-up modem. Widely used for file sharing and community/special-interest message boards in the 1980s and early 1990s.

COVERDISK/COVERDISC – A floppy disk or CD-ROM mounted on the front of a magazine. These would typically contain demos, shareware, utilities, and software updates.

DISK MAGAZINE – A subscription-based periodical that rather than a physical magazine would regularly send subscribers a floppy disk filled with software, articles, and other digital content. Notable examples include *Uptime*, *I.B.Magazette*, and *Big Blue Disk*.

ENHANCED GRAPHICS ADAPTER (EGA) – A 1980s PC computer graphics card standard. EGA cards were capable of displaying up to 16 colours on a compatible monitor.

FILE TRANSFER PROTOCOL (FTP) – FTP sites were used to upload and download files via online directories.

FREEWARE – Originally a trademarked name to describe software published by Andrew Fluegelman that was free to share and distribute but had an optional licence fee to use. Later became a generic term for describing all software released freely without source code.

LICENCEWARE – A twist on public-domain software whereby a PD library pays a licence fee to the developer for every disk sold.

MODDING/MODDERS – The practice of modifying a game (or some other hardware or software product) in a way not originally intended by its creator. In games this usually results in custom levels or graphics that replace or augment the published work, though sometimes modding involves changing game rules or behaviour or other elements of the experience.

NAG SCREENS – Used by many shareware authors to 'nag' the user, reminding and urging them to register or buy their software/game.

PUBLIC-DOMAIN (PD) SOFTWARE – Free software for which the author retains no copyright, though typically the source code remains protected. Often distributed at low cost by PD libraries and shareware disk vendors.

SHAREWARE – Also called 'user-supported software'. An assortment of related software licensing and distribution models in which authors explicitly encourage customers to try before they buy and to share the 'unregistered' program with others.

USENET – Short for Users Network. An assortment of online message boards organised into 'newsgroups' and distributed across servers around the world. Major source of news and discussion throughout the 1980s and '90s.

VIDEO GRAPHICS ARRAY (VGA) – A PC display controller and graphics standard first introduced in 1987 but not common until the 1990s. Supported a 640 by 480 resolution at up to 16 colours or 320 by 200 at up to 256 colours.

Index

Image Credits

Pages 4, 15 © PC Research, Inc.

Page 19 © Al Evans

Page 21 © Norland Software

Page 22 © Steve Lee/Shareware Marketing

Page 29 © Steve Lee/PC Shareware Magazine

Page 33 © David W. Meny

Page 34 © Steve Jacobs and Jim Boyd

Page 39 © Rob Eberhardt/Somak Software, Inc.

Pages 42, 61 © Michael Denio

Page 47 © John Calhoun

Page 50 © Alan Farmer

Page 54 © Robert Sanborn/Ninja Software

Page 57 © T. L. Winslow/Tommy's Toys

Page 64 © The Assassins

Page 69 © Matt Lafontaine and El Caracho

Page 75 © Simon Rush/Budgie UK

Pages 78, 87 © Scott Miller/Apogee Software

Page 92 © David Gray/Gray Design Associates

Page 95 © Todd Replogle/Apogee Software

Pages 96, 167 © id Software/Apogee Software

Pages 103, 202, 208 © id Software

Page 108 photo © Joe Siegler

Page 111 © Apogee Software

Page 119 © Wendell Hicken

Acknowledgements

I could not have written this book without the tireless efforts of those who preserve old magazines, websites, newspapers, games, software packaging, and other artefacts of our culture. History is built of stories of human ingenuity and endeavour, but it can be told only thanks to the survival of these artefacts produced along the way.

I am indebted also to the generosity of the many shareware industry veterans who answered my questions and shared their own histories. I hope I have done your stories justice. An extra special thank you to Scott Miller for promptly responding to my many follow-up emails, Joe Siegler for sharing loads of old photos, and the several interviewees who scanned or photographed things for me after we talked: Steve Lee, Robert Sanborn, Peter Steffen, David Gray, Chris Snyder, John Passfield, Rob Eberhardt, Bob Mancarella, Tom Warfield, and William Soleau.

A huge thank you must go too to each and every one of the people who supported this book on Unbound and Kickstarter. You made it happen. I hope you enjoyed the ride.

Thanks to former Unbound editor Beth Lewis for believing in this idea and pushing me to pursue it, and to DeAndra Lupu and Mathew Clayton and the rest of the Unbound team for once again ushering me through the process.

And, most importantly, thank you to my wife and cat and our little baby for putting up with me whenever I tuned them out so that I could focus on this getting this project done.

A Note on the Author

Richard Moss is an award-winning writer, journalist, and historian. He has written extensively about the history and culture of video games for leading games and technology publications, including *Ars Technica*, *Game Developer*, *Edge*, *Eurogamer*, *Mac/Life*, *Polygon*, *Rock Paper Shotgun*, and *Vice Motherboard*.

He also produces the narrative podcasts *Ludiphilia* and *The Life & Times of Video Games*, and is co-producer/writer on CREATORVC's documentary film *First Person Shooter*.

Unbound is the world's first crowdfunding publisher, established in 2011.

We believe that wonderful things can happen when you clear a path for people who share a passion. That's why we've built a platform that brings together readers and authors to crowdfund books they believe in – and give fresh ideas that don't fit the traditional mould the chance they deserve.

This book is in your hands because readers made it possible. Everyone who pledged their support is listed below. Join them by visiting unbound.com and supporting a book today.

Richard Bannister

Csongor Baranyai

Corbett Baratta

Jakob Barnard

Brian Barnes

David Barnett

Scott Barrett

Samuel Bass

Earl D. Baugh Jr.

Marc Beavan

Deft Beck

Kim Beck

Karl Becker

Max Beckman-Harned

Adrian Belcher

Laszlo Benyi

Dan Berends

Bryan Berg

Joanna Bergström

Antonio Bernardini

Tim Berry

Paolo Marco Bertoldi

Mark Biswas

Julien Blanchard

Robin Block

David Bloom

Xavier 'FenriX' Bodénand

Marc-Anton Boehm-von
    Thenen

Daniel Bohrer do Nascimento

Welmer Boiten

Grady Booch

Dimitri Boone

Davide Bottino

Katrina Bowen

Christopher Boyle

Corwin Brence

Peter Bridger

Frederico Brinca

Stuart Brown

Steve Browne

Nigel & Llewellyn Bruce

Brian Bruning

Hope Bryant

Samuel Bryant

Daniel Bungert

Adrian Burgess

Philip R. "Pib" Burns

Marcus Butcher

Grant Butler

Joey Butler

Mars Buttfield-Addison

Richard Byles

Olivier Cahagne

Carlo Caione

Taylor Campbell

Danilo Campos

Rob Caporetto

Frank Caratozzolo

Simon Carless

Rowan Carmichael

Jonathan Carpenter

Tim Carruthers

Tim Carruthers

Carter

Eric Case

Richard Case

Eric Casthart

Nick Chaimov

Derek Chandler

Chris Chapman

Paul Charlton

Justin Cheng

Tim Chmielewski

Kevin Christman

Allan Christophersen

Tommy Chu

Thierry Clavel

Peter Clay

Rob Clayton

Nicolas Clement

Hamish Clift

Elliot Clifton

Stephane Clonrozier

Ewen Cluney

Jason Coburn

Dan Cochrane

Blake Coglianese

Stephen Colgan

Christopher Collingridge

Ben Combee

Chris Comeau

Sal Conigliaro

Ryan Conway

Steve Cooper

Marc Copes

JD Cowell

Dan Cox

Paul Craddy

Jorge Crisostomo

Rob Crowther

Peter Curd

Tomasz Czaczka

Piotr 'pecet' Czarny

Kelly A. D'Ambrosio

Robert Daniels

Mátyás Dankó

Daveoh

Richard Davey

Drew Davidson

Matthew Davis

Lionel "Wildphinn" Davoust

Matt Dawidowicz

Tim Dawson

Roger de Boef

Elmar de Koning

Michael Dean

Christian A. Deitering, aka
  "Ferris Bueller"

James Densmore

Scott Densmore

Josh Deprez

Alain Deschenes

David des Jardins

G Dg

Matthew Diamond

Christopher Diaz

Nelson Diaz

Joel Nea Dinegri

John Doe

Phil Dokas

Nick Dominguez

Leah Dougherty

David S. Dowling

Cory Driscoll

Damian Duffy

Duncan

Carl Dungca

William Dunlap

Emory Dunn

James Dunn

Matt Dunn

Vivienne Dunstan

Flemming Dupont

Ian Easton

Andreas Edlinger

Henrik Edlund

Andy Eguia

Tonieh Ellis

Alex Engel

Jordi Escobar Bonet

Exit 23 Games

Evan F

Lorenzo Fantoni

Raphaël Fauveau

Daniel Felice

John C Fiala

Nathaniel Filardo

Joshua Fishburn

Sean Flannigan

Bruno Fonseca

Nick Forge

Jean-François Fortin

Kevin Foss

Olaf Fowles

Franklint

Klemens Franz

Hazel Fraticelli

Thomas Alexander Frederiksen

Jesse Freeman

Jordan Freeman

Paul Fruchey

Thomas Fuchs

Jeff 8bitrocket Fulton

Ken Gagne

Jesse Gallagher

Martin Gallo

David Ganz

Mike M. Garcia

Clay Gardner

Sam Gawith

Eilonwy George-Wallis

Greg Gerke

David Gian-Cursio

Mathieu Giannotta

Adam Gibson

Iona Gibson

Elizabeth Gilbert

Justin Gillenwater

John Ginsberg

David Goldsmith

Stu Gollan

Ben Gollmer

Joshua Gooden

George Goodfellow

Grant Goodine

Michael Goodine

Damian Gordon

Ian Gowen
Joe Gracyk
James Gregory-Monk
Sam Greszes
Mike Griffiths
Freddy Groen
GrosJoueurs
Jörn Grote
Tom Grundy
Dean Guadagno
Sergio Guerreiro Nuevo
Juan Guerrero
Olivier Guinart (•_•)
David Guiot
Sebastián Gavilan Gurvitsch
Matthew Gyure
Lasse H
Andrew Hagen
Gareth Halfacree
Mike MikeScott8 Hamilton
Giles Hamson
Nick Hamze
Mark Hardisty
Ken Hargreaves
Paul Hargreaves
Dinesh Harjani
Aaron Harpole
Alan Harris
Robin Harrison
Adam C. Hartling
Michael Harvat
Sam Harvey
Shaun Harvey

Oliver Haslinger
Haslup
Martin Hassett
Arno Hautala
Andrew Hayward
Bri Hefele
Henrik
David Heremans
Al Heuteux
Darren Hewer
Janosch Hildebrand
Jonathan Hildebrandt
Chris Hill
Craig Hills
Lucien Hoare
Paul J Hodgeson
Tim Hoekstra
JK Hollan
Richard Holt
Peter Hosey
Molly Howell
Stefan Huber
Marijn Hubert
Peter Humphries
Benjamin Hunting
Richard Hunton
Stephan Hüper
Grant Hutchinson
Bill Hutchison
M Matthew Hydock
Dom Ingersole
Simon Isakovic
David Isherwood

Andrew Jackson
Jonathan Jacobs
Jammy2049
Sean Jenkin
Andreas Johansson
Cody Johnson
Matt Johnson
Brian Jones
Dr. Ashley P. Jones
Luke D. Jones
David Jorge
Chris Jorgensen
James "SarshelYam" Joy
JSG
Dannel Jurado
Justin
Jesper Juul
Alexander Kaltsas
Aske Kammer
Indragie Karunaratne
Cole Kauffman
Harri Kauhanen
Otto-Ville Kaukoniemi
John Kavanagh
Jonathan Kay
Matsunga Kazushige
Jack Kelley
Jack Kelly
Florian Keßeler
Dan Kieran
Gary Kind
King Tom the Great
Tim Kingman

Jeffrey Kiok
Andre Kishimoto
Michael Klamerus
David Klco
Elliott Klein
Todd Klein
James Knowles
Dave Kochbeck
Christie Koehler
Paul Koerber
Kevin Konikowski
Tommy Kooi
Alexei Kosut
Jacob Krall
Zayin Krige
Michael M. Kroeker
Andre "kudrix" Kudra
Chris Kuivenhoven
Rajasekaran Senthil Kumaran
Zack L
Toni Lääveri
Joannic Laborde
LAK131
Nick LaLone
Ben Lambert
Matthias Lamm
Steve Landey
Jake Landis
Benyi "Grath" Laszlo
Tony Law
Alex Lee
Matt Lee
Nicole Leeyevna Zeltzer

Christopher Legg

Jarkko Lehtola

Heather Leijon

Sven Leistikow

Aaron LeMasters

Mike Leonardi

Volker Lerch

William K. Leung

Kelsey Lewin

Andy Libecki

Christoph "Sicarius" Licht

Henrik Lindhe

Breanna Lindsay-Murray

Peter Ljungman

Weston Locher

Andy Lochmann

Tony Loiseleur

John Loner

Chris Lowen

Carlo Luciano Bianco

LunarLoony

Donnie Luster

Rob MacAndrew

Isaac MacFarlane

Daniel Mackey

Loric Madramootoo

Andrew Madsen

Darcy Maguire

Brad Mahler

Jeremy Mahler

Rick Mallen

Zoran Malnar

Kyle Mandli

Rajiv Aaron Manglani

DJ Mangus

Michael Mannheim

Martin Markert

Mikel Marlin

Kelsey R. Marquart

Ynot (Tony) Martineau

Ilya Maryasov

Mattroid

Peter Mattsson

Aleksandr Matveev

Adam Mayhew

Dmitry Mazin

Mario Mazzoli

Patrick McCarron

Jaxsun McCarthy Huggan

Yvonne Carol McCombie

Robert McCue

Mike McGregor

Eamonn McHugh-Roohr

Skye McIntyre

Colin Mckellar

Lorna McKnight

Benjamin McLean

Bryan McLemore

Nadia McMahon

Kris McQuage-Loukas

Rod Mearing

Mehron loves Nefeli

Leonard Menchiari

Pierre Mengal

Joseph Merkel

Terence Merkelbach

Eric "djotaku" Mesa

Drew Messinger-Michaels

Daniele Metilli

Tony Meyer

Jason Middleton

Fiona Millar

Christian Miller

Scott Miller

Roland E. Miller, III

Alain Millet

Abe Mishler

Bryan Mitchell

John Mitchinson

Andrew Molloy

Leo Monelli

Spencer F Montgomery

John "MooseCantTalk" Moody

John D. Moore

Ian Moreno

Stephen Morris

Sean M. Morrow

Alexander Morse-Hambrock

Tyson Mote

Adrian Mroczko

Kristian Mroczko

Andreas Müller

Dennis Munsie

Dave Murray

Eugene Myers

Matt Myers

Hugh N

Ken Nagasako

Cody Nance

Giuseppe Navarria

Carlo Navato

Ross Neely

Anthony Nelzin-Santos

Marton Nemeth

Tegan New

Harry Newcomb

B Ng

Colin Ng

Peter Nicholls

Drew Nickels

Nico8

David Nielsen

Sylvain Nieuwlandt

Shawn Nock

Nordstroms

Børge 'NorthWay' Nøst

Tim Nugent

Sean O'Rourke

Kyra Ocean Rehn

The OCs

Chris Odorjan

Jose Olivenca

Par Olsson

Giovanni Orsoni

Angela Osborne

Don Osborne

Dave Oshry

Kyle Overby

Andrew Oyston

Geoff Pado

David Palomino

Giuseppe Pantaleo

Themistocles Papassilekas/ CPCWiki

Kevin Parichan

Alexander Parij

Jeremy Parish

Andy Parkes

John Passfield

Matt Patterson

Matt Payte

David Paz

Fabrizio Pedrazzini

Joseph Pence

Jeremy Penner

Stefano Peracchi

Elena Pereira

Rui Pereira

Xabier Pérez Del Val

Thomas Perl

Thomas Perrier

Brian Perry

Matt Perry

Sean Perryman

Cade "CadeRageous" Peterson

Diego Elio Pettenò

Christopher Phillips

Oliver Phipps

Collin Pieper

Florian Piesche

Felix Pietsch

Glen Piper

Maurizio Pistelli

Michael Pleier

Justin Pollard

Giorgio Pomettini

Bryan Pope

Sean Poynter

Jon Provencher

Stephen Quinlan

Gavi Raab

John Rademan

Alan Ralph

Nathan Raymond

John Raymonds

James Rayner

re4mat

Robert Anton Reese

David Reeves

Graham H Reeves

Dominik Reichardt

Nico Reichert

Caroline Reid

Kyle Reimergartin

Drew Ressler

Rick Reynolds

Paul Rigby

Kevin Riggle

Leo Riihiluoma

Brandon Riley

Dennis Riley

riv_mk

Aron Roberts

Whitney Roberts

Michael Rodriguez

Koen Roekens

Kevin Rohleder

Brenda Romero

Matt Ronge

John Rorland

Caleb Ross

Clay Ross

Dana Ross

Round2Gaming

Sylvain Rousseau

Tony A. Rowe

Huw Rowlands

Michael Rubin

Vilija Rubinaite

RufUsul

Frank Eivind Rundholt

Stephen Russ

Danny Russell

RVDV

Forrest Ryan

Anthony S

Stuart S

Nicolas Sabatier

Dan Sachar

Jeremy Sachs

Peter Safranek

Christopher Salomon

Phil Salvador

Antonio Pascual Sanchez

Rufo Sanchez

Sandro Sarang

Abhilash Sarhadi

Kevin Savetz

Nolen Scaife

Rolf Scheimann

Will Schenk

Jay V Schindler

John Schmidt

Rob Schmuck

Stefan Schneider

Peter Schubel

Stephan Schultes

Wes Schwab

Eric Schwarzkopf

Jason Scott

Sean W Scully

Selcuk

Kevin Seltmann

Reto Senn

Xenon Sharp

David Shaver

Pete Shaw

Bill Sheakoski

Steve Sheets

David Sheppard

Megan Sherret

John Shirlaw

Sean Sicher

Bruno Silva

Mark Simonson

Ben Sinclair

John Siracusa

Ruban Siva

sixhoursago

Ammon Skidmore

slashmastah

Donald Smeltz Jr

Ceilidh Smith

Ian Smith

Matt Smith

Thomas Smith

Tim Snow

Chris Snyder

Jeff Somers

Jake Sones

Mike Spall

Daniel Spreadbury

Dennis Spreen

Ben Squibb

Brandon Staggs

Rory Starks

Startrail

Keith Stattenfield

Dan Steadman

Markus Steck

Mike Stedman

Murray Steele

Matthew Stephenson

Matthew "Firefang"
  Stephenson

Michael Stevenson

Joe Stewart

Thomas Stidham

J. Ryan Stinnett

Dennis Stockhofe

Marcus Stöhr

Bernard Stolar

Sven Stoll

Michael Strange Jr

Jacob Strick

Peter Stubbe

Helen Stuckey

David Stutter

Michael Sullivan

Steve Sullivan

Andy Sum

Supercade

Ben Sutherland

Brian Sutorius

Noah Swartz

Alex Swift

Mark Sztainbok

Thom Tamayo

Eliza Tantivy

Harrison Tatem-Wyatt

S. Taushanoff

Andrew Taylor

Will Templeton

Julien Templier

Laurent Teyssandier

Dave Thomas

Andrew Thomson

James Thomson

Roy Tobin

Simon Todd

Scott Tooker

Per Torstensson

Christopher Toscano

Wade Tregaskis

Vasyl Tsvirkunov

Foone Turing

Jamie Turner

AK Turza

Dan Vallerand

Jeroen van der Velden

Thijs van der Vossen
Jay Van Doornum
Rune Vendler
Brandon Vessey
Andrew Vestal
Eric Vitiello
Maël Von Wiesel
Dante Vono
Josef Vorbeck
Ingve Vormestrand
Primož Vovk
David Wagner
waiwainl
Sammie Waldie
Mark Wales
Jamie 'reech' Walker
Christopher Walton
Chris Ward
Kennan Ward
Harley Watson
Michal Wawer
Thomas Weber
Jake Webster
Paul Webster
Wade Webster
James Weiner
Nat Welch
Robert 'Weaselspoon' Wells
P. Welsing
Fred Wenzel
Glen West
Shawn Wheatley
Paul Whelan

Brendan Whelton
Marcin Wichary
Owen Wiggins
Andreas Wiklund
Daniel Williams
Max Williams
Ross "Seiromem" Williams
Ryan Williams
Ronan Wills
Robert Wilson
David Winter
Dominik Wit
Ansel Witthaus
John Wood
Jamie Woodcock
Cory Woodrum
Steven Yau (yaustar)
Ido Yehieli
Fred Young
Serena Z
Jose P. Zagal
Tieg Zaharia
Steven Zakulec
Andreas Zecher
Pian Zhang
Vladislav Zheleznyak
Andy Zickler
Ben Zotto
Minier Zsolt